Slavery, Freedom, and Expansion in the Early American West

Jeffersonian America
Jan Ellen Lewis, Peter S. Onuf, and
Andrew O'Shaughnessy, Editors

Slavery, Freedom, and Expansion

in the Early American West

John Craig Hammond

UNIVERSITY OF VIRGINIA PRESS | CHARLOTTESVILLE AND LONDON

University of Virginia Press
© 2007 by the Rector and Visitors of the University of Virginia
All rights reserved
Printed in the United States of America on acid-free paper

First published 2007
9 8 7 6 5 4 3 2 1

LIBRARY OF CONGRESS CATALOGING-IN-PUBLICATION DATA

Hammond, John Craig, 1974-
  Slavery, freedom, and expansion in the early American West / John
Craig Hammond.
    p. cm. — (Jeffersonian America)
    Includes bibliographical references and index.
    ISBN 978-0-8139-2669-8 (alk. paper)
    1. Slavery—Political aspects—Southwest, Old—History. 2. Slavery—
Political aspects—Middle West—History. 3. Frontier and pioneer
life—Southwest, Old. 4. Frontier and pioneer life—Middle West.
5. Southwest, Old—Politics and government. 6. Middle West—Politics
and government. 7. United States—Territorial expansion. 8. Slavery—
United States—Extension to the territories. 9. United States—Politics
and government—1789-1809. 10. United States—Politics and
government—1809-1817. I. Title.
    E446.H27 2007
    306.3'6208996073076—dc22   2007012191

For Hallie, Hannah, and Addison,
and Pep and Lance, too

CONTENTS

ACKNOWLEDGMENTS

Many people and institutions have provided assistance and guidance that have helped me complete this book. Special thanks are due to the editors whose labors produced the many edited collections of papers that permitted prompt completion of this book. Librarians and archivists at the Historical Society of Pennsylvania, Library Company of Philadelphia, Library of Virginia, Kentucky Historical Society, Filson Historical Society, and the Cincinnati Historical Society helped me rummage through their archives. The extremely helpful staffs at the Ohio Historical Society, Indiana Historical Society, Margaret I. King Library at the University of Kentucky, and the Library of Congress's Manuscript Division deserve special mention. Molly was a great companion on many of my research trips. Although she ate my lunch while waiting for me in the car on a cold day in Columbus, she made the long day trips to archives much more pleasant.

This book began as a dissertation at the University of Kentucky, which provided support in many different ways. John Christopher and the physics department supplied two years of financial support while I made the transition from physics to history. The graduate school at the University of Kentucky provided me with a Dissertation Year Fellowship that facilitated completion of the dissertation and its transformation into a manuscript. Many fine graduate students and faculty members helped this project in numerous ways. Mark Summers's reams of good advice have improved this book significantly. David Nichols has been with this project since it began as a research paper. He has read almost as many drafts as I've written, and became a great friend in the process. Drew Fieght, Todd Estes, and Paul Newman contributed valuable last-minute readings of the manuscript.

Transylvania University provided a welcoming academic home after graduate school. My current academic home, Purdue University Calumet, has done the same. Saul Lerner and Dean Dan Dunn of the College of Liberal Arts and Social Sciences provided research release time and summer research funds that allowed me to complete revisions. Saul also gave a valuable late reading of the manuscript. Ms. Kris Mihalic has been an excellent department administrator. The unfailingly good advice and suggestions from my editors and outside readers for the University of Virginia Press, Dick Holway, Peter Onuf, and James Lewis, as well as Toni Mortimer, who copyedited the final manuscript, have made this book much better than it might otherwise have been.

Many others have given support that has proved especially valuable in completing this work. The kind guidance and advice of many people helped lead me toward academia. I owe much to my undergraduate institution, Temple University, and the many fine people who work there, especially Bill Cutler, Gerry Vision, Michael Tye, Stephen Zelnick, Ed Kaczanowicz, and Peter Goldstone. Had these professors not taken the time to cultivate my academic interests, I would be a steamfitter or a stockbroker, not a historian. Milo Aukerman made graduate school seem like a plausible idea in the first place, then came through again as I completed the manuscript. Karl Alvarez and Bill Stevenson have always helped me keep my work in perspective. I owe *all* you guys much. Friends in Lexington—Carrie, John, Stuart, Glenn, Whitney, Keri, and Rico—provided great Friday night diversions and friendship. At Purdue Calumet, Frank, Wendy, Mita, Miriam, Joe, Saul, and Kathy lent support, friendship, and someone to have a beer with on Friday nights. In Pittsburgh, my in-laws and the rest of the Pittsburgh crew can always be counted on to share good cheer and good times. They have made Pittsburgh a welcoming second home. On the other side of Pennsylvania (the good side), great friends from home, Billy in particular, provided much needed reprieve during my summer and winter trips to Philly. My parents and grandmother have given me more than I could ever ask for. Pep, you're the best. My father and Steamfitters Local Union 420, Philadelphia, helped teach me that dignity and honor are inseparable from honest labor; one of slavery's many tragedies is that it cast an air of disgrace on honest and honorable labor. Jeffrey Francis Maksym was a dear friend who is missed by all; together, we learned the redeeming value of hard work.

Hallie has been an endless well of patience, love, and support ever since I met her at Penn State all those years ago. Hannah and Addison have enriched our lives and love in ways that we never imagined. The passing of Lance Banning has made the completion of this book bittersweet. Lance was a great mentor and an even dearer friend. We miss you, Lance.

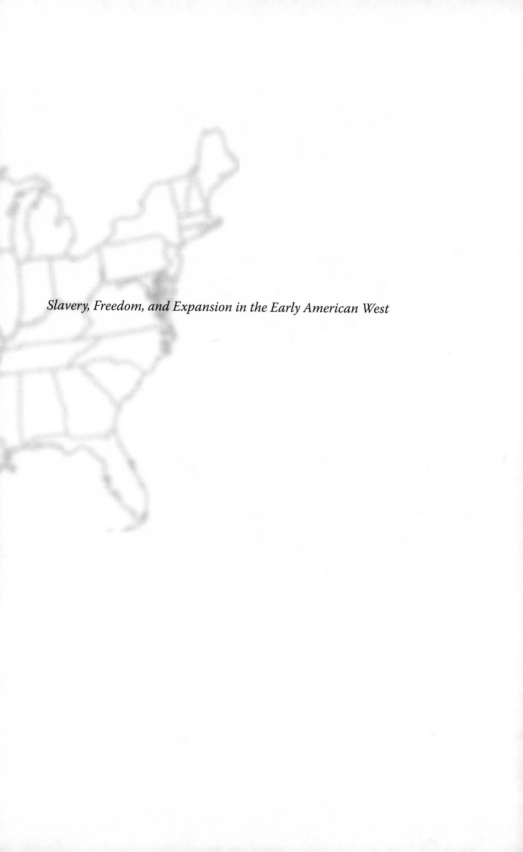

Slavery, Freedom, and Expansion in the Early American West

OREGON
COUNTRY
(U.S. and Britain)

42°

36°30'

MEXICO
(Independent, 1821)

(UPPER) LOUISIANA
UNORGANIZED
TERRITORY

MICHIGAN TERR.

MAINE
(1820)

VT
NH

NEW YORK

MASS.

CONN. R.I.

PENNSYLVANIA

N.J.

ILLINOIS INDIANA OHIO

MD. DEL

MISSOURI
(1821)

KENTUCKY

VIRGINIA

ARKANSAS
TERRITORY

TENNESSEE

NORTH CAROLINA

SOUTH
CAROLINA

TEXAS

MISSISS-
IPPI

ALABAMA

GEORGIA

LOUISIANA

FLORIDA
TERRITORY

Slave State

Slave Territory

Free State

Free Territory

THE UNITED STATES, 1820

Introduction

Slavery, Freedom, and Expansion in the Overextended Republic, 1787–1820

In February 1790 the Pennsylvania Abolition Society presented a set of petitions to the first federal Congress meeting in New York. The petitions, signed by an aging Benjamin Franklin, asked Congress to define the new government's relationship to the institution of slavery and to take measures promoting its gradual abolition. An initial committee report on the petitions suggested that Congress enjoyed wide powers to regulate the institution. The matter soon became embroiled with a controversy over funding the national debt, however, and already tremulous northern support for wide congressional authority to regulate slavery diminished even further. When congressmen from the Deep South threatened that disunion, civil war, and servile insurrection would follow in the wake of continued debate, support for the initial committee report all but disappeared.[1]

At the same time that Congress debated federal authority over slavery, they were also settling unrelated matters concerning federal territories in the West. Early in its first session, Congress re-passed the Northwest Ordinance of 1787. By accepting the Northwest Ordinance's Article VI, which stated that "there shall be neither slavery nor involuntary servitude in the said territory," Congress claimed the authority to regulate and prohibit slavery in federal territories. Congress next moved to settle North Carolina's claims to the lands that would become the Southwest Territory. North Carolina agreed to cede the lands only on the condition that slavery be permitted there. Congress conceded, and the Southwest Ordinance of 1790 exempted the territory from Article VI of the Northwest Ordinance.[2]

In readopting the Northwest Ordinance with Article VI, and by exempting the Southwest Territory from restrictions on slavery, Congress established its power to allow or prohibit the expansion of slavery in federal territories. The final committee report on the Pennsylvania Abolition Society petitions confirmed this authority. The report amounted to a list of prohibitions on congressional action against slavery in the states where it existed, but it said nothing about federal authority over slavery in the territories. When taken together, these developments established that the clause of the Constitution that granted Congress "power to dispose of and make all needful rules and regulations respecting the territory or other property belonging to the United States" included the authority to prohibit or permit slavery in the federal territories.[3]

When Congress passed the two ordinances in 1790, American slavery was largely confined to the Atlantic states, and its future—especially in the West—seemed in many ways uncertain. Georgia and South Carolina excepted, every state had banned the international slave trade, while the Constitution granted Congress the authority to close it permanently in 1808. Gradual abolition laws and economic changes clearly spelled the end of slavery in most northern states. The institution also faltered in the Upper South. The decline of the Chesapeake's tobacco economy and the Revolutionary animus against slavery had produced a flurry of private emancipations. Religious awakenings there seemed to threaten the institution even further. Only in the Deep South, it seemed, would slavery emerge from the American Revolution largely unscathed.[4]

In the West, slavery's future seemed more uncertain still. The Northwest Ordinance prohibited slavery north and west of the Ohio River. From Kentucky came serious murmurings about abolishing the institution at statehood. The Southwest Ordinance permitted slavery, but expansion was stalled by the Creeks, Cherokees, Chickasaws, and

Choctaws—numerous and well-armed Indian nations that controlled the southern interior from central Georgia to Tennessee to the Mississippi River. In the lower Mississippi Valley, spillover fighting from the American War for Independence further upset the small, delicate slave societies that French, British, and Spanish imperial officials had long neglected. Finally, among the polyglot groups of European American settlers in the trans-Appalachian West, the United States was already gaining a reputation as a power unfriendly to slavery. The Union, it seemed, might yet create an "empire for liberty."

Yet by 1819 the United States presided over an "empire for slavery" in the West. In the Old Southwest, the U.S. government sanctioned slavery in Tennessee, Kentucky, Alabama, and Mississippi. Congress failed to prohibit slavery in the immense Louisiana Purchase, and the institution stretched across the Mississippi River into Louisiana and the future states of Arkansas and Missouri. Article VI of the Northwest Ordinance clearly prohibited slavery north of the Ohio River, but its effectiveness seemed at best mixed. Congress did little, if anything, to enforce Article VI during the territorial phase of government in Ohio, Indiana, and Illinois. Only with great difficulty did settlers there manage to exclude slavery when those territories adopted constitutions at the time of statehood. Even then, the threat of slavery expansion into the Northwest remained real. When Missouri applied for statehood in 1819, slaveholders threatened to extend the institution still farther, not only from the Mississippi River to the Pacific Ocean but "backwards" into Illinois, Indiana, and Ohio. Worse still, slaveholding politicians now denied that Congress possessed any authority to block slavery in the federal territories.

In thirty years, American slavery had been transformed from a badly battered institution with an uncertain future into an expansive and aggressive force poised to cover much of the early American West. Why did the federal government fail to contain slavery's expansion despite the clear antislavery precedent set by the Northwest Ordinance? Why did the federal government sanction the rapid expansion of slavery in the Old Southwest, the lower Mississippi Valley, and the Missouri Valley? Why was it only with great difficulty that slavery had been excluded from north of the Ohio River, despite the antislavery provisions of Article VI? What, in sum, explains the peculiar expansion of both slavery and freedom through 1819, and what accounts for the supposedly sudden emergence of the slavery expansion question in the Missouri Controversy?

Historians generally agree that the interests of southern slaveholders prevailed whenever the federal government confronted the problem of slavery expansion in the early American republic. Upper South planters in Congress fought for expansion because it opened up new lands for slaveholders, along with new markets for their regions' "surplus" slaves. Deep South planters threatened disunion whenever slavery was discussed, lessening even further any possibility that Congress might restrict slavery's expansion. Despite their occasional antislavery rhetoric, southern Republicans led by Thomas Jefferson could temporize on restriction because northern Republicans proved unwilling to challenge their southern colleagues' mania for expansion. New England Federalists were supposedly the only group in the federal government that refused to acquiesce to slavery's expansion. But decimated by declining numbers in Congress, they could do little but pose occasional, ineffective opposition to the rapid acquisition of fresh territory for slaveholders. This status quo lasted until 1819, when "northerners seem to have awakened quite suddenly to a realization" that the expansion of the previous thirty years had created an empire for slavery in the West.[5]

The most significant work on the politics of slavery and expansion in the early republic focuses on the inconsistencies of a vaguely defined group of "founding fathers." According to the historian William Freehling, the "founding fathers" were "skittish abolitionists, chary of pouncing on antislavery opportunity," despite the ideological animus against slavery implicit in the American Revolution. Their "conditional antislavery" mentality limited slavery's expansion only when racism, climate, and other "crass motives" converged to pass the Northwest Ordinance. Even this was compromised by their unwillingness to implement the antislavery provisions of Article VI, thus inviting proslavery interests to evade and undermine Article VI while working for its repeal. The founders' racism, self-interest, ambivalence, and indifference fostered inaction on slavery expansion whether in the Northwest or the Southwest. Until 1819, slaveholders spread their institution westward, protected by a functionally proslavery "policy of silent sanction."[6]

The literature on the expansion of slavery and freedom in the early republic correctly highlights the failure of elite leaders like Jefferson and the dominant Republican Party to prevent the rapid expansion of slavery into western territories and states. But the strength of these interpretations is also their greatest weakness. Too often they degenerate into moralistic judgments about the failures of the founding generation: slavery expanded because Jefferson, Madison, and their fellow partisans made no effort to stop it. Except for a few New England Federalists, politicians and leaders in the early republic proved all too willing to jettison their antislavery professions whenever they conflicted with their personal, partisan, or sectional interests.[7]

The narrow focus on the "founders," along with sectional and partisan politics within Congress, ultimately produces a distorted understanding of the reasons why the federal government sanctioned slavery in the Southwest and did little to stop its expansion in the Northwest. It greatly overstates the power and influence that the federal government actually exercised in the West. Equally important, these interpretations tend to treat the early American West as "virgin territory," ignoring the presence, influence, and interests of the numerous groups already in the West. These interpretations thus incorrectly assume that slavery's fate in Ohio and Indiana or Mississippi and Louisiana could be decided from the comforts of the nation's capital. But this minimizes the critical role that western settlers themselves played in determining how slavery and freedom expanded. Furthermore, by focusing on party leaders such as Thomas Jefferson and Timothy Pickering, historians misread the partisan and sectional dynamics that shaped expansion policy. They also too readily overlook the numerous efforts of lesser politicians, especially northern Republicans, to contain slavery expansion prior to the Missouri Controversy. Finally, by assuming that the period between 1790 and 1818 was one long, unchallenged triumph for slaveholders, historians add to the erroneous conclusion that the Missouri Controversy was "a firebell in the night," caused by northerners' sudden and belated recognition that slavery had expanded so vigorously over the previous thirty years.[8]

What, then, explains the politics of slavery expansion in the early American republic, along with the seemingly sudden emergence of the Missouri Controversy in 1819? The early expansion of both slavery and freedom must be understood within the context of a weak but extended republic trying to establish its place on a North American continent where numerous parties and interests challenged the authority of the new nation in the West. As the United States acquired and organized western territories, concerns for halting slavery's expansion clashed with a separate set of considerations centering on the future of the trans-Appalachian West in the American Union. The failure of the federal government to stop expansion outside of the Northwest stemmed from the ability of southern politicians to protect the interests of southern slaveholders, to be sure. But it also reflected a determination to establish, maintain, and strengthen an American presence in the trans-Appalachian West, a project deemed crucial for the survival of the American Union.

From 1783 through 1815 the American Union remained fragile. The threat of a split between the Atlantic states and the trans-Appalachian West seemed much more real than disunion along northern and southern lines. Accordingly, potential East–West divisions figured prominently in conflicts over slavery expansion. The federal government and parties in the West both recognized that while the government possessed immense legal authority over western territories, it exercised little effective power there. In the West, the "extended republic" was an overextended republic, thus granting westerners extraordinary influence over federal policy, despite their meager numbers. The ability of the United States to govern effectively and compete in the "power politics of territorial hegemony" in the West dictated that Congress allow slavery where the white population demanded it and federal authority remained contested.[9]

Federal policymakers in the East recognized that while they might influence local decisions concerning slavery and freedom in the West, they alone could not decide the issue. The weaknesses of the federal government in the West meant that the decision to permit or exclude slavery became, by default, a local question. Consequently, slavery entered local politics in western states and territories far more frequently and intensely than it did national politics prior to 1819. Until the Missouri Controversy, interested parties in the West—settlers, slaveholders, and speculators of doubtful loyalties, minor federal officials, territorial politicians, French and British loyalists living in the West, potentially rebellious slaves, and hostile European and Indian nations on the far fringes of the extended republic—were more responsible for determining slavery's fate in western territories than were politicians in the East.

Whether in the Northwest or the Southwest, local popular politics determined if a particular state or territory would reject slavery.

Through the Missouri Controversy, slaveholders more often than not prevailed in contests over slavery's expansion. Yet at the same time they rarely lacked opponents. Through 1818, northern Republicans consistently challenged slavery expansion, whether in Ohio, Indiana, and Illinois, or in Missouri, Mississippi, and Louisiana. Except for important exceptions in the Northwest, these efforts failed because the federal government lacked the power to enforce meaningful restrictions on slavery in the far western reaches of the overextended republic. Nonetheless, these challenges—both the successes and the failures—revealed the limits and possibilities of federal action against slavery in the early American West, thus giving rise to the Missouri Controversy.

Until the Missouri Controversy, disputes over expansion typically pitted federal authority from the East against western interests and their threats of disunion. After the War of 1812, the West seemed unquestionably loyal, the Union itself stable and consolidated, thus settling the main problem that had thwarted past attempts to limit slavery expansion. For the northern Republicans who had sought restrictions on slavery in the past, it now seemed possible for Congress to halt slavery expansion permanently. Accordingly, when Missouri applied for statehood, northern Republicans proposed prohibiting slavery both in Missouri and "in the states or territories which may hereafter be admitted into the Union."[10]

With the crisis of 1819, North–South sectionalism overtook East–West conflicts over slavery in the West. Southerners and northerners now tried to project their own visions of slavery and freedom onto the West. Those visions would prove irreconcilable. More importantly, they insured that Congress would remain unable to address adequately the problem of slavery's future expansion, though for different reasons than in the past. The newfound southern defense of slavery and popular sovereignty provided the rationale for endless expansion. For white southerners, slavery was now an undoubtedly permanent institution. Its preservation in the Atlantic slave states required indefinite and unrestricted expansion in the West.

To counter this southern insurgency, northern politicians and voters created an antislavery past that justified far-reaching federal powers to halt slavery expansion forever. This new antislavery narrative demanded that Congress create a new Northwest Ordinance for the entire West, banning slavery's future expansion "in all states or territories, hereafter incorporated into the Union."[11] They failed because disunionist threats, used so effectively by westerners in the past, now came from a united and belligerent South. Those disunion threats assured the outcome of the Missouri Controversy. More important, the Missouri Controversy all but determined that the United States would never peaceably solve the problem of slavery's expansion, even if the Missouri Compromise provided a temporary solution.

1

Ordinances, Limits, and Precedents, 1784–1796

In 1783 the fledgling United States won both independence and Britain's former claim of sovereignty over the trans-Appalachian West. The following year the Confederation Congress began work on a series of proposals to establish some type of American government for the region. The first proposal, introduced by a committee headed by Thomas Jefferson, contained the provision that after 1800, there would be "neither slavery nor involuntary servitude in any of the said states" that the United States would create in its western possessions. Due to matters unrelated to slavery, Congress failed to adopt the 1784 proposal and its prospective ban on slavery in the entire early American West. Over the next three years, it would entertain but fail to pass several more such bans. Finally, in 1787 the Confederation Congress passed the Northwest Ordinance. Its Article VI provided that "there shall be neither slavery nor involuntary servitude in the said territory" and prohibited slavery's future expansion into all federal territories "north and west of the River Ohio." When the new federal Congress met in New York for the first time in 1789, creating viable territorial governments for the West was among the many pressing issues it confronted. As one of its first orders of business, Congress reauthorized the Northwest Ordinance of 1787.[1]

Congress next began work on a territorial government for what would become the Southwest Territory and ultimately the state of Tennessee in 1796. Circumstances there made it unlikely that Congress would attempt to apply Article VI. First, North Carolina claimed the territory, governed it as its own, and was under no obligation to cede either its jurisdiction or the land to the new federal government. In addition, while few white Americans lived in the Northwest, large numbers of slaveholders had already settled in the Southwest under North Carolina law, which permitted slavery. The 3,400 slaves and numerous slaveholders in the region made slavery an established fact rather than an institution that might be permitted or excluded at the discretion of Congress. Moreover, thousands of North Carolinians already possessed warrants for lands in Tennessee. They had acquired their claims under the assumption that slavery would be permitted, and they fully expected to settle those lands with the benefits of slave labor. Given these realities, Congress was already averse to apply Article VI to the Southwest; North Carolina made sure that it would not. The North Carolina Cession Act of 1789, which ceded North Carolina's claims to the new federal government, "*provided always* that no regulations made or to be made by Congress shall tend to emancipate slaves."[2]

Congress might have pressed North Carolina to drop its conditions, but that promised to exacerbate an entirely different set of problems centering on the federal government's limited power and authority. North Carolina was one of the last states to ratify the Constitution of 1787, it was a bastion of anti-Federalism, and it surely would have protested any federal demands that seemed at odds with its state interests. Equally important, Congress already found itself facing the disunion threats that would hamper future efforts to restrict western slavery in the early republic. Any demand that North Carolina drop its conditions would have delayed passage of the Southwest Ordinance, a situation the government strongly wanted to avoid. Leading men and land speculators in Tennessee had already grown frustrated with the government's weaknesses in the West. North Carolina senator William Blount and others possessed immense land claims in the Southwest. In order to cash in on their claims, they desperately wanted the new federal government to, among other things, encourage commerce and provide protection from the Creeks and Cherokees, measures that were needed to encourage white settlement. In order to speed passage of the Southwest Ordinance, and with it federal assistance, they deliberately spread rumors that settlers were plotting with the Spanish to break away from the United States; they even named (but misspelled) the main area of settlement around Nashville the "Mero District," after the Spanish governor of Louisiana.[3]

Lacking effective power to coerce North Carolina, and fearful of disunion schemes in the West, the federal government quickly acceded to North Carolina's demands. The Southwest Ordinance of 1790 permitted slavery in the Southwest Territory even as it deliberately avoided any mention of the institution or of Article VI of the Northwest Ordinance. The ordinance neither explicitly sanctioned slavery nor specifically exempted the Southwest from Article VI, as would be done in later ordinances. Instead, the Southwest Ordinance of 1790 merely stated that the government of the Southwest Territory would be the same as that for the Northwest, "except so far as is provided" in the North Carolina Cession Act.[4]

The interests of southern slaveholders and their representatives in Congress of course prevailed in 1790. But it is doubtful that the antislavery sentiments that permitted re-passage of the Northwest Ordinance in 1789 had disappeared by 1790. Instead, Congress's willingness to accept North Carolina's conditions and quickly establish a government for the Southwest reflected the weaknesses of the federal government in its western borderlands, weaknesses that greatly amplified the influence that westerners could exercise over the federal government.[5] Despite constant pleas and complaints, the national government had done little to address the concerns of white settlers in the Southwest, including access to the Spanish-controlled Mississippi River and protection from Indian attacks. Banning slavery would only increase the contempt many white settlers in the Southwest felt toward the far-off federal government. Congress knew better than to ban slavery in a region where the federal government lacked power, authority, and popular support. Pressing North Carolina or settlers in the Southwest to accept Article VI seemed futile at best, pernicious at worst.

If it was unlikely that Congress could have implemented Article VI in the Southwest Territory, it was impossible to do so in Kentucky. Through 1792, Virginia governed Kentucky as its westernmost counties, and Kentucky never was a territory of the United States. Virginia law and slaveholding settlers established slavery in Kentucky beginning in the 1770s. Slavery could be restricted or abolished only by Virginia, or by the people of Kentucky once Virginia permitted Kentucky to become its own state in 1792. Twice in the 1790s Kentucky held constitutional conventions where gradual abolition proposals were entertained. Both times, slaveholders and voters overwhelmed small antislavery coalitions led by evangelicals.[6]

In 1796 Congress admitted Tennessee with a constitution protecting slavery. Federalists, fearful that the new state's electoral votes would go to Thomas Jefferson in the upcoming election, used numerous tricks to try and delay its admission. Tellingly, they abstained from making an issue out of slavery.[7] If Tennessee's and Kentucky's passage to statehood with slavery was unproblematic, it was because the federal government lacked the power to challenge slavery there. Equally important, the failure of Kentucky's antislavery evangelicals demonstrated the severe limits on local, popular antislavery movements where slavery had already gained a foothold. The lessons from both pointed to the difficulties opponents of slavery expansion would face in the very near future. As the United States acquired, organized, and incorporated new western territories into the Union, the same problems that had bedeviled efforts to restrict slavery in Kentucky and Tennessee—weak federal power going up against popular, local support for slavery—would appear in new, far more menacing forms.

2

"That Species of Property Already Exists"

Natchez, Mississippi, 1795–1800

Responding to an urgent message from Secretary of State Timothy Pickering, the House of Representatives spent much of March 1798 framing a government for the immense stretch of land that would become the Mississippi Territory. As the end of the session neared, the House resolved a long-standing dispute over Georgia's claims to the territory. Immediately after the House voted to deny Georgia jurisdiction over the territory, George Thatcher rose and introduced a motion "touching the rights of man." Thatcher, a four-term Federalist from the District of Maine, had spent the better part of his congressional career inciting the ire of slaveholders. This time would be no different. At Pickering's request, the bill under consideration created a government identical to that "established for the Northwestern Territory . . . with the exception respecting *slaves*." Thatcher moved to apply Article VI of the Northwest Ordinance to the Mississippi Territory, which would have prevented American slaveholders from expanding their institution into the future states of Mississippi and Alabama. His proposal stood little chance of passage. A day's worth of angry debate winnowed away already meager support. In the end, only eleven other congressmen voted with him to prohibit slavery in the Mississippi Territory.[1]

The House's defeat of Thatcher's motion seems decisive enough. And as historians have argued, it seemed inevitable that Congress would permit slavery expansion into the Mississippi Territory. Yet the decision to sanction slavery there involved more than a coalition of interested Upper South politicians, disunion-threatening Deep Southerners, and weak-willed northern Republicans defeating a New England Federalist's antislavery proposal.[2] When it came to deciding slavery's future in Mississippi, the most crucial decisions were made not in the halls of Congress, or on Chesapeake and Carolina plantations, but in the lower Mississippi Valley itself. It was there, too, that the more serious peril of disunion lay. Slavery had long existed in what would become the Mississippi Territory. Under the Spanish regime that preceded the Americans, it was thriving. Ultimately, Congress permitted slavery in Mississippi because settlers who were already there demanded it as the cost of union. Months before George Thatcher reminded his colleagues that "the existence of slavery" was "an evil in direct hostility to the principles of our government," events and circumstances in Mississippi had already determined that Congress would sanction slavery there.[3]

I

The lower Mississippi Valley had long troubled American officials. A contested area coveted by the fledgling United States and European empires, in the 1790s this region was inhabited by powerful Indian nations, slaveholder speculators of ever-shifting loyalties, potentially rebellious slaves, and "men of no country." American and Spanish officials, British and French imperialists, and the inhabitants of the region all recognized that Spain was a decaying power whose hold on its colonial possessions was slipping. American officials remained cautiously optimistic that they could secure American possessions in the Old Southwest. This would require checking the imperial ambitions of Britain and France, and, more importantly, convincing the white inhabitants of the lower Mississippi Valley that American control of the region best served their interests.[4]

In the 1783 Treaty of Paris, American negotiators gained from the British terms favorable to American expansion into the Southwest. The Treaty of Paris drew the southern boundary of the newly independent United States along the 31st parallel (the present-day northern border of Florida) in the south, and the Mississippi River in the west. The treaty also granted American citizens access to the Mississippi River, providing western settlers with needed access to world markets through New Orleans. But Spain, seeking to protect the northern edge of its American empire, frequently denied American settlers navigation rights on the Mississippi. It also sought to move the border between Spanish West Florida and the United States northward, as additional protection against American encroachment into Spanish territory. From 1785 through 1794, American diplomats made scant progress in convincing their Spanish counterparts to sign a new treaty recognizing the terms of the Treaty of Paris. Finally, with war in Europe intensifying, Spain agreed to the 1795 Treaty of San Lorenzo, granting Americans rights to the Mississippi River and recognizing American claims to land that would form the Mississippi Territory.[5]

The United States now had to secure the territory gained in the treaty; this would prove no easy task. The Choctaws, Creeks, Cherokees, and Chickasaws controlled the bulk of land between the Mississippi River and Georgia. In the 1790s, they confined European American settlement to a few posts along the Mississippi River and some settlements in the interior. The "Natchez Country"—the town of Natchez and its hinterlands—was home to the majority of slaves and settlers: a diverse mixture of British Loyalists, expatriated Americans, slaveholding planter-speculators, and "men of no country," all governed by an English-speaking Spanish governor whose main task was to minimize American influence in the region, and stall, if not prevent, implementation of the Treaty of San Lorenzo.[6]

For better or for worse, federal officials believed they could best secure the southwest frontier by cultivating the loyalties of the settlers in and around Natchez. The "present inhabitants" of the Natchez Country—the white ones, at least—had three main concerns. Any government seeking to command their allegiance had to provide peace and security by reigning in the region's "banditti," organized bands of criminals who harassed settlers and stole slaves. Government also had to placate the Creeks and Choctaws, who increasingly resented encroachment on their lands. A stable government was also needed to provide good titles for land claims, which were entangled in a morass of overlapping British, Spanish, and Georgian grants. Finally, an acceptable government had to protect the inhabitants' property in slaves. American officials could secure the region by demonstrating to white settlers that the United States would best address these concerns. On all three counts, however, the Spanish, "habitually dexterious" in the art of borderland "intrigue," or the British, hoping to seize the lower Mississippi Valley, or the French, interested in regaining its lower Mississippi Valley possessions, might well offer better terms to the white settlers of the Natchez Country. Complicating matters further still, the Indian nations, slaves, and banditti in the region all had their own interests that conflicted with an American-controlled Natchez Country.[7]

With so many parties competing for control of the lower Mississippi Valley, and with so many different interests to satisfy, the United States found itself negotiating with the inhabitants of Natchez from a position of profound weakness. The single American official charged with securing Natchez for the United States in 1797 soon discovered that slavery could assume an important place at the intersection of interest, intrigue, and empire in the Southwest borderlands. The United States had gained possession of a region in the midst of intense change. A crucial transition to a plantation society had begun under Spanish rule in the 1780s, and the United States had acquired far more than an outpost in the lower Mississippi Valley.

II

The lower Mississippi Valley remained on the far fringes of the colonial plantation world for most of the seventeenth and eighteenth centuries. Around Natchez, slavery was only of marginal importance until the 1770s. French officials attempted to bring Natchez into the plantation world in the late 1720s, but uncooperative Indians and Africans quickly destroyed those efforts. In November 1729 a party of Natchez Indians arrived at the French fort, ostensibly to pay tribute to the French official who had warned them off lands marked for French tobacco plantations. The Natchez instead rebelled; at day's end, over two hundred French settlers lay dead, and three hundred African slaves had been carried off. The Natchez Indian Rebellion effectively destroyed French designs to establish plantations around Natchez, and it would be more than thirty years before any imperial power made a new effort.

In 1763, Britain gained control of the seemingly worthless Natchez Country as booty from the Great War for Empire. British officials offered generous land grants to entice settlers, in an effort to secure its new possession in the lower Mississippi Valley. Many who took the offer arrived with slaves or sought them once they arrived. The American War for Independence added to the trickle of settlers and slaveholders as the British resettled Loyalists from the Carolinas and Georgia in Natchez. By 1780, perhaps five thousand Loyalists and twelve hundred slaves inhabited Natchez and the surrounding plantations, laying the groundwork for the plantation revolution that soon followed.[8]

In 1783, Spain reclaimed control of the Natchez Country; the once languishing plantation economies in the lower Mississippi Valley quickly began to stabilize and expand. Spain's main interest in the 1780s was to create a buffer state protecting the far more valuable province of Mexico from Anglo-American expansion. Though intended to build up the Spanish presence in the lower Mississippi Valley, Spanish policy also encouraged the growth of slavery and threatened to undermine American influence in the region. To protect their Gulf Coast possessions from American expansion, Spanish officials tried turning American settlers into loyal Spanish subjects. In 1788 it became Spanish policy that any American willing to "take the due oath of allegiance" to Spain would receive, among other benefits, a free "tract of land from 240 to 800 acres," exempt from taxation. They also granted access to the Mississippi River and the market at New Orleans, and cut or eliminated export duties for Americans who settled in a Spanish province. Finally, Americans settling in Spanish provinces could expressly carry their slaves with them, a privilege the United States had recently prohibited in the Northwest Territory. As early as 1789, American officials in the West feared that Spanish inducements would lead American settlers "to imbibe the Spanish prejudices." Soon enough, "they will become Spaniards for all intents and purposes," wrote a worried Arthur St. Clair, governor of the newly established Northwest Territory.[9]

American officials had good reason to worry, as slaveholding and non-slaveholding Americans quickly took up the Spanish offer. In 1788, Virginian Peter Bruin and nine other families settled on 680-acre tracts of land granted by the Spanish. Two American families who made the same journey had with them thirty-six and sixty-seven slaves, respectively. In the spring of 1792, two families from settlements in Tennessee arrived at Natchez. Led by Henry Hunter, a "Colonel in the American Service in the last War" who had "taken the oath of fidelity" to Spain, they carried with them at least eighteen slaves, reported the satisfied Spanish governor. Many more Americans followed in their wake. "The

Rage among the poorer class of people here appears to be for the Spanish settlements and I believe numbers will emigrate to that place in the spring & next summer," wrote one concerned Kentuckian in 1797.[10]

Spanish immigration policy wavered through the 1780s and 1790s, at times encouraging American emigration, at other times actively discouraging it. Yet the very inconsistency of Spanish policy, along with the willingness of Americans to swear an oath of allegiance to the Spanish crown, only deepened American policymakers' suspicions that something was afoul in the Spanish borderlands. Making matters worse, Spanish policy seemed especially effective at attracting western Americans "who have been disappointed in obtaining land" in Kentucky and Tennessee. Spanish officials offered free tracts of lands to actual settlers, but actively discouraged the speculation and land engrossment that made it so difficult for Americans to secure land in Kentucky and Tennessee. On the whole, American settlers in the lower Mississippi Valley seemed generally content under Spanish rule, adding to the concerns of American officials and policymakers charged with bolstering the American presence in the West.[11]

Other Spanish policies, again designed to attract immigrants, also furthered the growth of a plantation economy. Spanish officials encouraged American slaveholders to settle in the Natchez Country by offering guaranteed prices for tobacco, indigo, and staples commonly produced with slave labor. They also encouraged an increase in the slave population by eliminating import duties on the international slave trade. Slaveholders in the Natchez Country soon used slave labor profitably, producing a variety of foodstuffs, such as cattle for markets in New Orleans and the Spanish Floridas and small crops of indigo and tobacco supported by Spanish bounties. As planters and Spanish authorities transformed the Natchez Country from a society with slaves into a full-blown slave society, Eli Whitney's cotton gin set off what the historian Ira Berlin has aptly termed a "plantation revolution."[12]

In 1794, Natchez's slaves, settlers, and Indians produced a little over 36,000 pounds of cotton for export. In 1798, three years after Natchez received its first cotton gin, the coerced labor of slaves had produced over 1,200,000 pounds of cotton for the New Orleans market, thirty-three times larger than the crop from just four years earlier. In that same year, slaves produced a remarkable 2,500 bales of cotton for a single Natchez planter.[13] Traveling through the Natchez Country in 1797, a Philadelphia merchant marveled that cotton "cultivation is the only thing the inhabitants of this area are involved in." Indeed, "the region for 50 miles around" Natchez was now "inhabited by cotton planters of whom a part seem to be rich." The "present inhabitants" of Natchez were well on their way to creating a plantation society based on an insatiable appetite for slave labor. All knew that just as Spanish rule at Natchez was ending, the plantation economy was booming.[14]

In the midst of a plantation revolution, the white inhabitants of the Natchez Country needed "a judiciously formed government calculated for our soil situation." In simple terms, that meant a government that protected their investments in land and labor. "The enemies of the United States" soon tried to convince the inhabitants that neither would be safe under American rule. In doing so, they all but insured that the United States would sanction slavery when it created the Mississippi Territory in 1798.[15]

III

It was not until March 1798 that Congress created a government for the Mississippi Territory. From February 1797 through late 1798, responsibility for securing American authority around Natchez fell on the shoulders of secretary of state Timothy Pickering, a Massachusetts Federalist, and Andrew Ellicott, a Quaker surveyor from Pennsylvania. Ellicott's main duty was to receive possession of the Natchez Country from Spanish officials. He was to govern Natchez until his replacements arrived, at which time he would survey the boundary between Spanish West Florida and the United States, in accordance with the 1795 Treaty of San Lorenzo. Ellicott's mission was seasoned with trepidation from the start; it would soon be engulfed in paranoia.

Before Ellicott left Philadelphia for Natchez in September 1796, President George Washington warned him that the British and Spanish might be conspiring with disloyal Americans to block his mission. Ellicott's concerns only deepened as he traveled to Natchez. Along the Ohio River, he picked up rumors of British conspiracies to break off the West from the United States. Along the Mississippi River, he encountered Spanish officials seeking to stall his journey and prevent American possession of Natchez. When Ellicott finally arrived at Natchez in February 1797, he found a swirl of peoples and intrigue in a place where American influence seemingly vacillated between weak and nonexistent. Ellicott

soon found himself entertaining rumors that everyone—from the British
to the French to the Spanish to the Creeks—was planning to drive out
the Americans and claim Natchez as their own. Though foreign influence and settler discontent never ran as deep as Ellicott's and Pickering's
fears, both had a reasonable dread that Natchez would soon descend
into chaos.[16]

Until Congress created a territorial government for the region, Ellicott and a small contingent of American troops were responsible for
governing Natchez. Ellicott hoped to increase "our influence in the
country" and secure American rule by demonstrating to the "present
inhabitants" that the U.S. government would protect their interests.[17]
The most important "friends of the United States" in Natchez sat on the
Permanent Committee, a self-created, planter-dominated body of leading local men who had taken it upon themselves to govern Natchez.
The committee welcomed American rule, so long as it preserved "peace
and good order" and protected their interests, including their property
in slaves. Ellicott worked diligently to keep them and other "friends of
the United States" in the "interest of my country," but he feared that
three groups stood ready to undermine his mission. "The officers of his
Spanish Majesty," "those attached to the British interest," and "another
class, who had nothing to lose," all allegedly sought to alienate the white
settlers from the United States so that their favored empire could take
control. Confirming his suspicions, Ellicott soon found himself battling
conspiracies—both real and imagined—hatched by "the enemies of the
United States."[18]

The Spanish governor of the Natchez District, Manuel Gayoso, allegedly stood at the head of "the enemies of the United States," but Ellicott
most feared the leader of the British Loyalist community in Natchez, former military officer Anthony Hutchins. According to Ellicott, Hutchins
"was well known to have been at all times an enemy" to the United
States and "to republican forms of government." Ellicott suspected
that Hutchins was deeply involved in the Blount Conspiracy, a British
plan to use Americans to seize the lower Mississippi Valley for Britain.
Hutchins also had personal and financial reasons to oppose American
control of the Natchez Country. During the Revolutionary War a group
of Americans destroyed his plantation and took him hostage. Though
the British had granted him 152,000 acres of prime cotton-growing land
in the early 1770s, his claims would surely be contested under American

rule. Finally, Hutchins's opposition to American rule had support from the Natchez Loyalists, who, "from both principle and habit," wished to see Great Britain regain control of the region. Hutchins hoped to facilitate a British conquest of the Natchez Country, and Ellicott feared that Hutchins possessed the connections, cunning, and popular support needed to make that happen. Adding to Ellicott's concerns, his few trusted associates in Natchez warned him that Hutchins was devising a scheme to destroy any lingering support for an American Natchez.[19]

Hutchins knew well that popular white support for black slavery ran deep in the Natchez Country. Hutchins also knew that the Northwest Ordinance had made Natchez's white inhabitants suspicious about what American rule might spell for Natchez slavery. Accordingly, he made slavery's still undetermined future central to "his plans" to destroy popular support for American rule in Natchez. In the late summer of 1797, Hutchins and the "enemies of the United States" began circulating rumors that American rule would result in "the abolition of slavery." According to Hutchins, Ellicott and the United States believed "that slavery ought to be prohibited here, as in the Northwestern Territory." Hutchins and his allies' effectiveness at spreading the rumor made matters even more difficult for Ellicott. The rumors were "brought forward with so much art, propagated with so much address," that even settlers friendly toward the United States "have given them credit."[20]

Though Ellicott was a Pennsylvania Quaker of antislavery convictions, he could not allow his conscience to dictate his actions. Rumors of impending abolition threatened to destroy any lingering attachments the white inhabitants felt toward the United States. Ellicott scrambled to quash the rumors. In doing so, he hoped to undo the damage done by Hutchins and restore the inhabitants' confidence that the United States would protect their interests, including their interest in protecting slavery. Ellicott promptly issued circular letters, sending additional copies to trusted associates throughout the region. In the letters, he assured the white inhabitants that under American rule, slavery would be permitted "upon the same footing, that it is in the southern states."[21]

According to the historian David J. Libby, whites in the Natchez Country were "more loyal to the market than any sovereignty, and the opportunity to sell their products mattered more to them than retaining any nationality." More precisely, they were willing to attach their loyalties to whatever empire could best provide the conditions under which plantation slavery would thrive. Six months before Congress considered the problem of slavery in the yet to be created Mississippi Territory, an antislavery Quaker from Pennsylvania had already assured the planters and settlers that the United States would protect their "system of slavery," which was so essential to their burgeoning plantation regime. In the Southwest borderlands, the politics of intrigue and empire, along with popular support for slavery, were already overtaking the possibility that the United States might use its meager powers to halt slavery's expansion there.[22]

IV

Ellicott's assurances were strictly provisional. The ultimate decision rested with Congress, which still had the power to prohibit slavery in the soon to be created Mississippi Territory. It therefore became essential for Ellicott, Pickering, and the Permanent Committee to see that Congress did no such thing.

The Permanent Committee and the white inhabitants expected Ellicott to convey their concerns to the government; Ellicott obliged. Though slavery was "disagreeable to us northern people," Ellicott explained to Pickering that Congress needed to address realistically the problem of slavery in Natchez. "Slavery not being tolerated in the north-western territory" formed an important "objection" to American rule in Natchez. The white inhabitants still feared that American rule might spell the demise of slavery, even though slaves were already "numerous" in the region, and despite Ellicott's pledge. If the United States wanted to secure the loyalties of settlers in Natchez, then it would be "expedient" to allow slavery "upon the same footing it is at present in the Southern States."[23]

In case Congress or Pickering failed to heed Ellicott's advice, the Permanent Committee sent its own petition. The petitioners, who deemed themselves the "rational moderate and respectable part of the Community," protested that they welcomed American rule but opposed any measures to restrict slavery. "As is in the southern states," the "great part of the labor in this Country is performed by slaves," they explained. Without protections for slavery, the "farms in this District would be but of little more value to the present occupiers than equal quantity of waste land." "From this consideration," the committee requested that under American rule, "the system of slavery may be continued as heretofore."

Coming from the leading men of Natchez, who had formed their own government and exercised considerable influence over the inhabitants, this petition was more a demand than a request. By late 1797, the most important authorities in Natchez who remained friendly to American rule had communicated to the federal government the importance of slavery. If the United States wished the transition to go smoothly, then Congress had to assure the white inhabitants that it would protect Natchez's "system of slavery."[24]

In January 1798, President John Adams presented Pickering's report on the Mississippi Territory to Congress. The report contained excerpts and summaries from Ellicott's letters along with Pickering's own recommendations. It also detailed the United States's precarious hold on the Natchez Country. Pickering suggested that Congress act immediately to frame a government for the territory. Otherwise, "the inconveniences and mischiefs which may result from leaving a population of five thousand persons, for any length of time, without the powers of government," would leave the Natchez Country vulnerable to foreign intrigue, as Ellicott had repeatedly warned. Pickering made sure to include Ellicott's recommendations on slavery. Like Ellicott, Pickering was a foe of both slavery and planters. But like Ellicott, too, Pickering believed that the United States could secure the Natchez Country only by protecting slavery there. Pickering counseled that Congress create a government the same as that "established for the Northwestern Territory . . . with the exception respecting *slaves.*" Basing his decision on the advice of an antislavery Quaker Federalist from Pennsylvania, Massachusetts Federalist Timothy Pickering recommended that Congress ignore the precedent of the Northwest Ordinance and permit slavery in the Mississippi Territory.[25]

In March 1798, the House of Representatives acted on Pickering's suggestion and began work on a bill to create a government for the Mississippi Territory. Ellicott's and Pickering's recommendations made it unlikely that Congress would prohibit slavery there; the circumstances under which Congress debated the issue made it even less likely. George Thatcher proposed prohibiting slavery in Mississippi in the aftermath of a series of tumultuous debates over slavery, just as fears about continued union between the East and West were rising to new heights and immediately after Congress received word that war with France was likely. These concerns about both slavery and union would profoundly affect the course of debate on Thatcher's proposal. It soon became clear that the question of slavery in the Mississippi Territory involved more than a simple decision to permit or prohibit slavery at the discretion of southern congressmen and their supposed northern allies.[26]

Immediately after Thatcher introduced and then defended his proposal, South Carolina Federalist Robert Goodloe Harper rose and went on the offensive. As long as the opponents of expansion debated the issue on the grounds that it involved the incompatibility of slavery and republican government, along with the simple question of permitting or prohibiting slavery, a case in their favor could be made. Harper recognized this and quickly shifted the terms of debate. According to Harper and the Federalists who followed him, at issue was not just an abstract conflict between slavery and freedom, or even a question of American slaveholders' interests in seeing slavery expand. Instead, Harper insisted that Congress had to consider the effects of Thatcher's proposal on popular support for American rule in Natchez.

Harper accepted that "in the Northwest Territory the regulation forbidding slavery was a very proper one." The settlers in the Northwest "were from parts where slavery did not prevail," and "they had of course no slaves amongst them." The situation in Mississippi was profoundly different. Because slavery was "that species of property [that] already exists" in the territory, "it would be improper to make such a regulation." At best, the ban "could not . . . be carried into effect," because it "struck the customs of the people," slaveholders who knew the value of slave labor on the Southwest frontier. At worst, it would "be a decree of banishment to all persons settled there," persons who would rather live under some other government if the United States insisted on prohibiting slavery.[27]

Massachusetts Republican Joseph Varnum answered Harper's concerns, asking Congress to show "a proper respect for the rights of mankind" by seriously considering Thatcher's motion. Federalist John Rutledge Jr. quickly laid waste to Varnum's creeping radicalism. Rutledge, also a South Carolinian, defended the honor of southerners who held others in slavery, denounced rabble-rousers like Thatcher and Varnum who "bring forward the Southern States in an odious light," and reminded Congress that free black and Quaker petitions had created "the most angry debate" just months before. Rutledge, like Harper before him, also offered more than typical South Carolinian proslavery belligerence when attacking Thatcher's proposal. Rutledge, too, raised concerns centering on American authority in Natchez. Congress would be "addressing these people" by saying: "We have made a treaty which puts you under the mild Government of the United States, but we must take from you your property; or, rather, we must set your blacks at liberty to cut your throats. The rights of man was the watch-word of the day, and Congress had determined that you shall not possess this property." According to Rutledge, Thatcher and Varnum allegedly proposed planting the seeds of a Haitian-style rebellion, policy that would sink the United States' sagging reputation in Natchez even further.[28]

Rutledge's speech was a tough act to follow; Massachusetts Federalist Harrison Gray Otis proved up to the task. Otis conjured up fantasies of black savages slaughtering innocent whites in a manner that surely made his fellow Federalists from South Carolina proud. "If the amendment prevailed," it would "of course declare that no slavery shall exist in the Natchez country," began Otis. This would not only be "a sentence of banishment," as Harper had warned, "but of war" against the slaveholding whites of Mississippi. Once word of the prohibition on slavery reached Natchez, "an immediate insurrection" against the United States "would probably take place," as the white inhabitants would find it impossible to live under a government that failed to protect their property in slaves. The "inhabitants would not be suffered to retire in peace," however. Instead, they would "be massacred on the spot" by slaves who would surely rise up and exploit the divisions, as had slaves in Haiti.[29]

Otis's warning, like those of his colleagues from South Carolina, cut two ways. On the one hand, he defended the unassailable rights of southern slaveholders and their claims on the Southwest. On the other, he strengthened his objections to Thatcher's proposal by further shifting the terms of debate. What began as a clash between slavery and freedom became a conflict between prohibiting slavery and weakening the Union in the strategically vital lower Mississippi Valley. According to the Federalists, the question confronting Congress was not whether to permit or prohibit slavery expansion but whether to incorporate Mississippi into the Union with slavery, or not at all.

Otis and the South Carolinians of course had other reasons for so fiercely opposing Thatcher's amendment. Their desire to see slavery expand into the Southwest meant they would have opposed Thatcher regardless of the circumstances. Yet the more important point is not that they masked their motives but that they could so easily exploit congressional fears of white disaffection in Natchez. Indeed, the concerns of Pennsylvania Federalist Thomas Hartley illustrate that even opponents of slavery expansion believed that the issue involved much more than proslavery or antislavery dispositions grounded in sectional and partisan interests.

Hartley had long opposed slavery; in the 1790s he worked closely with the Pennsylvania Abolition Society, and as a member of the Foster Committee, in 1790 recommended that Congress more stringently regulate the institution. Yet the undoubtedly antislavery Hartley joined his fellow Federalists from South Carolina and Massachusetts in opposing Thatcher's restrictions. Hartley had originally "intended" to introduce his own proposal for applying Article VI to the Mississippi Territory. "But, on inquiry" into the state of affairs in Natchez, he "found so many difficulties in the way that he was obliged to abandon it." The chief difficulty was that slavery was already well established in Natchez. Article VI "would be a serious attack upon, the property of that country," an attack that would only incite further discontent with American rule. Hartley, who was disinclined to conjure up fantasies of savage black slaves slitting the throats of their masters like his Federalist colleagues Otis and Rutledge, simply feared that the "present amendment, if carried, would be attended with bad effects" in Natchez.[30]

Pennsylvania Republican Albert Gallatin and Massachusetts Republican Joseph Varnum masterfully defended Thatcher's proposal, even as Thatcher's fellow Federalists abandoned him. Varnum pleaded with his colleagues to support the prohibition, launching into a free-soil argument and denouncing the gross inconsistency of slavery in the United States. Gallatin's support was all the more significant. By 1798 he had emerged as one of the House leaders of the Republican opposition. Like Varnum, Gallatin presented many good reasons to apply Article VI to Mississippi. Yet none addressed the issues raised by Hartley, Harper, Rutledge, and Otis. Indeed, the best Gallatin could do was plea for consistency on western slavery. "Having determined slavery was bad policy for the Northwestern Territory," he "saw no reason for a contrary determination with respect to this territory."[31]

Most of his fellow congressmen did. Thatcher, Varnum, and Gallatin tried to debate whether the expansion of slavery clashed with the ideals of the American experiment in republican government. Otis, Harper, and Rutledge refused to debate this question and instead turned it into a vote on inviting rebellion in Natchez. They did this so effectively because a Pennsylvania Quaker in Natchez, an antislavery Pennsylvania Federalist in the House, and the antislavery secretary of state from Massachusetts all agreed with the South Carolinians and their ally Harrison Gray Otis. It is perhaps most surprising that eleven representatives actually voted for Thatcher's proposal, given the dire warnings, suspicions, and concerns about American influence in the lower Mississippi Valley. In the end, Congress's decision reflected a desire not so much to open Mississippi to American slaveholders' expansion, but rather to accommodate those slaveholders already there.[32]

Though Thatcher's motion received only twelve supporting votes on Friday, March 23, some members of the House seem to have devised a plan to preempt Thatcher if he tried to force the issue when the House reconvened on the following Monday. When the House resumed debate, Georgia Republican John Milledge moved to add an amendment to the Mississippi bill. Milledge's motion acknowledged that "the people" of the Mississippi Territory "shall be entitled to and enjoy all and singular the rights, privileges, and advantages granted to the people" of the Northwest Territory, but it said nothing about slavery. Robert Goodloe Harper, mollifying politicians concerned about the growth of slavery, then moved to shut the international slave trade out of the territory. Thatcher then tried to change the wording of Harper's amendment to ban the further introduction of any slaves into the territory, but not a single representative seconded his motion.[33]

As passed, "An Act for the Government of the Mississippi Territory" authorized the president "to establish a government in all respects similar to that now exercised in the territory northwest of the river Ohio, excepting and excluding the last article."[34] Congress would permit slavery in the Mississippi Territory; Timothy Pickering could hardly wait to inform Andrew Ellicott of the good news.

V

On March 27, the day after the House voted down Thatcher's amendment for the second time, Pickering penned a brief note for Andrew Ellicott in Natchez. Pickering "intended to have sent" Ellicott "a long letter" with the dispatches leaving for Natchez, but other "business of great moment" meant that he could include only the two most important pieces of information. The first involved "intelligence" that Spain would remove its remaining troops from the Natchez Country. The second, "a bill for erecting a temporary government for the Natchez Country" was likely to become law within days. "The plan is the same as that for the North Western Territory," explained Pickering, "with the exception respecting slaves." To insure that there was no confusion about the status of slavery in the Mississippi Territory, Pickering reiterated for Ellicott that "the inhabitants may keep slaves." Of all the pressing matters involved with establishing a territorial government for the region—disputes over land, authority for negotiating with the region's Indian powers, and reconciling the inhabitants to American rule— Pickering saw fit to send Ellicott but one piece of information to relate to the white inhabitants; the U.S. government would give full sanction to slavery in the territory.[35]

When Pickering found the time to draft a lengthier dispatch to Ellicott a few days later, he again included information respecting slavery and the politics of competing empires. Mostly, the letter was a lengthy diatribe against the threat that France and war posed to the American Union. But Pickering did not forget to mention the law, now on the books, creating a government "the same as that for the territory N. W. of the Ohio, with the exception respecting slaves." Pickering sent a similar letter to Winthrop Sargent, secretary of the Northwest Territory. Pickering informed Sargent of his nomination as governor of Mississippi and expressed his hope that he "will not decline the acceptance of this office." The United States's tenuous hold on Mississippi made it "peculiarly necessary that a man of energy, of application to business, and a *military character,* should be charged with this new government." As for the details of that government, Sargent had to know only that it was "the same with that for the Territory northwest of the Ohio, except that Slavery is admitted." Pickering explained succinctly why Congress failed to extend Article VI to Mississippi: "Almost all the inhabitants are possessed of slaves."[36]

In August 1798, Governor Sargent presided over a ceremony marking the opening of the new territorial government. He reminded those gathered for the occasion that the U.S. government would protect slavery, "in special indulgence to the people of this Territory." With slavery secure, slaveholders and aspiring slaveholders in Natchez returned to fighting over other matters: speculating in land, battling over overlapping land claims, fighting over appointments to office, and indulging in general factional and partisan bickering. Leading men no longer divided into British, Spanish, and American cabals. Instead, they had broken into two factions, self-proclaimed Republicans and Federalists. Even Anthony Hutchins, the former British subject who had caused Andrew Ellicott so much trouble, proclaimed his Republican loyalties by 1801.[37]

While the white inhabitants fought over land claims, debts, offices, and party, their slaves were busily transforming the cotton frontier. By 1801 Secretary of State James Madison was receiving reports that "the whole district of Natchez is engaged in raising cotton and by report they will export to the value of 600,000 dollars, this year." By December, Governor William Claiborne expected the cotton crop to "exceed 700,000 Dollars." With the cotton boom on, "labor here, is more valuable, than in any part of the United States." American rule was undoubtedly safe for slavery.[38]

By 1802, Claiborne had grown quite confident that the Mississippi Territory was safely in American hands. Despite remaining obstacles such as faulty land titles, guaranteed access to the Mississippi River and New Orleans, and French and British designs on the region, he found "an opinion generally prevails in this District, that the Liberty, Peace, & safety" of Mississippi "greatly depend upon the preservation of our present National Union." Within two years, Claiborne would find himself governing the new territory of Louisiana. His ability to persuade white Louisianans that their interests were best served by American rule would be sorely tested, for Congress decided to overlook the lessons of Natchez and place severe restrictions on slavery in Louisiana.[39]

3

"Grant Us to Make Slaves of Others"

The Louisiana Purchase, 1802–1805

B y late 1804, the white inhabitants of the newly acquired Louisiana Purchase territories had grown quite discontented with American rule. That fall, "the representatives elected by the freemen of their respective districts" in Upper Louisiana met in St. Louis to protest their new territorial government, or as they deemed it, the "entire privation of some of the dearest rights enjoyed by *freemen!*" A motley assortment of French traders and farmers, expatriated Americans, and a few holdout Spanish officials, the "freemen" meeting in St. Louis especially feared that the United States might deprive them of their right to buy and hold slaves. They had good reason to worry. The host of restrictions that Congress placed on slavery in the Louisiana Purchase seemed "calculated to abolish slavery at a future day altogether."[1]

In 1804 a Republican-controlled Congress defied the testy demands of white Louisianans, the recommendations of Thomas Jefferson, and the interests of southern slaveholders to place severe restrictions on slavery in the Louisianas.[2] Congress only narrowly defeated a proposal to prohibit slavery expansion in the Louisianas entirely. Despite this setback, Congress outlawed both the international and domestic slave trades, limiting the further introduction of slaves to American citizens "removing into said Territory for actual settlement, and being, at the time of such removal, *bona fide* owner of such slave or slaves." The laws for Louisiana also provided stiff penalties for violations of the prohibited slave trades. Slaves sold in or into the Louisianas by American citizens received immediate freedom, as did any slaves imported through the international slave trade.[3]

To white Louisianans, these laws seemed tantamount to a plan of gradual abolition. From planter grandees in New Orleans to small farmers in St. Louis, white Louisianans expressed outrage at slavery laws that heralded the destruction of "our country." They also hinted at rebellion and disunion if Congress insisted on restricting their right to buy and hold slaves.[4] Fearful that white Louisianans might act on their threats, Congress quietly failed to renew the bulk of the restrictions on slavery the following year. As in Natchez, the problem of slavery in the Louisiana Purchase involved more than Congress and the president making a simple decision to permit or prohibit expansion. Instead, Congress realized that they had to decide whether to accept Louisiana with slavery, or lose Louisiana entirely if it insisted on maintaining the anti-expansion laws.

I

In October 1803 the Philadelphia *Aurora and General Advertiser* published a "letter from a gentlemen . . . relating to Louisiana." The writer counseled Congress to exempt the entire Louisiana Purchase from Article VI of the Northwest Ordinance. The United States could best accommodate the "interests and conveniences" of white Louisianans, including their interest in slavery, by establishing a government "similar to that of the Mississippi Territory." The staunchly Republican editor of the *Aurora*, William Duane, published the letter but scorned the writer and his plea. Under American rule, "the gradual abolition" of slavery in Louisiana would be "a measure confidently to be looked for." American settlers would prove that "three or four hundred white farmers" were capable of producing more sugar "than a negro estate with two thousand slaves." According to Duane, American republicanism and the prosperity generated by free American settlers would banish the aristocratic and archaic slave regime from Louisiana forever. Unlike Duane, however, white Louisianans themselves proved far less enthusiastic about a free-soil Louisiana.[5]

In Upper Louisiana, slavery was an important institution. The French, Spanish, American, and British inhabitants in Upper Louisiana had long used slave labor in their mixed agricultural and fur-trading economy, as had the region's many Indian nations.[6] In the 1790s two developments spurred the growth of the institution in the ancient French settlements strung along the Mississippi and Missouri rivers in present-day Missouri. The expansion of plantation slavery in Lower Louisiana increased demand for foodstuffs and other commodities downriver at New Orleans. As New Orleans planters devoted more attention to the production of cash crops like cotton and sugar, they and their slaves gave less attention to the production of staples, opening new markets for farmers, traders, and slaveholders in Upper Louisiana. Meanwhile, the American exclusion of slavery in the Northwest drove some American and French slaveholders from the Illinois Country to "the Spanish side of the Mississippi." When the United States took possession of Upper Louisiana in late 1803, slaves accounted for between one-fourth and one-third of the population in the main settlements at St. Louis, St. Genevieve, and Cape Girardeau. Though long neglected by successive French and Spanish rulers, Upper Louisiana had become a small but thriving slave society in the 1790s.[7]

On receiving word of the cession of Louisiana to the United States, white Upper Louisianans immediately expressed apprehension about the future of slavery under American rule. One American official in the region advised Thomas Jefferson that most settlers in Upper Louisiana remained "averse" to American rule if it was accompanied by "the liberation of their slaves (of which they have great numbers)." Other Americans familiar with Upper Louisiana sent similar letters eastward. Louisianans were "very much interested in obtaining an unlimited slavery," wrote one American official from the West. That interest left them "very much divided on the score of becoming American citizens . . . lest their slaves should be liberated." The "sooner their minds can be quieted on that subject the better," he added, forewarning Congress to address the concerns of white Louisianans who remained ambivalent about their future in the American Union. Meriwether Lewis wrote of a more menacing situation. On arriving in Upper Louisiana, Lewis found circulating "a report that *the Americans would emancipate their slaves immediately on taking possession of the country*." These concerns extended beyond a small slaveholding class, encompassing almost the whole of white society in Upper Louisiana. "There appears to be a general objection not only among the French, but even among the Americans not slaveholders," continued Lewis, "to relinquish the right which they claim relative to slavery in its present unqualified form."[8]

Because "many of them hold a considerable part of their estate in that species of property," restricting slavery in Upper Louisiana was just about the worst thing the U.S. government could do if it expected annexation to go smoothly. Upper Louisiana remained worlds away from the plantation revolution remaking the lower Mississippi Valley. Yet even in Upper Louisiana, the turmoil over slavery in Natchez threatened to play itself out all over again. Before Congress even considered the future of slavery in Upper Louisiana, the white inhabitants, who were at best indifferent about American possession, were already demanding that the United States protect their right "to slavery in its present unqualified form."[9]

Even more than their counterparts to the north, white Lower Louisianans tied their future to unimpeded access to slave labor. Like Natchez, for much of the eighteenth century Louisiana remained only marginally incorporated into the trans-Atlantic economy. The Natchez Indian Rebellion of 1729, in which several hundred African slaves either participated or were taken captive, was but the most spectacular incident of slave and Indian rebellion that persistently thwarted French efforts to create a plantation society in Louisiana. Slavery remained an important institution after 1730, but as Ira Berlin notes, "There was no confusing Louisiana with a plantation regime." The Spanish gained control of Louisiana in 1763, but the slave regime soon suffered another blow. The American War for Independence carried sporadic fighting into the region, accelerating the growth of the free black population through manumissions, self-purchases, and running away. As in Natchez, however, the stagnation of slavery in Louisiana took an abrupt turn in the 1780s, when Spanish officials adopted policies to attract planters and spur the growth of a plantation economy.[10]

Spanish policies promoted a modicum of stability and nurtured the slow but steady growth of Louisiana slavery after 1780. Spanish bounties for cash crops, tighter regulation of free and enslaved blacks, and a new emphasis on the international slave trade in the 1780s combined to set the stage for the explosive growth of plantation slavery in the mid-1790s. North of New Orleans, settlers with land, labor, and capital focused on cotton production. South of New Orleans, a longer, warmer growing season led some planters to experiment with sugar. Sugar production required considerable expertise, capital, and labor. In the mid-1790s Louisiana received all three from French planters fleeing rebellious slaves on Saint Domingue. When the United States acquired Louisiana in 1803, French Creole planters and Spanish officials were well on their way to creating a plantation society that rivaled the Caribbean in both its potential for profit and its insatiable demand for slave labor.[11]

Travelers in the lower Mississippi Valley expressed astonishment at the rapid growth of sugar plantations around New Orleans. "This city and all the countryside" offered "a brilliant and easy fortune to be made through the sugar refineries which are multiplying every day," recorded a Philadelphia merchant in 1799. Seeking their own "brilliant and easy fortune," planters and aspiring planters quickly put uncultivated land into production. In 1802 the American traveler John Sibley observed an unbroken string of sugar plantations along a 250-mile stretch of the river. Though sugar had been planted for only a few years, Sibley was astonished at how effectively planters had shifted production to cultivating their new cash crop while devoting their profits toward acquiring more land and slaves. Indeed, sugar production so consumed planters that Sibley speculated "a person might make a fortune" by producing vegetables for the market at New Orleans; the planters were too preoccupied "to attend to so small matters" as the production of food. The planters' fortunes simply awed Sibley, who noted that in 1801 the seventy-two plantations in the immediate vicinity of New Orleans had produced a sugar crop valued at over $300,000 at market.[12]

Observers invariably drew the connection between the plantation revolution and a constant influx of slaves from the international slave trade. One seasoned French traveler concluded that the demand for slaves was "higher in Louisiana than in any other French colony." With "so much land to cultivate," planters could not find "enough" slave labor to work it. Traveling through the Mississippi Valley between 1801 and 1803, another French observer remarked that slavery "must continue many succeeding ages" in Lower Louisiana if France hoped to make it profitable. Unaware of events in Madrid and Paris, he hoped that France would soon reclaim Louisiana and erect a new mid-continent colony, which would include "the Western States of America." If France wished "to derive advantage" from his planned supercolony, then slavery "must either subsist, or the colonies be lost."[13]

The importance of slavery in Louisiana would not be lost on American policymakers. In late 1803, Daniel Clark, the unofficial American consul at New Orleans, drafted a lengthy letter for officials in Washington, detailing the importance of cotton, sugar, and slaves in Louisiana. The widely circulated "Description of Louisiana" cited Clark's figures and provided an even clearer picture of the connections between planters and slaves, sugar and cotton. The most ambitious planters in Lower Louisiana estimated that anywhere from one-third to one-half of the land there "might be planted in cane." The "Description" also noted that extensive sugar lands held under French and Spanish grants had yet to be cultivated because planters lacked slaves to work them. Finally, with farmers upriver providing "a regular supply of provisions," planters could devote their slaves' labors even more fully to the production of sugar. Clark's letter and the "Description" sounded ominous warnings about the plantation revolution remaking Lower Louisiana.[14]

Other widely read American accounts of Lower Louisiana furthered expectations that the United States—like its French and Spanish predecessors—must protect slavery there. In 1802 the American minister to France Robert Livingston drafted a memorial encouraging Napoleon to sell part of France's newly acquired lower Mississippi Valley holdings to the United States. The memorial warned French officials that Lower Louisiana could be made profitable only by laying out massive amounts of capital for the purchase of slaves, capital that France could ill afford to expend if it wished to hold on to its already battered empire. Livingston hoped to scare France away from Louisiana by playing up the expenses of a far-off plantation colony dependent on slave labor, but his larger point was not lost on his American readers. American newspapers reprinted Livingston's memorial; few doubted its maxim that Louisiana's "cultivation is to be carried on, as in all warm climates, by slaves." Federalist critics who harped on Livingston's memorial to justify their opposition to the Purchase only fed convictions that "a still more numerous race from *Africa* must be violently brought in, to toil and bleed under the lash" in Louisiana. The list of crops detailed in newspaper descriptions—everything from sugar to rice to tobacco and cotton—made the connections between Lower Louisiana's future and the growth of slavery inescapable.[15]

No congressman in Washington could doubt that the United States had acquired far more than an outlet on the Mississippi River. Lower Louisiana seemed second to none when it came to the production of plantation staples, and the region was clearly in the midst of a plantation boom. Indeed, when the Senate began debating the future of slavery in Louisiana, John Quincy Adams spent his evenings reading accounts not of Louisiana or the Mississippi Valley, but of the West Indies, the international slave trade, and the production of cash crops in the tropics.[16] The host of reports, letters, and descriptions circulating established that the future of slavery in the Louisiana Purchase involved considerations far more complicated than any simple decision to permit or prohibit the institution's expansion. The Louisianas were no Northwest Territory lightly settled by European Americans and only barely touched by slavery. In both Louisianas, the once neglected institution was booming; white Louisianans were already expressing concerns about the institution's future.

II

With white Louisianans clamoring for the "importation of slaves," Thomas Jefferson sensed an opportunity to implement his evolving notions of "diffusion." Diffusion would work best if the United States prohibited the international slave trade to Louisiana, but permitted the domestic slave trade. Without access to the international slave trade, white Louisianans would prove ready buyers of American slaves from "overstocked" slave regions, like the Chesapeake. The domestic slave trade to Louisiana would also boost Chesapeake planters' declining fortunes and thin out the Chesapeake's growing black population, which seemed especially large and dangerous in the wake of Gabriel's Conspiracy in Virginia and the slave rebellion in Haiti. Finally, the process of diffusion offered some hope to planters still troubled by slavery. If the domestic slave trade and migration to the Louisianas drained off enough of their black population, Upper South states might be able to enact gradual abolition laws.[17]

In November 1803, Jefferson asked Senator John Breckinridge to introduce in Congress a territorial bill implementing his vision of diffusion. Provided that Congress would go along with his plan, Jefferson's proposal would placate edgy Louisiana planters, serve as a panacea for the ills of the Chesapeake, and satisfy expansionist American slaveholders who looked forward to settlement in the West. Congress, however, had its own agenda. As Pennsylvania Republican Samuel Maclay explained to his Senate colleagues, Louisiana "was purchased to serve as an outlet for the U.S.—to admit slaves there will defeat that object."[18]

On January 23, 1804, the Pennsylvania Abolition Society presented a petition to the Senate requesting that it prohibit both the domestic and international slave trades to the Louisiana Purchase. The following day, Connecticut Federalist James Hillhouse proposed prohibiting the international slave trade to the territory. No South Carolinians were present to disrupt the debates with threats of disunion, and the Senate found itself engaged in a far-reaching discussion of the future of slavery in the West and the place of the Louisianas in the Union. In the end, worries about securing Louisiana in the Union shaped the laws governing slavery expansion as much as competing proslavery and antislavery interests in Washington.[19]

Vigorous objections to Hillhouse's proposed ban came from rather unlikely quarters in the Senate. Republicans Samuel Smith of Maryland and Israel Smith of Vermont both expressed their undying hatred of the international slave trade. Both, however, feared that prohibiting it would only anger white Louisianans, exacerbating an already precarious situation in the lower Mississippi Valley. Yet the most strenuous objections to Hillhouse's proposal came from an even more unlikely alliance. Georgia Republican James Jackson and New Jersey Federalist Jonathan Dayton enthusiastically and repeatedly voiced their support for the international slave trade. The Senate needed to lay its moral scruples aside if it hoped to gain fabulous Caribbean-style riches from Louisiana, they explained. They also made sure to exploit fears about the weakness of American authority in the lower Mississippi Valley. Louisiana planters would gain access to the international slave trade with or without congressional sanction, they explained. At best, the restriction would be ineffective. At worst, it might just incite rebellion among white Louisianans clamoring for unfettered access to more slaves.[20]

For all their admonishments and dire warnings, Dayton and Jackson made little headway with their colleagues. Delaware Federalist Samuel White denied that there was any reason to permit the international slave trade, let alone recognize slavery there. Indeed, White believed it was the United States's "duty to prevent as far as possible, the horrid evil of slavery" in Louisiana. Not only could Congress assist Louisiana in "avoid[ing] the fate of St. Domingo" by prohibiting the international slave trade, they could bring to Louisiana all the benefits of free labor, which White detailed in an extended free-soil argument. Regardless of whether senators agreed with White's vision of a free-soil Louisiana, revulsion against the international slave trade and fears that Caribbean-style riches meant Caribbean-style slave revolts were reasons enough to prohibit it. The Senate outlawed the international slave trade by a vote of 21 to 6. Despite Louisianans' well-documented dependence on it, along with Jackson's, Dayton's, and the Smiths' well-founded warnings that a prohibition would only incite white Louisianans, the Senate cut Louisiana off from its most important source of slave labor.[21]

During the debates over the international slave trade, several senators expressed concerns that planters and merchants would find loopholes to import foreign slaves to the territory. The Senate quickly moved to close them. Hillhouse proposed prohibiting the carrying to the territory of any slave that had arrived in the United States after 1798. This motion, aimed at South Carolina and Georgia's continued importation of slaves, passed 21 to 7 with little debate. Though Congress lacked the authority to prohibit the international trade to Georgia and South Carolina until 1808, they proved willing to restrict what slaveholders and slave traders from the United States could do with the slaves they imported. Georgians and South Carolinians could continue importing foreign slaves. They could not, however, use or sell them in the Louisiana Purchase territories.[22]

Another source of slaves and planter grandees was the Caribbean. Rocked by slave rebellions and watching their economy decline during the wars of the French Revolution, in the early 1790s French Caribbean planters had begun migrating to Louisiana, where they were instrumental in furthering the plantation revolution. The Senate dealt another blow to the burgeoning slave regime in Louisiana by expressly prohibiting foreigners immigrating to Louisiana from carrying their slaves with them. This prohibition, of course, served multiple purposes. It kept potentially rebellious slaves from the French Caribbean from carrying the infection of rebellion to American shores. It also would limit the growth of the French Creole population, hastening the "Americanization" of Louisiana and its eventual incorporation into the Union. But the prohibition also reflected larger concerns for limiting the growth of slavery. No planter grandees from the Caribbean would be allowed to make a new start in Louisiana, as they had been doing for over a decade.[23]

With the prohibition of the international slave trade and the closing of loopholes, Congress cut Louisiana off from any foreign slaves or slaveholders. Historians tend to slight the prohibition on the international slave trade, but this overlooks Louisiana's dependence on it. Neither Congress nor white Louisianans expected that a barely established trading system carrying slaves from the Chesapeake to Louisiana would replace the already well-established international slave trade. If fully implemented, the prohibitions on the importation of any foreign slaves would deny white Louisianans their most steady and important source of slave labor. Both Congress and white Louisianans recognized that this would retard, if not reverse, the plantation revolution that was remaking the lower Mississippi Valley.[24]

Prohibiting the international slave trade was an important first step toward curbing the growth of slavery in Louisiana. Yet any serious plan to limit slavery in the early American West required that Congress address the expansion of American slavery into the Louisianas. The Senate debated what was, in effect, a plan of gradual emancipation to be applied to American slaveholders settling in the Louisiana Purchase territories. Under the Senate proposal, any adult slave carried by an American into the Louisianas would receive his or her freedom after living in the territory for one year. Younger slaves brought there by Americans would receive their freedom at the ages of twenty-one and eighteen for females and males, respectively. While the Senate proposal failed to go as far as the Northwest Ordinance's Article VI, it would have severely limited American slaveholders' expansion into the Purchase territories. The Senate, however, failed to pass the measure; Federalists Timothy Pickering and John Quincy Adams and Ohio Republican John Smith joined a nearly solid South to defeat it by a vote of 17 to 11.[25]

Despite the defeat of the Senate amendment, the House took up the matter in the midst of a rancorous debate over South Carolina's reopening of the international slave trade. Historians often point out that a Connecticut Federalist introduced the defeated and limited Senate proposal; however, they overlook the fact that a northern Republican actually guided a complete prohibition on slavery through the Republican-controlled House. New Jersey Republican James Sloan proposed "inhibiting the admission of slaves into Louisiana, as well from the

United States, as from foreign places." By a narrow 40 to 36 margin, the House passed Sloan's proposal to stop the further introduction of any slaves into the Louisianas, whether via the international slave trade, the domestic slave trade, or by actual American settlers. The House bill, however, failed to become law, as the Senate would not agree to a complete prohibition.[26]

Congress's ultimate failure to adopt these two proposals illustrates some of the limits of antislavery politics in the early republic. Certain senators refused to endorse any plan limiting American slaveholders access to the Southwest, or to vote for a federally sponsored plan of gradual emancipation. The interests of southern slaveholders certainly contributed to the defeat of these two proposals. But another consideration weighed heavily in the decision allowing American slaveholders' access to the Louisiana Purchase.

The United States had purchased Louisiana because it needed to secure for western Americans access to the Mississippi River and the port at New Orleans. As the entire commerce of the trans-Appalachian West flowed down the Mississippi, whoever controlled the lower Mississippi Valley could also control the West, a fact that kept alive French and British ambitions for a new mid-continent empire that included the western parts of the United States. The security of the entire trans-Appalachian West rested on a secure Louisiana. That, in turn, rested not on the good will of southern planters in Congress, but on the intentions—already too obvious—of empire builders in Paris, Madrid, and London. It also rested on the willingness of white Louisianans and western Americans to be seduced by European imperialists proposing more favorable terms than anything the United States might be willing or able to offer. Ultimately, the antislavery wishes of some congressmen had to compete with larger concerns for incorporating the Louisianas peacefully and permanently into the now dangerously overextended republic.[27]

Congressmen, federal officials, and political observers expected little commitment to the American Union from either footloose American westerners or white Louisianans. French Louisianans inspired a fit of intemperance in the normally temperate secretary of the treasury, Albert Gallatin, the influential Jeffersonian Republican from Pennsylvania. They were "but one degree above the French West Indians, than whom a more ignorant and depraved race of civilized men did not exist," wrote

Gallatin. "Give them slaves and let them speak French (for they cannot write it)," he continued, "and they would be satisfied." Others dismissed white Louisianans for being "unacquainted with our language, customs, laws, and all the ordinary principles of the policy of our government." One senator warned his colleagues that "those people are absolutely incapable of governing themselves." Another feared that "they are not yet bound to us by any ties." It was "monstrous," quipped the *Philadelphia Port Folio,* to suppose that white Louisianans, "being chiefly Spaniards and French, and totally unaccustomed to republican institutions, should all of a sudden be expected to forget their former allegiances and turn United States-men." The "mixture of American, English, Spanish & French," the "5,000 militia, all foreigners & Frenchmen," and the "two thousand boatmen from the back country" with "dissipated habits, unruly tempers, & lawless conduct" hardly seemed fit material upon which to build a lasting presence in the farthest reaches of the early American West.[28]

Officials and Americans in Lower Louisiana communicated similar concerns. John Sibley was "astonished at the misrepresentations" about the United States that Louisianans opposed to American rule had spread. More threatening, Daniel Clark warned Secretary of State Madison that the United States should not count on white westerners, including Americans, to bring the region under American control. "If even the slightest advantage were held out" to western Americans by European powers, or if "they could be made to believe they would find their Interest in seceding" from the United States, the "majority of them" would do so. Far too many westerners were "indifferent about their Country or at least indifferent about the effect French measures may produce on the Union provided they derive a temporary benefit from them." This problem seemed especially troublesome, because "every Frenchmen in Office in this Country" looked for opportunities to encourage discontent with the United States. The former monarchical subjects of the Louisianas seemed unfit for republican government and incapable of understanding the benefits of the American Union, leaving them especially susceptible to British, Spanish, and French intrigues. Worse still, their American counterparts were apparently little better. American officials endlessly worried that "ignorant" white Louisianans and western Americans might "be easily imposed upon" by men whose agenda would not be served by an American Louisiana.[29]

Securing the Louisiana Purchase demanded that Congress create a "torrent of emigration" led by "loyal" American settlers who already understood the benefits of the American Union. Officials in the Mississippi Valley wrote repeatedly of the importance of encouraging "numerous Americans" to settle in Louisiana. The Louisianas would "be the source of continual trouble" for the United States so long as the inhabitants were "from all Countries" and "a variety of sentiment and discordant opinion prevails among them." American control of Louisiana remained in peril "until a majority of Americans settles in that Country," wrote an American judge in Natchez to his son in Congress. "The American population must be increased, . . . it must be made to overbalance that of every other description of persons," wrote another official. "The character, the manners, the language of the country must become American if we wish the Government to be such."[30]

This need forced Congress and federal officials to pass and implement policy that would rapidly increase the American population in Louisiana. As the secretary of the treasury, Albert Gallatin explicitly shaped his land survey-and-sale policies to bolster American authority in Louisiana. Writing to a federal land agent in Louisiana in 1806, Albert Gallatin conveyed the federal government's overwhelming interest in seeing that Louisiana lands not claimed under the Spanish and French regimes be quickly surveyed so that they could be sold to American settlers. Rapid survey and sale was "intimately connected with the welfare & even safety of that newly acquired territory," explained Gallatin, "for it is the only portion where any great increase of American population can take place, and I need not comment on the importance of that object." Some congressmen even proposed offering 160-acre land grants to entice thirty thousand American militiamen, "not at present residing in [Louisiana] or in the Mississippi Territory," to settle there. The same concerns that shaped federal land policy—a desire to settle Louisiana with American citizens—would similarly rein in Congress's willingness to shut slavery out of Louisiana entirely.[31]

Ultimately, how far Congress could afford to restrict slavery hinged on which group of Americans would most rapidly settle the Louisiana Purchase: slaveholders, non-slaveholders, or both. Senator James White and the _Philadelphia Aurora_'s enthusiasm notwithstanding, the history of western settlement through 1804 did not bode well for a free-soil Louisiana growing the fastest. By the time of the Missouri Controversy in 1819, large free populations in Ohio and Indiana vindicated the Northwest Ordinance's prohibition on slavery. But fifteen years earlier, few free-soil examples existed to challenge the connection between slavery and the rapid settlement of the West by Americans. By 1804, American slaveholders had already settled significant parts of western Virginia, Kentucky, Tennessee, upland South Carolina, and parts of the Georgia interior. North of the Ohio River, however, Article VI seemed to have stalled American settlement. Indeed, even as Congress considered the fate of Louisiana slavery, it received two petitions from the Indiana Territory declaring that Article VI of the Northwest Ordinance had retarded settlement and development there. The 1803 pleas from Indiana, like the many that preceded and would follow, explicitly linked legal sanction for slavery to western settlement, economic development, and integration into the Union. According to the Indiana petitioners, non-slaveholders had done a fine enough job turning Ohio into a free state. It was slaveholders, however, who comprised "the numerous Class of Citizens disposed to emigrate" westward. As Congress knew, they settled only "where they can be permitted to enjoy their property."[32]

Congress was in no position to disagree, especially with the plain facts of western settlement so clear; slaveholders stood at the vanguard of American expansion. Slaveholders, more than any other group of Americans poised to emigrate westward, possessed the private capital and coerced labor that was crucial for rapid settlement and development in the early American West. With Kentucky, upland South Carolina, most of the Georgia interior, the Mississippi Territory, and the Spanish Floridas all permitting slavery, American slaveholders could easily avoid settling in the Louisianas at no loss to themselves. Congress had to permit American slaveholders access if it wished to establish an American presence in the vast Louisiana Purchase. As John Breckinridge explained to the Senate, "If you do not permit slaves from the United States to go there, you will thereby prohibit men of wealth from the southern States"—good, loyal republican slaveholders such as himself—from "going to settle in that country." Breckinridge, like other American policymakers, believed that white Louisianans would follow the lead of distinguished, propertied men like himself. Faced with the proposition that slaveholding men of property rank would avoid settling in the Louisianas, the Senate defeated Hillhouse's proposal to free all slaves carried to the territory. Again, concerns for securing Louisiana were as important as proslavery interests in defeating restrictions on slavery.[33]

This would be illustrated further by Congress's prohibition on the domestic slave trade to the Louisiana Purchase. Though it failed to prevent the migration of American slaveholders to the Louisianas, Congress prohibited the domestic slave trade entirely and placed a *"bona fide* settler" restriction on American slaveholders. The bona fide settler restriction limited the future introduction of slaves into the Louisianas to those brought there by actual American settlers. These slaves could not be sold once the settler arrived in Louisiana, and the law also provided freedom for any slave sold in or into the Louisianas in violation of the restriction.[34]

During the debates over the bona fide settler proposal, some senators opposed the prohibition on the domestic slave trade as detrimental to slaveholders' property rights and interests. The "near 900,000" slaves in the United States were "worth $200,000,000," according to David Stone of North Carolina, a slaveholder who clearly knew the worth of Upper South slaves in Louisiana. "Why should the sellers of this kind of property be prohibited from sending and selling their slaves in Louisiana?" asked a baffled Stone. Other senators spoke strongly of their fears that without rapid diffusion of the type that only the domestic slave trade could provide, a rebellion on the order of Haiti's seemed almost inevitable in the Atlantic states. Despite these concerns, the bona fide settler restriction and its prohibition of the domestic slave trade passed the Senate, 18 to 11.[35]

On both the gradual emancipation and bona fide settler proposals, opposition and support came from what seems to be unlikely quarters. One could not have picked a supposedly more antislavery or antisouthern senator than Federalist Timothy Pickering of Massachusetts, now serving in the Senate. A longtime foe of planters, he had led two aborted New England secessionist movements in reaction to southern dominance of the Union, and his writings inspired a young William Lloyd Garrison to embrace abolitionism. But Pickering had learned much about the importance of slavery in the Mississippi Valley while serving as secretary of state in the late 1790s. During the Senate debates in 1804, he showed that he was still aware of the importance of slavery to securing American control in the region, and that he was equally unconcerned about slavery. Pickering voted against both the proposal to free all slaves carried to the territory and the bona fide settler limitation. He also expressed serious misgivings about prohibiting the international slave trade.[36]

Pickering's unqualified support for slavery expansion put him in good company with fellow Federalists John Quincy Adams and Jonathan Dayton, who also voted against both restrictions. Northern Federalist support for expansion was not enough to sink the bona fide settler restriction, however. Seven of nine northern Republicans joined with the Senate's five other Federalists to support it. Though Federalist James Hillhouse proposed the restrictions, it was northern Republicans who provided the crucial votes needed for passage.[37]

Equally important, six southern Republicans voted for the bona fide settler restriction, placing limits on their own ability to sell their slaves into the Louisianas. John Breckinridge, a close confidant of Jefferson and a considerable slave owner, had strongly cautioned against banning the domestic slave trade. He repeatedly expressed his "fear" that "our slaves in the south will produce another St. Domingo." Like Jefferson, Breckinridge was "alarmed at the increase of slaves in the southern states." He wished to "free the southern states of part of its black population, and of its danger" through diffusion via the domestic slave trade. North Carolina Republican Jesse Franklin also frequently raised concerns that "unless we mean to aid the destruction of our southern States, by laying the foundation for another St. Domingo," Congress must prohibit the international but permit the domestic slave trade. Yet both Franklin and Breckinridge voted to prohibit the domestic slave trade to the territories. So did Maryland's two Republican senators, Robert Wright and Samuel Smith. Southern slaveholders, who stood to lose the most by prohibiting the domestic slave trade, provided needed votes to pass the prohibition on the domestic slave trade.[38]

In their final form, the 1804 laws governing slavery in the Louisianas prohibited the further introduction of any slaves into the territory, except by "a citizen of the United States, removing into said Territory for actual settlement, and being, at the time of such removal, *bona fide* owner of such slave or slaves."[39] The laws failed to go as far as some congressmen had sought. If successfully implemented, however, they held out promise for severely curbing the growth of slavery in the western reaches of the new American empire. Unfortunately, the success of those restrictions rested in the hands of the very people they were designed to restrain. Congress soon learned that passing restrictions on slavery and gaining white Louisianans' consent to those laws were two entirely different matters.

III

Nobody understood the severity of the congressional restrictions better than white Louisianans themselves. To white Lower Louisianans, U.S. rule threatened to do more than abolish the importation of slaves; it seemed dangerously destructive to the plantation society only recently born in the lower Mississippi Valley. Indeed, with a plantation boom underway, white Louisianans of all ranks feared that American possession might destroy both plantation slavery and the racist hierarchy that underwrote it. As Louisiana governor Claiborne wrote to James Madison, mere word that the Senate had prohibited the foreign slave trade caused "great agitation in this City and in the adjacent Settlements." The agitation only worsened once white Louisianans became aware of the full set of restrictions. "The importation of negroes there is abolished point blank," wrote Pierre Clement de Laussat, French prefect for Louisiana; "the present inhabitants of Lower Louisiana could not have been attacked in a more vulnerable spot." And once attacked, white Louisianans fought bitterly for their right to enslave others.[40]

The Haitian Rebellion, three small rebellions in Louisiana itself, the introduction of large-scale cotton and sugar production, and the corresponding increase of African slaves all put white Louisianans on guard long before American possession. Beginning in the 1780s, whites of all classes worked to transform Lower Louisiana into a plantation society bottomed on ever-greater "subordination" of free blacks and slaves. In the wake of "the disasters which have ruined the French colonies," Spanish officials and French planters redoubled their efforts. In the 1790s, they devised a new, extensive set of slave codes to "alienate them from the wish of acquiring freedom." They also ordered all officials "to direct their whole attention to the internal police of the plantations." By the time of the Louisiana Purchase, French planters and Spanish officials had implemented the full set of codes, laws, and force needed to build a plantation society founded on black subordination.[41]

In sharp contrast, the United States appeared gravely abolitionist in its tendencies. The Northwest Ordinance, gradual abolition laws in northern states, the ban on the international and domestic slave trade, and their provisions for freeing illegally purchased slaves all pointed in dangerous directions for white Louisianans. American policy seemed poised to reverse if not destroy white Louisianans' ongoing efforts to subordinate blacks, whether slave or free. Indeed, the territorial governments framed by Congress appeared expressly designed to destroy a thriving but still fragile and developing plantation society.[42]

The relationship seemingly forged between the "free people of colour" and American officials only exacerbated these fears. The free blacks and mulattoes of New Orleans, who faced increased marginalization prior to the Louisiana Purchase, were one of the few groups in Orleans Territory who welcomed American rule. At the same time that white Louisianans were restricting the rights of free blacks, the "free people of colour" praised annexation to "the American Republic," because "our personal and political freedom" would be "assured to us forever." They also expressed their "fullest confidence" that the United States would extend "justice and liberality . . . towards every class of citizens which they have taken under their protection." Governor Claiborne acknowledged their loyalty by granting a "Stand of Colours" to the Mulatto Militia Battalion, thus granting them American military recognition. In a public address, he also assured them "that their rights would be protected, and that their confidence in the government of the United States would increase as they became acquainted with its principles." This exchange could not have been reassuring to white Louisianans. Fraying their nerves further still, Thomas Paine wrote an unmistakenly hostile letter to the inhabitants of Louisiana, citing their attachment to slavery as proof of their unfitness for self-government.[43]

American settlers and officials soon enough demonstrated that they were as committed to slavery and racial subordination as their French and Spanish predecessors. Jefferson recorded "that the Militia of Colour" was "treated favorably" only until "a better settled state of things shall permit us to let them neglect themselves." American officials soon winked at the international slave trade so long as slavers first touched port at Charleston, South Carolina. Congress would rescind the restrictions on the domestic slave trade in 1805. In 1806, American officials helped draft and enforce a new Black Code, placing even more stringent regulations on free and enslaved blacks. Finally, the planters of Louisiana selected Claiborne as governor when the territory became a state in 1811. But in the confused circumstances of 1804, American rule seemed to herald the destruction of white Louisianans' plantation society.[44]

Almost immediately after receiving word of the laws passed by Congress, the white inhabitants of Orleans began petitioning their new government. White Louisianans had grown quite accustomed to living under far-off imperial powers who neglected their needs and interests. In this sense, the United States differed little from its French and Spanish predecessors. White Louisianans could undoubtedly live with another government that left them to their own devices. American rule seemed far worse than neglectful, however. "Slavery" was the "one subject extremely interesting to us," wrote the New Orleans petitioners in their "Remonstrance." The domestic slave trade was unjustly denied to them. More importantly, the international slave trade was "absolutely prohibited." These restrictions were especially harmful because "the necessity of employing African laborers" was "all important to the very existence of our country." Without a constant supply of slaves, explained the petitioners, "cultivation must cease, the improvements of a century be destroyed."[45]

Claiborne assured officials in Washington that many of the grievances in the "Remonstrance" were of little interest to the majority of the white inhabitants. Indeed, Congress could reject most of the petitioners' requests with little harm, "unless it respects the African trade." As he explained, the petitioners' main purpose was "the opening of the African trade, and upon this point, the people in general take a lively interest." Claiborne's warnings pointed to a larger problem confronting congressmen and other officials concerned with restricting the expansion of slavery. "The people generally," and not just a clique of planter grandees and merchants, demanded uninterrupted access to enslaved black labor. On the Southwest sugar and cotton frontier, all ranks of white society—the "present inhabitants," the "people generally," the "Citizens," and even "the Farmers"—eagerly participated in the plantation revolution. All seemed equally outraged at American restrictions on slavery. "On this point," wrote a worried Claiborne, "the people here have united as one man!"[46]

Adding to Claiborne's woes, ostensibly loyal Americans in New Orleans joined and even led the protests against the prohibitions on the slave trade. Claiborne was at first pleased that Edward Livingston of New York had moved to New Orleans immediately after the cession.

Claiborne expected that Livingston, a distinguished, propertied, well-born American, whose brother had negotiated the Treaty of Cession with France, would help "render my administration more pleasing and the present state of things more acceptable to the people." Livingston instead joined a group of "designing men" inciting the "uncommonly credulous" people of New Orleans against the United States and the restrictions on slavery. It seemed that Americans in Louisiana subverted American authority as badly as their French counterparts. "A spirit of adventure has already induced quacks, pettifoggers, and starvelings, from every part of the Union, to migrate to that country," complained one observer. "Never was a government so imposed upon by renegado rascals as ours," wrote another frustrated American from Natchez. "A fellow comes to Louisiana, professes attachment to the administration," and "receives an appointment." Soon enough he "goes about exciting discontent, and exerting every nerve to injure that government." With Americans joining in, the protests grew noisier, and a "general discontent" spread "throughout Louisiana." By the summer of 1804, newspapers throughout the United States were printing the "Remonstrance," along with reports that "the French at New Orleans" were "discontented, troublesome, and insolent."[47]

Under French and Spanish rule, white Louisianans had exactly what they wanted: a government that served their interests by protecting their property in land and slaves. Should the United States prove less responsive to their needs, it seemed that white Louisianans might resort to measures more drastic than petitions. One American official warned "that there are men who speak seriously of appealing to France & requesting the first Consul [Napoleon Bonaparte] to give them aid." Claiborne became convinced that the "most sincere Admirers of Bonaparte" had "tinged with foreign influence" the inhabitants and their petitions. According to another dismayed American official, there was one best way of placating white Louisianans: repeal of the slavery restrictions "would go farther with them, and better reconcile them to the Government of the United States, than any other privilege that could be extended to that Country." Incorporation into the Union would be on their terms or not at all. As white Louisianans made clear, their terms included protections for their property in slaves and access to more.[48]

In September 1804 an anonymous American mocked white Louisianans' cries that American rule spelled the end of their right to enslave others in the aptly titled poem, "The Louisiana Memorial Abridged."

> Power despotic is infernal
> Freedom is a right eternal
> Unchangeable in every time
> For every people, & for every clime
> This truth your ancestors profess'd
> And led to make their Country bless'd
> Why unto us the boon denied?
> Oh spread lov'd freedom far & wide
> Receive us to your arms as Brothers
> And grant us *to make slaves of others.*[49]

Satirical poetry aside, Congress could not ignore Claiborne's pleas, white Louisianans' huffy demands, and the increasingly unsettled situation in Louisiana had they wanted to.

The 1804 Territorial Acts included a provision that they expire in 1805. Distracted by other business, in early 1805 Congress hastily passed new territorial ordinances based on the report of a committee charged with framing new governments for the Louisianas. The committee insisted on continuing the prohibition on the international slave trade. However, the committee report and the final 1805 Territorial Acts said nothing about the South Carolina restriction that prohibited slave traders from touching port in Charleston to evade the prohibition on "international" slaves. By failing to close the South Carolina loophole in 1805, the ban on the international slave trade became effectively meaningless. The committee and the 1805 act were similarly silent about the domestic slave trade, which was now permitted because it was no longer prohibited by law. The absence of these two restrictions now sanctioned the commerce in slaves to Louisiana. So long as slave traders first touched port in Charleston or some other American port, the international slave trade would then become part of the domestic slave trade. Finally, the act failed to address the expansion of American slavery and slaveholders into the territory. In its final version, the 1805 Act for Orleans Territory said nothing about slavery or the 1804 restrictions. It simply provided that "the sixth article of compact," which referred to the Northwest Ordinance's prohibition on slavery, be "excluded from all operation within the said Territory of Orleans." The plantation boom—never really interrupted by the 1804 restrictions in any case—was on once again.[50]

Why had the United States accepted slavery in Lower Louisiana, thus further transforming the American empire in the West into an empire for slavery? According to historians, the meager and diffused northern commitment to doing something about slavery expansion was far too weak to compete seriously with the threat of disunion between the North and the South, the power of southern slaveholders, and the indifference of northern Republicans.[51] White Louisianans had built a thriving plantation society prior to American possession. The best the United States could do in 1804 was cut off the constant supply of slaves that was crucial for the continued existence and expansion of Lower Louisiana's plantation boom. Congress's efforts to do just that collapsed when white Louisianans refused to accept any meaningful limits on their right "to make slaves of others." In the end, it was the ability of slaveholders in Lower Louisiana to exploit the weaknesses of the U.S. government in the lower Mississippi Valley that triumphed over Congress's very real efforts to restrict the growth of slavery there.[52]

IV

At first glance, the situation to the north would seem more likely to favor freedom over slavery. As the historian William Freehling notes, "The future state of Missouri no less than the future state of Louisiana was in the Louisiana Purchase Territory." But, according to Freehling, Jefferson's "inclinations not to dare a controversy over slavery" with "slaveholding apologists" in Virginia, South Carolina, and Georgia, "permitted the institution inside one area where termination was feasible." Focusing on Congress, Don Fehrenbacher also speculates that the "prohibition of slavery" north of present-day Louisiana "might well have won majority support, especially if linked with acquiescence in slavery south of that line."[53] Arguably, Jefferson and Congress might have agreed to a compromise allowing slavery in Orleans but banning it in Upper Louisiana. For the "freemen of the District of Louisiana," however, the decision was not for Jefferson or Congress to make. The white inhabitants of Upper Louisiana knew the importance of slavery to their society. No more than their neighbors to the south would they obey any laws impinging on their right to possess and traffic in slaves.

Many white Upper Louisianans had been wary of the U.S. government since at least 1787, when Article VI of the Northwest Ordinance prohibited slavery in the territory just across the Mississippi River from Upper Louisiana. From 1787 through 1803, Article VI drove a significant number of French slaveholders from the Illinois Country across the Mississippi River into Upper Louisiana. Upper Louisianans understandably expressed concern that American rule in Upper Louisiana would threaten slavery, just as it had in the Northwest Territory.[54] With good reason, the 1804 laws for Upper Louisiana exacerbated concerns about the sanctity of slavery under American rule. For administrative purposes, the 1804 Act for Upper Louisiana appointed the officers and judges of the Indiana Territory to the Louisiana Territory. The bill maintained that the two territories were separate and distinct, and the laws and regulations of one did not apply to the other. The white inhabitants of Upper Louisiana nonetheless suspected that this was a prelude to an eventual merger of the two territories and the eventual imposition of Article VI of the Northwest Ordinance on Upper Louisiana. When taken together, the Northwest Ordinance, the growing reputation of the United States as a nation hostile to slavery, and the territorial government of 1804 all made white Upper Louisianans fear that the United States intended to abolish slavery west of the Mississippi.[55]

Writing to Senator John Breckinridge in the summer of 1804, American William Carr warned that "people" of Upper Louisiana were "very much agitated" in "regard to this district's being annexed to the Indiana Territory & the regulations which Congress might adopt relative to slavery." As in Lower Louisiana, the agitation involved more than the orchestrated protest of leading men trying to protect their own interests. Carr found nearly all of the residents "apprehensive that slavery" would soon "be prohibited" under American rule. The greatest concerns came from small slaveholders who "were fearful least those already in their possession would also be manumitted." Like the white inhabitants of Lower Louisiana, white Upper Louisianans had learned to prosper under French and Spanish governments that provided little more than neglect; they, too, could live under an American government that promised much the same. They would not, however, accept American rule if it was accompanied by laws that seemed designed expressly "to abolish slavery altogether."[56]

After meeting in St. Louis in September 1804, "the representatives elected by the freemen" of Upper Louisiana sent Congress a strongly worded "remonstrance and petition." The petitioners warned that the slavery laws seemed "calculated to alarm the people with respect to that kind of property." Indeed, they appeared "calculated . . . to create the presumption of a disposition in Congress to abolish slavery altogether" in Upper Louisiana. Congress had erred badly by placing stringent restrictions on slavery, and then joining Upper Louisiana to the Indiana Territory. "The laws" of Indiana and Louisiana "must be very dissimilar in a number of respects," they explained. Most important, though "slavery cannot exist in the Indiana Territory," it "prevails in Louisiana." These circumstances demanded that the United States recognize their right "to the free possession of our slaves." But the "freemen" of Upper Louisiana wanted more than "free possession" of slaves already in the territory; they also requested "the right of importing slaves." Though willing to accept restrictions on the international slave trade, they were unwilling to forego the slave trade entirely, especially if this measure was a prelude to a broader program of abolition. Congress could easily rectify the situation by granting them a territorial government "similar in many respects to the one formerly made for the Mississippi Territory." For Upper Louisianans the terms of union required sanction for black slavery and its continued growth.[57]

Lacking the power to enforce unpopular restrictions on slavery in the farthest reaches of the American empire, in 1805 Congress quietly failed to renew the more severe restrictions on slavery in Upper Louisiana. The 1805 Territorial Act for Upper Louisiana made no mention of slavery, either directly or indirectly, by exempting the territory from Article VI, as was done with the Mississippi and Orleans territories. As of 1805, slavery existed in Upper Louisiana by force of local law and territorial statutes and was not explicitly sanctioned by the territorial ordinance. And though Congress failed to sanction slavery explicitly, its inability to prohibit it set the stage for the growth of slavery that would set off the Missouri Crisis in 1819.[58]

According to William Freehling, "President Jefferson's early failure to bar potential slavery in Missouri Territory" led to the Missouri Crisis of 1819. Paul Finkelman similarly points out that Jefferson "might have used his influence to prohibit slavery throughout the territory, or at least limit it to what became the state of Louisiana."[59] Yet their focus on Jefferson and Congress obscures an equally important point. There was nothing "potential" about slavery in Missouri in 1804, and there was little even a Jefferson could do to halt its growth, let alone "bar" it. While Jefferson certainly could have influenced Congress to pass more-stringent restrictions on slavery, white Upper Louisianans surely would have disregarded them with impunity.

The events in the Louisiana Purchase between 1803 and 1805 revealed that the federal government could do little to restrain the growth of the institution in far-flung western territories. They could accomplish even less when a long history of slavery predated American possession. In 1804 Congress had framed an elaborate set of restrictions that balanced concerns about incorporating the Louisianas into the Union with the desire to check slavery expansion in the farthest West. From nabob planters in New Orleans to farmers and traders north of St. Louis, white Louisianans made it impossible for Congress to maintain those restrictions, let alone enforce them. By 1805 Congress had no illusions about the reality of white westerners' infatuation with slavery or the overextended republic's ability to restrict its growth in the West.

4

Slaveholders' Democracy, the Union, and the Nation

Missouri, 1805–1820

In May 1819 the residents of Franklin, Missouri, gathered to celebrate the arrival of the steamship *Independence*. One reveler, Nathaniel Patten, offered a toast to "the Missouri Territory—Its future prosperity and greatness cannot be checked by the caprice of a few men in Congress, while it possesses a soil of inexhaustible fertility, abundant resources, and a body of intelligent, enterprising, independent freemen." The glaring omission in Patten's toast was not lost on his fellow revelers. "Intelligent" and "enterprising" though they might be, the "independent freemen" meant to tap those "abundant resources" with a far-from-independent source of labor. A Major Wilcox followed with his own toast to Missouri's citizens: "May they never become a member of the Union under the restriction relative to slavery," undoubtedly to hearty cheers. Lest anyone in the crowd doubt their seriousness about slavery, a third celebrant offered his toast to "the Missourians," who would "defend their rights"—including their right to hold others as slaves—"even at the expense of blood."[1]

Congress's 1804 attempt to restrict the growth of slavery in territorial Missouri failed when American and French settlers insisted that protections for slavery be included in the terms of union. As the above toasts demonstrate, white Missourians had lost little of their enthusiasm for black slavery in the fifteen years between cession and statehood. Indeed, by 1819 they had become militantly proslavery.

Between 1805 and 1819, thousands of Americans, hailing "almost exclusively from the states south of the Ohio and Potomac," streamed into Missouri with "many slaves" in tow.[2] The steady stream of masters, aspiring slaveholders, and slaves who found their way to a Missouri Country with no legal restrictions on slavery demonstrated that slavery was anything but a dying institution. Even before the congressional restrictions on statehood led Missourians into a new defense of slavery, the process of settlement convinced white settlers that the slave society they were creating in Missouri would be different from those in the Atlantic states and the Southwest. The Tallmadge restrictions challenged slaveholders and aspiring slaveholders in Missouri to articulate further a vision of society that reconciled the reality of slavery with their own notions of republicanism, democracy, and prosperity. The process of state-making, culminating in the election of delegates to frame a constitution, forced them to codify their beliefs about the relationship between race, slavery, and expansion. What white Missourians wrote, said, and threatened revealed just how thoroughly they had tied permanent black slavery to their vision of democracy in the West.

As the Missouri Controversy played out, white Missourians increasingly imagined themselves as part of a larger slaveholding nation defined by divisions between the North and the South, rather than the East and the West. They also convinced themselves that they were on the cusp of creating a perfect slave society, encompassing all of the benefits of slaveholding and none of its drawbacks. Slavery in their corner of the West would become neither an undemocratic institution monopolized by domineering planters nor an unrepublican institution that drained society of its vitality. Instead, Missouri's slave society would be free of planters, frightfully large concentrations of slaves, troublesome free blacks, meddling "Yankees," and menacing "emancipationists." Aspiring and small slaveholders in Missouri envisioned creating a society that fostered democracy for white men and prosperity for white families— all resting on the backs of African Americans whose slavery would be permanent. Independent of the tutelage of great planters in the East, ordinary white families in search of western freeholds proved quite capable of creating their own "positive good" theory of slavery. Their unshakeable commitment to slavery ensured that white Missourians would resist any congressional attempts to reign in the institution's expansion in the West.

I

By 1805, congressional efforts to restrict the further expansion of slavery in Upper Louisiana had clearly failed. When Congress prohibited the domestic slave trade and attached Upper Louisiana to the Indiana Territory in 1804, white Missourians feared this was but the first step toward some plan of gradual abolition, and they reacted with predictable outrage. Congress rescinded the restrictions in 1805, but the laws for the new territorial government of Upper Louisiana made no mention of slavery whatsoever. A proposed version of the bill would have acknowledged slavery, at least indirectly, by creating "a government in all respects similar to that now exercised in the Mississippi Territory." The final version of the territorial ordinance, however, omitted all references to slavery. As of 1805, the institution existed in what would become Missouri by force of local law and territorial statute, rather than by territorial ordinance, as was the case in other territories where slavery was permitted.[3]

By 1810, the territory's population had increased, prompting a congressional committee to present a bill for raising Upper Louisiana to the second stage of territorial government. The proposed bill would have created a government "in all respects similar to that now exercised in the Mississippi Territory," thus indirectly recognizing slavery in Missouri by twice removing it from Article VI of the Northwest Ordinance. The bill failed to make it to the floor in 1810 and the proposal died. The following year, Pennsylvania Republican Jonathan Roberts tried to prohibit the further introduction of slaves into the territory when the House considered another proposal to raise Upper Louisiana to the second stage of territorial government. With war on the horizon, and with other pressing business to consider, Roberts voluntarily withdrew his proposal and the bill again failed to make it to the floor for consideration. In 1812, with war even more imminent, the bill made it to the floor. Another Pennsylvania Republican, Abner Lacock, moved "to prohibit the admission of slaves into the said territory," but the motion mustered only 17 supporting "Ayes." Though Congress raised Upper Louisiana to the second stage of government and renamed it the Mis-

souri Territory, the territorial ordinance again failed to make any mention of slavery, either directly or indirectly. Slavery continued to exist in
Missouri only by force of local law and territorial statute. So it would
remain until 1820.[4]

Ultimately, a mix of indifference, fear of upsetting settlers on the
farthest fringes of the overextended republic, and a continuing desire
to slow slavery's expansion all contributed to Congress's failure either
to restrict slavery's expansion into Missouri or to give it explicit sanction.[5] Ordinary settlers could of course look past the legal niceties that
left the future status of Missouri slavery in limbo to the one point that
really mattered: slavery was prohibited in Ohio, Indiana, and Illinois;
it was allowed in Missouri. With Congress's failure to renew the 1804
restrictions on slavery, the institution there grew slowly. Then, after
the War of 1812, it began expanding rapidly. Slaveholders and aspiring
slaveholders from Kentucky, Tennessee, Virginia, and the Carolinas all
continued their migration into Missouri, where they joined the motley
population of white westerners already there.

Southern migrants headed to Missouri left behind states where
economic and political developments had brought changes to the relationship between slavery and society. Planter classes from Virginia to
Kentucky to the Carolinas consolidated their rule after the Revolution,
thwarting middling farmers' efforts to gain a greater share of political
power. At the same time, declining soils and a tight land market put
new pressures on the South's middling slaveholding class. Finally, the
population of free and enslaved blacks continued to grow, adding to
white fears that all blacks were a menace to white society, a powder keg
waiting to explode in a dramatic, Haitian-style rebellion on American
shores.[6]

Missouri offered middling slaveholding families something dramatically different from slave states in the East and the emerging plantation
societies in the Southwest. The Missouri River Valley's rich bottomlands, its ready access to markets via the Missouri and Mississippi rivers, and its cheap and abundant lands promised prosperity to families
who owned but few slaves. Equally important, its temperate climate,
deemed unsuitable for plantation crops, promised to forestall the
growth of a powerful planter class as well as dangerously large concentrations of enslaved blacks. Much as the process of settlement in the
free Northwest led settlers to rethink notions of slavery, prosperity, and

republican society, the experiences of white settlers in Missouri forced them to rethink the future of slavery in a place that seemed worlds away from the Chesapeake, the Carolinas, or territories in the Southwest. And while Missouri slavery would supposedly be different from slavery in the East, it would be no less important.

In an 1813 letter to his brother, Indian agent George Sibley explained that his "almost insufferable objection to" settling in Lower Louisiana was "the great number of Slaves now there." The gangs of slaves forced to labor on Louisiana's cotton and sugar plantations, "who only want a safe opportunity to cut the throats of their masters in whom they have little dependence," hardly "comport[ed] with" Sibley's "ideas of comfort and worldly happiness." But, according to Sibley, in Missouri "we have but few slaves," and those few "are all well fed & clothed & kindly treated." Louisiana slaves daily faced the lash as overseers squeezed ever-greater profits from their gangs of laborers. In Missouri, slaves "are not so much employed to amass wealth for their owners as to provide substantial comforts" and to "render life easy, comfortable and happy." The difference supposedly showed in the deportment of Missouri slaves. Sibley claimed his slave George was "faithful, industrious and attentive." Missouri's climate, which favored small farms over large plantations, meant that there would be no gangs of slaves ready to rebel. Supposedly less harsh conditions in Missouri eased the burdens of slaves, "ameliorating" not just the lives of slaves, but the consciences of slaveholders. Missouri might not offer the fantastic profits available on the Southwest cotton and sugar frontier, but it did offer "substantial comforts," security, and peace of mind.[7]

The experiences of Virginian Frederick Bates further illustrate how settlers from the East came to rethink old notions about slavery in Missouri. In 1801 Bates's father, a middling, slaveholding Quaker, lost everything—including his five slaves—due to ill health and mounting debts. Bates's brother bailed out their father by purchasing the family's slaves and land, but Frederick lost his inheritance as a result. Bates now sought his fortune in the West, where he occupied a variety of minor offices for the federal and territorial governments in the Northwest Territory. Then, in 1807, Jefferson appointed him secretary of Upper Louisiana, where he also became recorder of land titles.[8]

In August 1810 the non-slaveholding Bates responded to his friend John Michie's inquiries about the prospects for slaveholders in Mis-

souri. Michie, who still resided in Virginia, must have been delighted
with Bates's information. Slaves sold for anywhere "from $300 to $500,"
indicating a high demand for slaves. The great demand for slave labor
in Missouri meant that "Negro men hire at the [lead] mines from $10
to $15," and on farms at "$8 & $10 Per Mo." But the slack periods where
Michie could hire out his slaves would be few. When slaves were not
used for clearing land, slave owners used them for mixed farming, producing everything from corn and whiskey to peach brandy, bacon, and
lead, all of which commanded high prices in Missouri and downriver in
New Orleans. Finally, Bates expected that slaves could produce small
but valuable crops of tobacco and hemp. Territorial Missouri had much
to offer Virginians and other slaveholders who hoped to exploit more
fully the labor of their slaves in the West.[9]

Thus inspired, Michie made plans to settle in Missouri, and one year
later Bates was acting as his land agent. Bates, slaveless and thus less
wealthy than his friend, soon became despondent, envious, and dismayed with his own misfortune. Without slaves, Bates was confined to
a life of "sweat and toil and drudgery." But "at the same time," he knew
that if he had "lands and slaves and cattle and money," his lot would
be less difficult. Though Bates had spent the better part of four years
enjoying both a salary and the fees he collected from public office, without slaves he could only curse his failure to prosper. That would soon
change. The following year Bates joined the ranks of Missouri slaveholders, when he purchased a family of three slaves for $900.[10]

Bates immediately became ecstatic about his changing fortunes. In
a letter to his mother, he recalled her advice "to never have a slave, because, for the most part nothing but discipline could make them profitable." Mother Bates apparently held no moral scruples about slavery.
Instead, she shied away from slaveholding because the difficulties of
forcing slaves to work outweighed any financial gains. Frederick assured her that slaveholding in Missouri would prove easier than in the
Chesapeake. Bates's slave "family" was "raising" for him "a most promising crop," and he assured his mother that "plantation business was
more to my permanent advantage than anything else I could pursue."
Now the owner of two adult slaves, Bates boasted how "my blacks . . .
have done wonders." As Frederick's fortunes continued to improve,
his family's prospects continued to decline in the Chesapeake. In 1818,
Bates's family, including his brother, Edward, who had purchased their

father's five slaves, headed out for the Missouri Country to recoup their fortunes.[11]

Others shared Bates's belief that slave ownership provided a fast and certain road to prosperity in the West. Alexander Stuart was a federal officeholder in the Illinois Territory who sought a transfer to Missouri. Like Frederick Bates, Stuart's office provided him a guaranteed income. Yet he too feared going broke unless he could exact greater profits from his slaves. Article VI left Stuart reluctant to use his slaves in Illinois, and he found himself unable to meet his "annual expenses" as a result. But if he could "go to Missouri" and "take my Slaves with me," he could solve his "embarrassing" financial problems. Recent Yankee transplant Justus Post similarly lauded the prospects for slaveholders in Missouri. "There is one thing you must reconcile your mind to when you get to this region," he warned his brother from Vermont. "That is the owning of slaves." Post owned five himself and planned to purchase two more in the immediate future. Marginally paternalistic at best, Post would give his slaves but "victuals, clothes & work in abundance." Even for the hearty sons of Vermont, prosperity in territorial Missouri involved slavery for others.[12]

Various observers in territorial Missouri also saw the link between slavery and bounty. As one of the earliest accounts of post-cession Upper Louisiana noted, in 1811, "The excellence and cheapness of the lands, besides the holding of slaves, will cause this territory to be preferred by emigrants from the southern states, to any part of the western country." Timothy Flint, an itinerant Yankee preacher who found his way to Missouri in 1816, also recognized the importance of slavery to settlers. "The most respectable people" from Kentucky, Virginia, and the Carolinas found "their imaginations were warmed by" the prospect of settling in Missouri. Unlike his fellow Yankee traveler Justus Post, Flint was less cheerful about the future of a Missouri Country populated by slaves and slaveholders; the slaveholding settlers failed to realize "that evils of all sorts can exist in the most beautiful countries." The "physical advantages" that slave labor heaped on slaveholders might have been "but a poor compensation for the loss of moral ones," but Flint could not deny how considerable those physical advantages were. Indeed, slavery seemed central to Missouri's postwar economic boom; while the "progress of Illinois" was comparable to Missouri, Illinois still "labored under the inconvenience" of its laws interdicting slavery.[13]

Fueled by cheap money, abundant land, good titles, and a more secure West after the defeat of the British in the War of 1812, slaveholders
and non-slaveholders from slave states poured into postwar Missouri.[14]
Gazettes and geography books promised readers that they would find
"incalculable riches" in the Missouri Valley, which was "probably the
easiest unsettled country in the world to commence farming in." Equally
important, good land titles made Missouri attractive to families who
had originally settled in Kentucky and Tennessee. Families had settled
in those states during the first great western movement in the 1790s
and purchased land in good faith. But "instead of wealth, independence, or even a home," a settler instead "frequently paid his money for
a chain of law suits that entailed poverty upon him and his posterity."
Conversely, Missouri land titles, whether purchased from the government or private sellers, provided "land unencumbered by prior claims,
and consequently uninvolved in the masses of litigation." In Virginia,
these descriptions of Missouri combined with word of mouth and the
squeezing out of middling families to produce a "rage" for settlement
in Missouri. Similarly, in postwar Kentucky "the rage for emigration is
now towards the Missouri" and the "Boone's Lick" settlements along the
Missouri River. Indeed, the "rage for emigration" was so great, observed
Missouri's single newspaper in 1816, that "a stranger would imagine that
Virginia, Kentucky, Tennessee and the Carolina's had made an agreement to introduce us as soon as possible to the bosom of the American
family."[15]

With the bonanza on, Missourians imbibed "the rage for speculating
in their lands," as an onslaught of settlers and slaves arrived after the
War of 1812. To secure their own land—and to make a small fortune in
the process—settlers increasingly purchased a tract of land, cleared and
improved that land, and then sold all or part of it to the next wave of settlers. Under the Harrison Land Act, the federal government facilitated
this practice. The government sold land at $2 per acre. One-twentieth
was due at the time of purchase, and another four-twentieths was due in
forty days. However, the next payment, for one-quarter of the purchase
price, was not due until two years from the date of sale. A family could
purchase a 320-acre tract for $32 down and an additional $128 due in
forty days. Families would then spend the next two years improving the
land, hoping to sell both their land and the improvements before the
next payment was due. In addition to purchasing government lands,

squatters claimed—and the federal government recognized—"preemption rights." Hence, a family could squat on land and improve it before bidding was open to the public, with squatters having first claim on the lands they had improved. By early 1819, improved lands along the Missouri and Mississippi rivers averaged from $4 to $12 dollars an acre, with some lands around St. Louis commanding prices as high as $26 an acre.[16]

Other families preferred to remain on their land and gain clear title rather than selling out to new migrants. The terms of the Harrison Land Act might have been generous, but they still required families to come up with $480 in four years to gain clear title. This obviously required families to begin production for the market immediately—no easy task in a newly settled country.[17] Writing in 1812, Amos Stoddard noted that "the first care of a settler" in Missouri "is to raise the necessities of life." After this, families sought to produce for the market and generate the cash needed to gain full title to their land. But as Stoddard noted, those who were "destitute of slaves" found it more difficult to produce a surplus for the market and thus to secure a coveted freehold.[18]

The Rochester, Carroll, and Fitzhugh families were just the type of middling slaveholders who found Missouri so alluring. In 1809 the three families and their slaves left Virginia to settle in New York's Genesee Valley. When New York passed an accelerated gradual abolition law in 1817, the three families looked to settle elsewhere. This time, they would avoid the mistake of settling in a place where the future of slavery remained in doubt. "The absence of this necessary evil, to a person of southern habits," precluded settlement in states and territories north of the Ohio River. The families would settle in Kentucky or Missouri, because there, "slavery is permitted." In 1818 Charles Carroll set out to scout lands in the West. He quickly decided that Kentucky's high land prices and confused titles made the Missouri Valley "a much more desirable country to settle in."[19]

Carroll's glowing descriptions conveyed many of the inducements that drew small slaveholders to Missouri. "The admission of slaves gives you that kind of labor that we southern people know how to get along with & we feel at home with this servitude," Carroll admitted. Furthermore, the Missouri Valley "embraces the finest body of rich land in any country." He knew of "no portion of the US which' holds forth as fair prospects to the man of enterprise and industry" as did

Missouri. The three families could make a killing by speculating in and improving land, and by selling improvements and supplies to new settlers. Missouri also provided expatriated slaveholding Virginians with a familiar social environment. "Slavery being permitted in this Territory" attracted the South's respectable, middling slaveholders; it also discouraged settlement by "the Yankees." In 1819 Carroll and his family, along with the Rochesters' two sons and a nephew, settled in Missouri.[20]

With its white population having swollen to over 40,000 after the war, and with settlers and slaves arriving daily, Missouri was ready for statehood. By 1818, various settlers began petitioning Congress to admit Missouri into the Union. In November, the territorial legislature formally requested admission through its nonvoting delegate to Congress.[21] Nothing seemed capable of interrupting Missouri's rapid march to prosperity and statehood. Nothing, that is, except for a New York congressman who convinced a majority of his colleagues that it was now time to stop slavery's westward march. As a condition for statehood, James Tallmadge of New York proposed that Missouri prohibit the further introduction of slaves into the state and provide emancipation for all slaves born after statehood at the age of twenty-five. White Missourians would have none of it. The early settlers had already stared down the U.S. government over slavery in 1804; the new settlers would prepare themselves to do so again.

II

To many in Missouri, the Tallmadge Amendments threatened the ability of small slaveholders to enjoy the economic boon inseparable from the use of slave labor. They expressed their outrage at the Tallmadge "restrictions" in a host of public gatherings, celebrations, newspaper articles, and protests. In the process, they strengthened their commitment to entering the Union as a slave state and imagined themselves as part of a larger slaveholding nation at war with jealous, cunning, hypocritical "Yankees," which soon became an epitaph for anyone who opposed slavery. This made it all but certain that Missouri would never consent to restrictions on slavery. It also forced white Missourians to define the place of slavery in Missouri and the United States. White Missourians were after something more than just a state that permitted slavery. In the words of Nathaniel Beverley Tucker, their population would be "more homogenous," composed exclusively of whites committed to slavery and blacks whose slavery would be permanent.[22]

The first popular protests against the Tallmadge Amendments came from grand juries sitting in St. Louis, which turned into mass rallies against restrictions. "Although we deprecate anything like an idea of disunion," the jurors nonetheless felt "it our duty to take a manly and dignified stand for our rights and privileges." Widely circulated accounts of the St. Louis rallies set a defiant tone for the protests that followed. At their ever popular Fourth of July celebrations, Missourians in settlements across the territory seemed intent on threatening their way into the Union as a slave state. "Missouri—May she be admitted into the Union on an equal footing with the original States, or not be received in any other way," went one toast. Another insisted that "the citizens of the Missouri Territory" were "a population who understand their rights, and know how to maintain them." Congress could pass whatever restrictions on slavery they saw fit; white Missourians did not intend to abide by them. Popular protests generated a consensus in favor of slavery, insuring that "the Territory will never go into a State under those shackles."[23]

In part, Missourians' sensitivity about the Tallmadge restrictions stemmed from the popular belief that the Tallmadge restrictions were part of a larger conspiracy aimed at southern and western slaveholders. When the Missouri Controversy first erupted in early 1819, Representative John Taylor of New York expressed his wish that his relatives be able to settle in a Missouri Country unscathed by slavery. John Scott, Missouri's delegate to Congress, did not extend a welcome. Rather, he "begged" Taylor "to relieve him from the awful prospect." Scott "did not desire" any northerner with qualms about slavery "in that land of brave, noble, and independent freemen" who owned slaves. Taylor's wish about antislavery settlers to settle in Missouri fed popular suspicions that the real motive behind restrictions was to drive out southern settlers and secure Missouri for "our northern guardians." Overwhelming northern support for the Tallmadge restrictions had to be a conspiracy. Like Taylor, other restrictionists allegedly hoped that "emigration from the southern and westerns states will be checked, through fear of losing their slaves." In place of slaveholders, "emigration from the New England states will increase, under hope of gaining supremacy in this country." According to another essayist, Taylor, Tallmadge, and their allies "wish to expel *our* slaves" so "that *their* brothers and sons, and nephews, and cousins," all presumably hostile to slavery, "may enter upon the possession of this magnificent country."[24]

From the standpoint of proslavery Missourians, only politicians with an agenda, fools, or lunatics would try to check the growth of slavery in the West; restrictionists in Congress were apparently all three. Missourians labeled "eastern politicians" dangerous fanatics. One toast, to James Tallmadge and John Taylor, the two leading restrictionists in Congress, declared them "politically insane." The author of the toast continued by recommending that "the next Congress appoint them a dark room, a straight waistcoat and a thin water gruel diet." Another toast consigned them to "a dark room and strait jackets." Tallmadge's and Taylor's notions of restriction and gradual abolition demonstrated that they were dangerous lunatics who needed to be locked away for the safety of Missouri—and presumably of slaveholders throughout the nation. Missourians' convictions that a conspiracy was afoot only increased their commitment to defeating these schemes. With or without the Tallmadge restrictions, slaveholders would continue to migrate to Missouri and "emigration will continue in giant stride." Northerners might hope to slow the western march of slaveholders, but white Missourians refused to grant even that small victory to their Yankee enemies. The rapid settlement of Missouri would signal the emerging power of the West and southern slaveholders' influence over it.[25]

Though the specter of disunion had defeated previous efforts to restrict Missouri slavery, white Missourians understood that their own disunion threats would ring hollow in the strengthened, post-1815 Union. Accordingly, they now turned to the slave South for allies. The threat posed to slavery by the Tallmadge restrictions led Missourians to envision a new alliance forming among slaveholders from "the Western and Southern States." By 1819, both possessed a common interest in slavery; they shared a common "enemy" in northern restrictionists; and Missouri was peopled largely by recent settlers from the slave states. This diminished older, East–West conflicts, but it also heralded a new, equally menacing form of North–South sectionalism that made Missourians even more militant in their defense of slavery. From the outset of the Missouri Controversy, Missourians latched on to the slaveholding states, which, like Missouri, were "vitally menaced" by the Tall-madge restrictions.[26]

Immediately upon receiving word of the Tallmadge restrictions, Missourians appealed for help in a series of letters written to Thomas Ritchie, the editor of the South's most important newspaper, the *Richmond Enquirer.* The Tallmadge restrictions have "united all nations and tongues here in favor of slavery," explained one of Ritchie's correspondents from Missouri. Settlers already in the territory would never consent to restrictions. "The only thing we have to fear is that migration from the southern States will be checked." This "would bring in a flood" of settlers opposed to slavery, making Missouri's future as a slave state doubtful. Indeed, unless southern emigrants poured into the territory, one Missourian explained, the entire trans-Mississippi West would become "a Yankee country, governed by the sniveling, sanctimonious doctrines in politics and religion which, as a Virginian, I early learned to abhor."[27]

Missourians' pleas paid off. Letters from southern newspapers exhorted Missourians to "repel" the restrictions "with firmness." In return, southern whites, politicians, and newspapers would adopt "their cause as the cause of the nation." So long as Missourians insisted on statehood with no restrictions on slavery, the slave states would resist passage of the Tallmadge restrictions in Congress and "the emigrants from the southern states will continue to flock to you." Flocked they supposedly did. The settlers who streamed into Missouri in the summer and fall of 1819 "are principally from Kentucky, Tennessee, Virginia, & the states further south," boasted Thomas Hart Benton's *St. Louis Enquirer.* They "bring great numbers of slaves, knowing that Congress has no power to impose the agitated restriction, and that the people of Missouri will never adopt it." Indeed, "not withstanding the great number of persons who are held in check by the agitation of the slave question in congress," slaveholders' continued migration to Missouri proved "astonishingly great." Missourians, assisted by planter politicians from the South and slaveholding families on their way to Missouri, would defeat the Yankee conspiracy.[28]

In many ways, it was irrelevant whether Missouri really was "peopled almost entirely by slave-holders" before the crisis, whether slaveholders really answered the call and flocked to Missouri, or whether the population had become "more homogenous." White Missourians believed that they had, and they increasingly identified themselves as part of a larger nation dominated by "Virginia and her sister slave-holding states." Non-slaveholding states of course had the right to live without slavery, but the United States was a slaveholders' republic. The fact was, Americans lived under "a constitution not only permitting, but partly based on domestic slavery." The right to enslave others was a right, as well "our privilege, our advantage, as Americans." As such, Congress could do nothing to impair the exercising of that right in Missouri or anywhere else. Here was something dramatically new from western slavehold-ers. In previous conflicts over slavery expansion, western slaveholders had claimed that by protecting slavery the federal government could demonstrate its commitment to serving the interests of western set-tlers. White Missourians turned what had once been a privilege and an indulgence into a new doctrine of slaveholders' rights that extended to Missouri and all of the West.[29]

Nathaniel Beverley Tucker furthered Missourians' notions that the Missouri Country and the West were now part of a larger slaveholding republic rightly dominated by "southrons." In a letter to the *Richmond Enquirer,* Tucker pledged white Missourians' determination to create a slave state that would do honor to his native Virginia. "Instead of the southrons being discouraged and giving Jonathan an opportunity of slipping in and throwing open our doors to his brethren (the sons and brothers of Mr. Taylor)," the Missourians "have backed him out com-pletely," Tucker boasted. "Scarcely a Yankee has moved into the country this year." Even "the more designing and ambitious" ones were "giving up the game" and leaving Missouri. With Yankees staying away, "Vir-ginia, the Carolinas, Tennessee, and Kentucky, are moving on in great force" to Missouri. Undoubtedly satisfied at the accomplishments of his irascible band of "southrons" in Missouri, Tucker gloated that "our population is daily more homogenous."[30]

To make their population "more homogenous," Missourians had to silence or drive out any secret "emancipationists" or northern sympa-thizers who remained among them. Missourians' "deep rooted preju-dice" and "scarce toleration" for suspected "emancipationists" came to the surface as soon as word of the Tallmadge restrictions reached Missouri in late March 1819. In early April, "A Farmer of St. Charles County," claiming to represent the sentiments of his "neighbors," wrote an antislavery plea to the *Missouri Gazette.* The "Farmer" denounced slavery, defended the Tallmadge restrictions, and called on his fellow Missourians to do the same. Writers to the St. Louis newspapers spent the better part of the next month denouncing the "self-styled Farmer" for claiming to speak for anyone in Missouri. "The writer is not a St. Charles farmer," declared one sleuth, who also discovered that "there was not a single neighborhood" in the county, let alone the territory, that favored restrictions on slavery. According to "A MISSOURIAN," the "Farmer" merely "pretended that he has neighbors, into whose mouths he puts sentiments, too contemptible and servile" to have come from Missourians. Yet another writer traversed the entire county to prove that the "Farmer" was a fake.[31]

Having proved that no person in St. Charles County would admit to supporting restrictions, white Missourians turned their attention elsewhere. Like a horde of Vandals, northerners allegedly stood ready to inundate Missouri from Illinois. One Missouri paper raged against a Fourth of July celebration held just across the river in Edwardsville, Illinois. On July 3, a comet streaked through the night sky, inspiring the following day's celebration at Edwardsville.

A comet appear'd last night in the sky
To give us a *toast* for the fourth of July
May she sail up *Missouri*—and slavery end it
And scorch with her tail those who wish to defend it.

In addition to wishing a scorching lesson for Missouri slaveholders, the gathering also made the following toast: "If slavery must there be tolerated, let it be on these terms, that master and slave change conditions every seven years." The indignant editor of the *Missouri Intelligencer* warned Illinois "emancipationists" to steer clear of Missouri, and proposed sending out Missouri preachers to set Illinois right.[32]

Other slaveholders preferred to take care of problems in Missouri first. Humphrey Smith, a preacher from New Jersey, apparently took doctrines about the equality of men too seriously, much to the chagrin of his neighbors in the Boone's Lick settlements along the Missouri River. Smith unwisely revealed his dislike of slavery and his support for the Tallmadge restrictions. He was soon accused of planning a slave uprising, and found himself "beset in the night by a mob of slaveholders, who dragged him out of his bed, beat him with clubs, and inflicted from twenty to thirty lashes upon his body." The crowd then "declared their intention 'to kill, or drive out of this country,' any man who should open his mouth against slavery." By April 1820 the *St. Louis Enquirer* was warning its readers that "an immense number of preachers who have arrived from the North within two or three years" had "silently taken root among us," apparently intent on spreading their abolitionist doctrines. When Yankee itinerant John Mason Peck faced allegations that his sermons had too much of an antislavery bent, he denied that he had ever so much as "preach[ed] on slavery," no doubt with his own personal safety in mind. Like Peck, Missourians who harbored sympathy for restrictions soon learned to silence or disavow those beliefs. With the threat and reality of mob violence silencing dissent, proslavery Missourians could rightly proclaim "their *unanimity* of sentiment."[33]

Codifying the place of slavery and African Americans in Missouri was as important as driving out Yankees and encouraging slaveholder settlement. The protest of the Mount Pleasant Baptist Association illustrates how thoroughly white Missourians had reconciled slavery as a permanent institution along with their political, economic, and religious aspirations. Eager to defend Missouri slavery, the Baptist association drafted a set of resolutions and published their protest against restrictions in the *Missouri Intelligencer* and *Niles' Weekly Register*. They first refused to recognize any claims that blacks might have to freedom. They next defined slaves exclusively as property, and they insisted that their own "liberty" included the right to purchase, sell, and hold slaves free from any government interference. The association framed the issue facing Missouri and the nation in poignant terms that revealed their unshakable commitment to slavery. "The constitution does not admit slaves to be freemen; it does admit them to become property, and guarantees to the master an ownership, which his fellow-citizens, living in another state, holding other principles, cannot legislate from him." They reiterated that the Constitution bound the federal government "to protect us in the free enjoyment of our liberty and property—and therefore, not only our right to admission into the union, but our right to hold slaves."[34]

Like so many other apologists for Missouri slavery, the Baptist association addressed every qualified criticism of slavery with an unqualified defense of their right to hold slaves—forever. They assured readers "that, as a people, the baptists have always been republican." Along "with Washington, Jefferson, and every other person," they claimed to "regret the existence of slavery at all." They favored "amelioration," bettering the conditions under which slaves labored for others. They "hail[ed] with Christian gratitude" measures that purportedly lessened the burden on slaves, and they pledged to "always aid any measures tending thereto." But like every other proslavery Missourian, they had nothing to say about emancipation, no matter how gradual or how far into the future. For the benefit of tender consciences in the East—and perhaps their own—the Mount Pleasant Baptists welcomed amelioration through expansion and diffusion. Yet they adamantly refused to consent to any restrictions on slavery, let alone entertain even the most gradual of abolition plans, as the Tallmadge Amendments proposed. Jefferson and others who extolled diffusion might have hoped that expansion could some day lead to gradual abolition. White Missourians harbored no such fanciful delusions.[35]

III

In Ohio and Indiana, popular politics would prove the deciding factor in determining slavery's future. In Missouri, the already widespread acceptance of slavery made popular politics far less crucial in determining the institution's fate there. Even as debates in Congress stalled statehood, politicians in the territory proceeded with plans to hold elections for delegates to a constitutional convention. After Congress agreed to admit Missouri "without restrictions" in 1820, the campaign for delegates to the state constitutional convention began. The debates over slavery that had taken place in the year between Missouri's application for statehood and Congress's decision to admit the state only deepened white Missourians' commitment to entering the Union as a slave state. It also destroyed any possibility that they would voluntarily place restrictions on the institution, as a few hardy souls in Missouri proposed. As one recent settler noted, "the attempts to exclude slavery & make the exclusion a condition of admission into the union" produced "great excitement" throughout Missouri. That "great excitement" led white Missourians to unite solidly behind proslavery candidates for the constitutional convention. The few "restrictionist" candidates who proposed placing at least some constitutional restrictions on slavery in Missouri hardly stood a chance.[36]

A successful restrictionist campaign would have to exploit small slaveholders' and non-slaveholders' animosity toward allegedly imperious planter grandees, just as it had in Ohio and Indiana. "You are now called upon for the last time to say whether aristocracy and tyranny shall prevail—whether a few nabobs selected by a secret caucus shall be forced upon you," declared the restrictionists. Leading restrictionist candidate John Lucas warned voters that "great slaveholders" would soon be "coming amongst us with their gangs of plantation slaves: assuming airs of nabobs; superciliously looking upon our plain and unassuming farmers." Missouri would become either a small farmers' democracy, touched lightly by slavery's blighting hand, or a planter-dominated aristocracy.[37]

Despite their strong words, the restrictionists recognized that farmers could not be brought around to gradual emancipation as a policy, no matter how couched or cushioned with conditions. They assured voters that the restrictionists would make no attempt to "impair any existing right, even the right to hold slaves or their offspring, to the most remote generations." Slaveholders already in Missouri would own their slaves and their offspring, forever. The restrictionists also refused to push for an immediate ban prohibiting settlers from carrying any additional slaves into Missouri, as the Tallmadge restrictions proposed. They instead adopted a platform that called for a prohibition to go into effect in ten years, a milder proposal with a slightly better chance of passing. They would lessen "the evil" of slavery only by the most gradual steps. They would do so "without interfering with the existing rights of property." Equally important, the ten-year window for slaveholder migration would allow slavery and southern emigration to revive Missouri's prosperity, which had suffered a serious blow in the Panic of 1819.[38]

Demonstrating the dearth of antislavery sentiment, the restrictionists' proposals made little headway with Missouri voters. One longtime resident of the Boone's Lick settlements along the Missouri River estimated that "nine tenths of the people" there were "in favor of slavery" with no restrictions. With voter sentiment so solidly against restrictions, one aspiring candidate expected that "no man will be elected from these counties unless he declare himself for slavery," and it might very well "require a property in slaves" for election. He also knew that any candidate who mistakenly declared his "sentiments against slavery" would immediately find his "political career is ended." This was exactly the fate of John Lucas, a longtime prominent resident of St. Louis and the leader of the restrictionists. The "ardent friends of slavery" labeled him "an emancipator, the worst name that can be given in the state of Missouri." Despite his prominence, Lucas's political fortunes plunged once the "emancipationist" tag was hung on him. The proslavery forces spared no opportunity to excoriate the nominally antislavery candidates, despite their exceedingly mild proposals. They also attacked candidates deemed insufficiently proslavery. The so-called Independent Tickets, candidates who were not aligned with the strongest proslavery factions, had to defend themselves against charges that they were secretly in favor of restrictions. Even candidates who declared themselves in favor of slavery faced charges that their proslavery militancy was too soft.[39]

Not a single restrictionist made it to the constitutional convention. The restrictionists' greatest strength was in St. Louis County. Yet even there, the proslavery candidate with the smallest number of votes, 562, ran 162 votes ahead of the popular restrictionist John Lucas. And while St. Louis County voters cast 7,265 votes for proslavery anti-restrictionists, there were only 2,026 votes for the restrictionists.[40] Thomas Hart Benton was certainly prone to fits of overstatement, but his *St. Louis Enquirer* spoke the simple truth when it declared that "there is not a single *confessed* restrictionist elected throughout the Territory, nor a *disguised* one that will venture to confess himself in the convention." With their protests against the Tallmadge restrictions and their election of a unanimous anti-restrictionist slate to the state constitutional convention, white Missourians had spoken in unmistakable tones.[41]

Meeting in 1820, the state constitutional convention passed a host of provisions protecting slavery as a permanent institution. The constitution prohibited the legislature from interfering with slaveholder's property rights. Only a constitutional amendment, ratified by the voters, could enact a gradual emancipation program in Missouri, and whatever the popular margin, Missouri slaveholders had to give their consent to the amendment before the state could implement it. Finally, the state was obligated to pay full value for any slave so emancipated, making it prohibitively expensive. Gradual abolition thus became a virtual impossibility. Nor did Missourians have to worry that their fellow brethren from other southern states might be deterred from settling in Missouri. The constitution expressly prohibited the legislature from denying settlers the right to carry their slaves into Missouri. Many Missourians had emigrated from Upper South states with relatively large free-black populations. Hated free blacks would never trouble free white Missourians. The constitution directed the state legislature, "as soon as may be, to pass such laws" to "prevent free negroes and mulattoes from coming to, and settling in, this state, under any pretext whatsoever."[42]

IV

In recent years, historians have established that conflicts between planters and farmers were an important dynamic shaping antebellum southern politics, along with class, gender, and racial relationships. As they have pointed out, non-slaveholding whites complained of the excessive political power of planters, despised blacks whether free or slave, and cursed slavery's detrimental effects on economic development.[43]

In the Upper South, it is indisputable that the notion that slavery retarded economic prosperity and burdened society received a fresh hearing among planters and farmers alike. Complicating Upper South planters' notions of "conditional antislavery" was their belief that most whites remained but half-committed to an institution that they saw as something of a menace. Consequently, planters and farmers continued to express hope that somehow, someday, the Upper South might be able to rid itself of both slavery and blacks, as was debated during the Virginia constitutional convention of 1829–30. In the Deep South, slavery and planters came under assault as "egalitarian republicans" challenged domineering planters whose hold on power stood at odds with the principles of democracy for all free white men. In addition, the insatiable demand of planters and aspiring planters for slave labor meant that the Deep South's dangerously large slave population continued growing, adding to the complaints of non-slaveholders and small slaveholders against planters. It was in response to this new vulnerability that planters began to formulate notions of "Herrenvolk democracy," codifying the belief that white freedom and equality were inseparable from black slavery and subordination. By the early 1830s, a shared commitment to white man's republicanism and permanent slavery for blacks bridged the class chasm between planters, small slaveholders, and non-slaveholders in the South.

This may apply to the Old South as a whole, but it does not seem to fit Missouri. White Missourians evinced little concern that slavery might prove detrimental to economic prosperity or democracy in their corner of the nation. On the contrary, Missouri's future prosperity and greatness seemed tied inextricably to slavery as a permanent institution. Few whites displayed ambivalence, let alone hostility, toward the institution; many expressed unabashed enthusiasm for it. Indeed, it is quite possible that historians may have overstated slavery's vulnerability and underemphasized its resilience. The same might be said for the Missouri Crisis in Congress. The militancy that Missourians demonstrated had its counterpart in Washington, where southern politicians, encouraged by Missourians, for the first time took a bold, unequivocal, and aggressive stand against any national restriction of slavery's expansion. They did so, not on fears of an underpopulated, disaffected, and vulnerable West, but on the interests of an expansive and burgeoning South.

5

"Hot Times about Slavery and Republicanism"

Ohio, 1799–1802

Voters and politicians in Ross County, Ohio, knew Elias Langham well. Formerly a Virginia planter, Langham was an inveterate politician and office monger who hungered for popular acclaim. Though his political opponents denounced him as "a man lost to every sense of honesty or honor," they also acknowledged his mastery of electoral politics. When electioneering, Langham "could take a drink of grog and smoke a pipe, and 'kick up a fight' and make it up again." Another opponent, frustrated at Langham's skill, labeled him "the great author of bustle and confusion" among the voters of Ross County.[1] Despite his mastery of politics and his electioneering shenanigans, all was not well for Langham in the fall of 1802. As the election for delegates to Ohio's constitutional convention neared, his popularity plunged because of his alleged support for slavery and his past association with the deeply unpopular territorial governor, Arthur St. Clair.

Langham turned to the press both to redeem his candidacy and to denigrate his opponents. He charged that the two most popular candidates in the county, Edward Tiffin and Thomas Worthington, had supported a group of Virginia officers' 1799 petitions to open the Virginia Military District of Ohio to slavery. Langham also claimed that he had led the opposition to efforts to permit slavery in Ohio. As proof, he reprinted—but badly misrepresented—his and his opponents' votes on the 1799 petitions. Finally, Langham charged that Worthington and Tiffin opposed his candidacy because he knew of and opposed their secret plan to use the upcoming constitutional convention to legalize slavery in Ohio. According to Langham, he was the lone candidate in Ross County with a proven antislavery record. He alone could be trusted to keep slavery out of Ohio. "Here, my fellow citizens, you find me on record opposed to slavery under any colour or pretence, at a very early day in this territory."[2]

Langham's plan to regain popular favor failed badly. Rather than opposing slavery in 1799, he supported and probably wrote the bill to permit the indenturing of black slaves in the territory. The week after Langham championed his fictitious antislavery record and attacked Worthington and Tiffin, his opponents struck back. They reprinted the correct proceedings of the 1799 bill to introduce slaves, exposing Langham as "the alone candidate for slavery, or for a servitude little better than slavery." The essayists then praised the antislavery credentials of Worthington and Tiffin, former slaveholders who had emancipated their slaves before moving to Ohio. As one of his more biting critics would have it, Langham's distortion of his own and his opponents' records on slavery "proves the author to be either a drunk or a fool."[3]

Langham's conversion to antislavery politics reveals much about the failure of slavery expansion in Ohio and the Old Northwest. In 1799 Langham was the driving force behind efforts to open Ohio to slavery. Three years later, as he stood as a candidate for office, he boasted of his fictitious antislavery record to any voter willing to listen. In the Virginia Military District of Ohio, former slaveholders were outdoing themselves in extolling their opposition to slavery before a largely southern-born electorate. The heated public debates over slavery galvanized once indifferent Ross County voters into a potent antislavery political force. Squabbles among ambitious office seekers turned into a referendum on the place of slavery, republicanism, and aristocracy in the future state of Ohio. Langham, the candidate with the most equivocal record on slavery, lost the election. Ross County voters instead selected only candidates who had publicly pledged their opposition to any effort to permit slavery in Ohio.

In 1847 aging Ohioan Jacob Burnet recollected that "the public feel-

ing, on the subject of admitting slavery into the Territory, was such that
the request would have been denied, by a unanimous vote, if the Legislature had possessed the power of granting it." Burnet was, of course,
correct; there was no chance that Ohio voters or politicians would have
legalized slavery in their 1802 Constitution. Yet the deep animus against
slavery expressed by Ohio voters in the 1802 campaign was in many
ways a product of that campaign itself. Competitive democratic politics, especially in the two most densely settled portions of Ohio, around
Cincinnati and Chillicothe, made slavery a salient political issue. It also
gave voters a meaningful way to express their opposition to it.[4]

In the 1802 election for delegates to the state constitutional convention, Ohio voters overwhelmingly selected Republican candidates
pledged to oppose any efforts to permit slavery in their new state. When
the delegates met at Chillicothe in November, they placed Article VI of
the Northwest Ordinance into their constitution, prohibiting slavery
in any form. Ohio's voters and politicians had successfully preserved
Article VI of the Northwest Ordinance. Ohioans quickly elevated their
state's reputation as a bastion of freedom to near-mythical status. As
the "freeborn Sons" of Ohio boasted in 1806, they were "true to the
rights of humanity, and the principles of liberty." They would "never
permit the foul form of slavery to tread on their sacred soil." If the "free-
born Sons" of Ohio were indeed "true to the rights of humanity, and
the principles of liberty," it was in no small part because Ohio politics
became highly competitive and issue-oriented in the years leading to
statehood.[5]

I

By 1790, three years after the passage of the Northwest Ordinance, massive land claims already covered nearly half of what would become the
state of Ohio. From Connecticut's Western Reserve in the northeastern
corner to the Miami Purchase in the southwest, surveyors and speculators drew lines on maps anticipating the onslaught of land-hungry
settlers from the East. Migration proved sluggish, however, as the allied
Indians of the Northwest posed a threat to European American settlers
in both Ohio and Kentucky. Exorbitant demands from American officials made negotiated settlement with the Northwest Indians impossible.
When those Indians responded by stepping up attacks on encroaching
American settlers, the army set out to destroy the core towns of the

most hostile Northwest Indians. The expeditions proved disastrous, as American officials badly overestimated American might while underestimating their foes. Northwestern Indians ambushed, defeated, and scattered larger forces led by Josiah Harmar in 1790 and territorial governor Arthur St. Clair in 1791. With much of the Ohio Country exposed to Indian raids in the early 1790s, the few settlers clustered at settlements around Cincinnati and Marietta and their nearby army forts.[6]

In August 1794 General Anthony Wayne and the Legion of the United States defeated the Northwest Indians at Fallen Timbers and then burned their settlements along the Maumee River in northwest Ohio. Three months later, an American treaty with Great Britain stipulated that the British must evacuate their forts in the American Northwest, forts that had provided crucial support for the Indian nations allied against American encroachment. These circumstances made it increasingly more difficult for the Northwest Indians to hold onto their lands in Ohio. In August 1795 they signed the Treaty of Greenville, ceding much of southern and eastern Ohio to the United States. Much of what would become the state of Ohio was now free from Indian threats and land claims. Almost immediately thereafter, settlers from New England, the mid-Atlantic states, the Chesapeake, and Kentucky began to migrate to the part of the Northwest Territory that would become the state of Ohio.[7]

Settlers from Virginia and Kentucky tended to migrate to the Virginia Military District of Ohio, a great swath of land in the south-central part of Ohio set aside by Virginia as payment to its Revolutionary War veterans. The Virginia Military District proved especially attractive to Virginians wary of settling in Kentucky, and to Kentuckians looking for more secure land titles elsewhere. By the early 1790s, Kentucky's troubled land market was already undermining its reputation as a "good poor man's country." Even in the mid-1790s, the average price of land in Kentucky ranged from $3 an acre for remote tracts to $6 or $8 an acre for land in the already developed Bluegrass region. Making matters worse, in their rush to claim land and settle Kentucky in the 1770s and 1780s, early settlers and speculators from Virginia had hastily surveyed their grossly inflated land claims, often resulting in overlapping, multiple claims to the same piece of land. Instead of a secure land title at a good price, settlers in the 1790s found costly, confused, and overlapping land titles tied up in costly lawsuits.[8]

Once cleared of Indian threats, Ohio became far more promising for settlement than Kentucky. In Ohio itself, settlement in the Virginia Military District seemed more favorable than settlement on lands owned by the federal government. Federally owned lands in Ohio sold at a costly $2 per acre on 640-acre tracts, with credit unavailable until the Harrison Land Act of 1800. The price, size, and stingy credit terms for federal land put it out of the reach of many families. In the Virginia Military District, however, lands could be purchased from speculators with the tract price, size, and terms of credit negotiable. Settlers could also purchase warrants issued to Virginia military veterans, good for a specified quantity of unlocated land in the Virginia Military District. The warrants traded on the open market in Virginia, Kentucky, and Ohio, and settlers who purchased one could exchange their warrant for a piece of land in the Virginia Military District of Ohio. In the 1790s, the Virginia Military District was still a fresh land market. Unlike Kentucky, it provided affordable, secure land titles, along with ample opportunity for small-time speculation. Beginning in 1795, Virginians and Kentuckians poured into the Scioto Valley of Ohio.[9]

Settlement in Ohio presented a problem for one group of southern migrants, a promise for another. Many antislavery Virginians seeking settlement in the West first went to Kentucky. Despite some anticipation and ample effort on their part, Kentucky's 1799 constitutional convention failed to adopt any plan for gradual abolition. Disappointed antislavery Virginians and Kentuckians then looked to Ohio, hoping that it would adhere "strictly to the idea that was first held out concerning this territory, that hereditary slavery should not exist there." Though the great rush of southern antislavery evangelicals would not begin in earnest until after Ohio statehood, beginning in 1795 they crossed the Ohio River into free territory in ever-increasing numbers. Other Virginians and Kentuckians proved far less enthusiastic about the Article VI prohibition on slavery. For slaveholding Virginians and Kentuckians, Article VI created a serious impediment to settlement in the Virginia Military District of Ohio, despite its clear advantages over settlement elsewhere.[10]

The legislature of the Northwest Territory met for the first time in September 1799. Almost immediately thereafter, a group of Virginia military officers presented a petition "praying for the toleration to bring their slaves into" the Virginia Military District of Ohio. The

legislature referred the petition to a committee of three. William Goforth Sr., a New Yorker active in the Republican Corresponding Societies of Cincinnati, chaired the committee, which also included Thomas
Worthington, a former Virginian living in the Military District who had
emancipated his slaves before removing to Ohio. It was doubtful that a
committee including these men would do anything but reject the petition. Perhaps hoping for a more favorable hearing for the petitioners,
some member, most likely Elias Langham, motioned to place himself
on the committee. If Langham hoped to influence the committee's decision and open the Virginia Military District to slavery, he must have
been disappointed. The committee deemed the petition "incompatible"
with Article VI of the Northwest Ordinance. After the committee read
its report, the house "resolved, unanimously" to accept its recommendation.[11]

Slaveholding Virginians and Kentuckians were not yet finished. Two
months later, as the assembly concluded its business for the session, a
larger group of Virginia veterans and warrant holders presented a second, more carefully worded petition. The timing and wording of the
second petition suggest that the petitioners had help from someone familiar with the reservations of the assembly, most likely Elias Langham.
The petitioners requested only that "persons holding slaves under the
laws of the state in which they acquire that species of property, and removing to this territory" be permitted "to bring their slaves with them,
under certain restrictions." Rather than opening the territory to slavery,
the petitioners requested that the assembly allow a limited form of slavery, more akin to indentured servitude than permanent slavery. Here
was a request that the representatives might grant. The petition asked
only for a limited admission of slaves as indentured servants into a labor-starved and underdeveloped territory.[12]

Langham chaired the second committee, which was rounded out by
John Smith, a former Virginia slaveholder and Baptist preacher from
Cincinnati, and Paul Fearing, a Federalist lawyer from Marietta. The
following day, Langham presented a bill that sounded like a proposal
to keep slavery and servitude out of the Northwest Territory. Actually,
it was a cleverly worded attempt to permit indentured servitude while
prohibiting chattel slavery. After various efforts to modify the bill, the
legislature finally seemed to have caught on to Langham's plan to cir-
cumvent Article VI. The assembly promptly killed his proposal by a vote

of 15 to 2. There would be no slavery or indentured servitude in territorial Ohio. That would not be the end of the slavery issue, however.[13]

II

Langham and the Virginia officers' attempts to dodge Article VI in the Virginia Military District helped make slavery an important political issue in the years leading to statehood. Federalists led by Governor Arthur St. Clair had ruled the territory since 1788. Beginning in 1798, with the population and number of settlements increasing rapidly, the Federalists faced frequent challenges to their power, authority, and influence. Their unpopular and allegedly self-interested policies drew resentment from various interests, settlers, and settlements across the territory. Political squabbles and the Federalists' inability or unwillingness to address the diverse interests in the territory frequently turned into deeper ideological and cultural clashes that hurt Federalist reputations further. After 1800, Federalists faced steady allegations of "corruption," "aristocracy," and "colonial rule," charges they found increasingly more difficult to overcome. With Republican victories in the national elections of 1800, the numerous anti-Federalist factions in the territory began to congeal under the Republican banner. Republicans now demanded statehood for Ohio, partly as a means to overthrow Federalist domination of the territory. By 1801, the Federalists badly needed an issue to revive their sagging political fortunes; they found it in slavery. Soon enough, Ohio Federalists began to charge that the Ohio Republicans' push for statehood was part of a larger, secret plot to legalize slavery in Ohio.[14]

Federalists and Republicans were matched most closely in Cincinnati and its hinterlands. Federalists there tried to stall the statehood movement by denouncing it as a scheme cooked up by the "Chillicothe junto"—the allegedly self-appointed oligarchy of Virginia-born Republicans who dominated politics in the Virginia Military District. The Federalists charged that once in power the "junto" and their lackeys, the Cincinnati Republicans, would quietly repeal Article VI of the Northwest Ordinance and open the state to slavery. By 1802, the Federalists had clearly failed to stop the movement for statehood, despite their efforts to defeat it with the slavery issue. Rather than fight a losing battle, they now sought the election of Federalist candidates to the constitutional convention that, if the voters approved, would meet in Chillicothe in November 1802. To do so, they tried to make slavery one of the more important issues in the statehood campaign in Cincinnati and its hinterlands.[15]

Opposition to slavery gave Cincinnati Federalists a symbolic but potent issue they could use to rehabilitate their reputation with Ohio voters. For one, it afforded them an opportunity to shake their reputation as incorrigible aristocrats. Challenging the Republicans' claim that Federalists were unrepublican aristocrats, St. Clair dubbed every man in the territory a republican, *"except, perhaps, a few people who wish to introduce negro slavery amongst us."* In another Federalist essay, a "Hamilton Farmer," who knew "what's what as well as the best of them," addressed his "Neebours" with misspellings and a condescending homespun voice that could only have come from a gentleman unable to disguise himself as a farmer.[16]

The "Farmer" nonetheless did his best to encourage real farmers to vote Federalist. The "Farmer" warned his readers that if the Republicans prevailed, "we should have gentlemen enough, and their negroes too, and that's what they want to be at—if they could only get their negroes brought here." Blatantly racist, the Federalist "Farmer" warned that if slavery were permitted in Ohio, ordinary men would suffer most: "If one of us were starving we would not get a days work, nor a civil word from one of them" aristocratic planters. Farmers and workmen would "be obliged to go out along" with the planters' "negroes to make roads." While free white men suffered the indignities of working side by side with enslaved blacks, the aristocratic planters would degrade free white men even further by "riding over us with their coaches." According to the "Hamilton Farmer," to keep taxes low, land accessible, and gentlemen out—and their "negroes too"—voters had to oppose the Chillicothe gentry and their Cincinnati minions.[17]

As the election neared, Federalists stepped up their attacks, supplementing their fake letters from farmers with fictitious toasts supposedly given by Virginia Republicans in Ohio. The former Virginian "Republicanus" purportedly offered one of his Fourth of July toasts, "To myself." All he and his ilk wanted were "Virgin's bottom" and "forty negro slaves, a good living and I am content." Self-interested Virginia planters would supposedly flock to an Ohio that permitted slavery. Once there, they would gobble up "virgin" bottomlands (valley land best for farming and access to markets), work it with the coerced labor of their black slaves, spread slothfulness across Ohio, and denigrate slaveless freemen while confining them to isolated regions with poor soils. "Virgin's bottom" had its sexual connotations as well, suggesting that lewd and licentious planters would defile the daughters of freemen. When Federalist political celebrations offered real toasts, they also included statements against slavery. The "Dayton Association" ended a celebration by offering that "SLAVERY *shall not be known on this bank of the Ohio.*" Another Federalist essayist denounced the whole statehood movement as a scheme concocted by "certain members of congress" who "wish to introduce slavery among us." By selecting Federalists of sound antislavery principles for the convention, however, voters could "forever blast the illiberal expectations of the slave scourging junto in Congress, with that of their territorial adherents," the proslavery Ohio Republicans.[18]

For all of its rhetorical flourish, chicanery, and outright racism, however, the Federalist campaign fared poorly. Many of the Republicans from Cincinnati and its hinterlands genuinely abhorred slavery. Moreover, they had no intentions of losing the election over a shadow issue conjured up by Federalists. Writing "to the Republican Corresponding Society at Cincinnati," one Republican leader expressed outrage that the Federalists "have been hardy enough to aver that our society are favorable to the admission of slavery into the new state," despite the Republicans' "full, candid and public declarations" opposing slavery. In Cincinnati and its hinterlands, the Republican corresponding societies would lead the campaign against both Federalism and slavery. To do so, they did not resort to racism, turning a campaign against slavery into a campaign to denigrate African Americans and keep them out of Ohio. Though some historians have argued that it was Republicans who resorted to racism when opposing slavery, defining the slavery issue as an effort to distance whites from blacks, in Cincinnati it was actually Federalists who tried to excite and exploit animosity toward African Americans.[19]

In 1802, nineteen Republican corresponding societies dominated the Republican Party in Cincinnati and its hinterlands. Similar to the Democratic-Republican societies that appeared in New York and Philadelphia in 1793, the Ohio Republican corresponding societies dedicated themselves to preserving the "principles of genuine republicanism" against the allegedly aristocratic Federalists. Property-holding farmers, shopkeepers, and mechanics filled the ranks of the corresponding societies, which were led by wealthier, politically ambitious men like the printer John Browne and the merchant William Goforth. In the 1802 election, they would use their rudimentary party machinery to answer Federalist charges and bury Federalist opposition.[20]

Opposition to slavery soon became one and the same with opposition to Federalism and support for republicanism. Before the Republican corresponding societies met to endorse candidates, two avowedly antislavery Republican essayists demanded that candidates declare their opposition to slavery if they hoped to receive the Republican societies' support. Republican candidates for the convention quickly obliged. Some Republican candidates undoubtedly joined the chorus of voices damning slavery to further their own political ends. Other Republicans seemed intent on purging their party of slavery independent of any Federalist allegations. Joining them was a small group of gifted essayists who penned eloquent and moving antislavery tracts for consumption by voters. Regardless of the origins of the Republicans' express dislike of slavery, their antislavery campaign all but insured that Republican candidates would declare their unbridled opposition to slavery in Ohio. It also made it that much more likely that voters would select those same Republican candidates. By defending themselves against the Federalists' accusations, the Republicans forged a devastating critique of slavery. In the process, they became the defenders of small producers and farmers against the forces of hierarchy, aristocracy, slavery, and inequality, forces that found a welcome home with Federalists and slaveholders alike.[21]

The antislavery Republican campaign appealed directly to voters' notions of republicanism and equality. As many Cincinnati Republicans understood their world, republicanism and aristocracy, equality and hierarchy, were in a constant struggle. At stake was the independence of men and their families, as opposed to degrading dependence on the wealthy, the powerful, and the well-born. For Cincinnati Republicans, the American Revolution was both a political and a social revolution, an important victory for republicanism and equality. Yet Federalist dominance in the 1790s demonstrated that true republicans must remain vigilant. Cincinnati Republicans thus understood their battle against slaveholders and Federalists as part of a larger struggle that pitted equality and republicanism against hierarchy and aristocracy. Federalists and slaveholders possessed a shared and unshakeable affinity for aristocracy and inequality. Slavery, by its nature, stood in stark opposition to republican equality. Furthermore, slaveholding inevitably made men petty but powerful tyrants, aristocrats who would use their wealth and power to lord over slaves and freemen alike. During the campaign, Cincinnati Republicans displayed an obsession with maintaining the dignity and propertied independence that the American Revolution promised to bestow on ordinary people. Thus, an unmistakable hatred of slavery permeated the Republican campaign.[22]

After lashing out against the aristocratic machinations of the St. Clair administration and the Federalists, "A Republican" launched into a polemic denouncing the "aristocratic" schemes for permitting slavery in Ohio. Slavery was simply inconsistent with the principles of "a republican government," where "every citizen has rights one with another, standing on the same footing, on the ground of equality." In a true republican government, "no man can assume" the right to rule "over another." Other essayists deepened the Cincinnati Republicans' ideological animosity against slavery. "Slavery is contrary to the rights of man," avowed "A Farmer." According to "The Friends of Humanity," if readers would apply "the leading principles of genuine republicanism" to "the subject of SLAVERY," they would of course find the two incompatible. Republican candidates incorporated the same reasoning into their campaign statements. "If there is any thing that is opposite in its nature to republican principles, or disgraceful to the professions of republicanism, it is the abhored system of slavery," declared candidate John Browne in his statement to the voters.[23]

Andrew Badgley, John Gossett, and George Medsker, three middling farmers who deemed themselves the "New Market Township Republican Society," published their own plea to the voters and delegates. Their vision of republican society recognized the agonizing plight of ordinary men who struggled to maintain their dignity and independence against the ever present threat of aristocracy. Their opposition to slavery in Ohio stemmed from a larger set of concerns for destroying the social, political, and constitutional conditions that sustained aristocracy in America and now threatened the future state. Slavery promoted the worst kind of aristocracy, and their opinion on slavery in Ohio was clear: "We do not want a constitution to deprive any of the sons of liberty of their natural rights, to constitute them slaves and entitle their fellow citizens to live on the fruit of their fellow labor." The New Market

Republicans' antislavery convictions contained a firm ideological commitment to equality for all men, irrespective of race. Their equally fierce hatred of hierarchy, subordination, and aristocracy—of men "puffed up with pride, who look upon their fellow citizens as a rank of animals beneath their notice"—intensified their opposition to slavery and their commitment to keep it out of Ohio. Only by excluding all forms of aristocracy, including slaveholding, could Ohio expect a constitution that would "cherish, support, and strengthen the laboring man with all the sweets and advantages of liberty."[24]

Like Badgley, Gossett, and Medsker, the Hamilton County Republicans defined the slavery issue as part of a larger struggle between honest producers and worthless aristocrats who held all labor in contempt. Aristocracy in any form would invariably corrupt the promise of republicanism, equality, and individual opportunity in Ohio. Importantly, their dislike of distinctions helped keep any latent racism under tight wraps. No other writer went as far as the Republican author of "Some Short Observations on Slavery," which called for the offspring of enslaved blacks to receive immediate freedom and have all rights and privileges restored to them. Badgley, Gossett, and Medsker simply demanded "a constitution that will set the natural rights of the meanest African and the most abject beggar, upon an equal footing with those citizens of the greatest wealth and equipage." The New Market and Cincinnati Republicans might not have been racial egalitarians who would warmly welcome African Americans to Ohio. Nonetheless, the Republicans called for a constitution that would extend all rights and privileges to African Americans in Ohio, including the right to vote. And while Republicans proposed extending the vote to African Americans, Federalists denigrated blacks and promised that their opposition to slavery would free white Ohioans from planters and "their negroes too." For radicals like Badgley, Gossett, and Medsker, social and legal distinctions among men—even those based on race—smacked of aristocracy and were unacceptable to any "true" republican.[25]

This dislike of distinctions and the heat of the campaign led the Republicans to a radical denunciation of slavery. The Republicans published "Some Short Observations on Slavery" in the July 3 issue of Cincinnati's *Western Spy and Hamilton Gazette.* Anything but short, the essay and commentary covered the entire front page of the paper and almost all of the second. The Republicans wished readers to know that this was a Republican production through and through. Thomas Brown, "Chairman for the Republican Corresponding Society" of Anderson Township, had prepared the essay and presented it for publication. John Browne, "Chairman for the Republican Corresponding Society of Cincinnati," proudly announced that he and the Republican societies had sponsored its printing. Published the day before Republican societies all over the county gathered to celebrate American independence, it would deliberately set the tone for the Fourth of July festivities held by the Republican societies.[26]

Though the essay had nothing to say about slavery in Ohio, it had much to say about the place of slavery in a republic committed to liberty. "Some Short Observations on Slavery" contained a ringing denunciation of racial prejudice and an equally forthright plea that blacks enjoy the same rights, liberties, and privileges as whites. "Does not justice loudly call for LIBERTY being restored to them?" asked the author. Was it not "the duty of every dispenser of justice . . . to remember that they are men, and to declare them free[?]" Only when the nation invited slaves to become free men could the United States "expect to flourish, under the blessing of him who delights in justice and mercy." And by giving freedmen "an interest in their own labour . . . those talents and ingenuity, which are now depressed by slavery," would instead be used "for the general good." Here was a radical call for full black citizenship produced and endorsed by the Republican corresponding societies.[27]

The following day, "the Republican citizens of the town of Cincinnati and its vicinity" publicly expressed the antislavery principles found in the "Short Observations." At their Independence Day celebrations they voiced hostility toward slavery and the doctrine of inequality that underwrote it. After toasting and singing a song dedicated to "Columbia's brave sons," they offered another toast to "the enslaved sons of Africa— may the time [come] when every son and daughter of Adam shall enjoy the sweets of freedom." By deeming Africans to be the sons and daughters of Adam, the Republicans repudiated the belief that Africans were the sons of Cain. In doing so, they reiterated the denial put forth in the "Short Observations" that the biblical "curses denounced against Cain or Cannan" justified slavery. Good Christian Republicans simply could not countenance slavery in Ohio.[28]

The few arguments favoring Ohio slavery claimed that it would accelerate the economic development of the state by supplying an inexpensive source of much-needed labor. They also claimed that constitutional limits could be placed on the duration of Ohio slavery, making it more a form of temporary servitude than a permanent institution. Finally, "diffusion" would supposedly provide more comforts for slaves themselves, while providing the conditions necessary for slaveholders to emancipate their slaves. According to the Cincinnati Republicans, however, diffusion and constitutional limits on the duration of Ohio slavery were nothing more than the schemes of "devils, acting under the banners of christianity and republicanism."[29]

Kentucky's failed attempt to place constitutional limits on slavery in 1799 made it that much more important to elect only candidates committed to shutting slavery completely out of Ohio. That the "chains of slavery were riveted afresh" in Kentucky's constitution demonstrated the folly of believing that Ohio slavery would be temporary. As soon as Ohio "permitted slavery with a limited term," slaveholders would begin "forming every practicable scheme to evade the same, and every artifice will be tried to defeat the design of every emancipating provision." The claim that Ohio slavery would somehow be more humane than southern slavery was equally bankrupt. "Tyrannical holders" would subject slaves to "unknown tortures." The expansion of slavery would only serve to encourage "the vile and inhuman traffic" in slaves. So that voters could better understand just how "vile and inhuman" that traffic was, the *Western Spy* carried numerous articles explicating all the horrors of the international and domestic slave trades, reminding readers that they would implicate themselves in those horrors if they permitted slavery in Ohio. There would be nothing temporary or humane about Ohio slavery. Only by stopping slavery at the constitutional convention could voters insure that slavery would never blight the promise of a free Ohio.[30]

Hamilton County Republicans were not content with merely denouncing slavery and inequality in their essays, toasts, and addresses to the voters. Antislavery Republicans had to get elected to the constitutional convention; thus, they had to denounce their Federalist opponents. Though Federalists had given token statements against slavery, they simply could not be trusted. Aristocrats at heart, Federalists would prove unable to resist proposals to permit slavery, if only because it promised to breed the inequality and hierarchy they allegedly held so dear. Only men of genuine republican principles could be counted on to "meet the sophistical insinuations of the advocates for slavery, and the fawnings and frowns of aristocratic policy." Voters had to "discard the man from your confidence, however popular he is, who would take any step to the introducing of slavery among us," another essayist instructed. Only candidates who pledged "to establish a permanent barrier against the introduction of slavery in any degree whatsoever"—meaning Republican Society candidates—were acceptable to true republican voters.[31]

As the election neared, "a number of citizens" suggested that the candidates make their positions on important issues publicly known. Of the five questions posed, one asked the candidates to address whether they were "men strenuously opposed to the introduction of involuntary slavery." The Republicans jumped at the opportunity to pledge their undying opposition to slavery. One candidate promised to "use my utmost endeavors to prevent the introduction of slavery in any manner or degree into this country." John Browne, who chaired the Hamilton County Corresponding Society's nominating committee, pledged "to oppose its introduction in to this country in any manner or degree whatsoever, and use my utmost endeavors . . . to raise an insuperable barrier against it in the first principles of the constitution."[32]

Though Federalists expressed their doubts about Republican "talk . . . against slavery," Cincinnati voters did not. Of the ten delegates chosen from Hamilton County, eight were Republicans nominated by the corresponding societies, with most bound by pledges to vote against slavery in the convention. And any delegate who considered doing otherwise was sure to be rebuked. "The Friends of Humanity" vowed "to sound the alarm, and use our utmost efforts" to destroy the political career of any delegate who voted in favor of slavery. Their warning left little doubt about how Cincinnati's Republican delegates would vote on slavery at the convention.[33]

III

It is less clear why slavery became an important political issue during the campaign for delegates in Ross County, home to the majority of settlers in the Virginia Military District. The Federalists had far less of a presence in Ross County, and Republicans were less successful at applying party discipline to the nominations. With no regular party nominations, twenty or so candidates nominated themselves and the election revolved around what Republicans the voters would elect. Candidates and politicians filled the *Scioto Gazette* with their pronouncements, and the town itself was "glutted with hand-bills and long tavern ha-rangues" extolling the virtues and detailing the shortcomings of each candidate. After various anonymous articles denouncing slavery appeared in the *Scioto Gazette* in August, the leading Republicans from Chillicothe called on all candidates for the constitutional convention to give answers to a set of five questions. One of those questions asked "whether they are, or are not, in favor of slavery being admitted into the country." Of the twenty Republican candidates, at least sixteen declared their opposition to Ohio slavery, while two Federalists pledged to support efforts to allow slavery.[34]

As in Cincinnati, the most prominent Ross County Republicans inveighed against slavery in the strongest terms. As they were pitching their campaign to a largely southern-born electorate, however, they were less harsh in their indictment of slaveholding planters than their Cincinnati counterparts. They instead resorted to a simple free-soil argument that appealed to settlers' memories of the slave societies they had left behind in the Chesapeake, western Virginia, and Kentucky. Like the Federalist candidate who claimed that "wealth" will be "brought to our country" by slaveholders, most Republican candidates were willing to admit that slavery would "at present, and for some time hence, contribute to improve our country." It was difficult to deny the benefits of slave labor on the frontier. But even if slavery "would operate as a temporary convenience," Republican candidates were sure to denounce it as a "permanent evil" that would ultimately do far more harm than good.[35]

Just as a pledge to "prohibit all involuntary slavery" became a necessary part of every candidate's address to the voters, candidates seemed intent on outdoing their opponents' hatred of the "bad policy" of slavery. Edward Tiffin, a former slaveholder who would become president of the constitutional convention and later Ohio's first governor, declared that slavery would be "the greatest national curse we could entail upon our country." Thomas Worthington, a former Virginia slaveholder who would become one of Ohio's first senators, "was decidedly opposed to slavery long before he removed to the territory." Indeed, Worthington explained, like the voters themselves, he had settled in Ohio because of "the prohibition of slavery in the territory." Worthington continued by offering what quickly became a standard trope in the election: "If slavery be admitted into this country, it will be entailing one among the greatest curses on the succeeding generations." When Elias Langham attacked Tiffin's and Worthington's antislavery credentials, anonymous essayists came to their defense, strengthening the Republicans' identification with opposition to slavery. It was well known "that Mr. Tiffin, from principle emancipated sixteen valuable slaves, which he might have sold for upwards of one thousand pounds." Worthington, too, "has been as uniformly opposed to slavery."[36]

Campaigning to a largely southern-born audience, Ross County Republicans evoked memories of all the iniquities that plagued slave states like Virginia. One deemed slavery "unjust and cruel—prejudicial to the community in general, and an encouragement to idleness and luxury." Candidates who opted to avoid listing the consequences of slavery simply referred to it as "bad policy," reminded voters of "all the impositions" slaveholders would place on freemen, or warned that "posterity" would "curse the memory of those who entailed upon them" all "the difficulties arising from slavery." In other missives, candidates warned that slavery would "discountenance labor" and "create greater distinctions in society." Inevitably, the "equal distribution of property" that characterized territorial Ohio would be "destroyed." In turn, "labor and industry would be brought into contempt," and "idleness luxury and dissipation" would infect once industrious men and women. In true free-soil fashion, "A Citizen" instructed his readers to "compare" Virginia and Pennsylvania. With "Virginia being more than one third slaves," it was scarcely surprising that "agriculture and the mechanical arts" flourished in Pennsylvania but languished in Virginia.[37]

As in Hamilton County, candidates in Ross shied away from equating their opposition to slavery with white supremacy and racial exclusionism. The denouncement by "Yellow Jacket" of the "negro feds"—Ross County Federalists who supported slavery—was as far as most Ross County Republicans were willing to associate their antislavery views with racism. But "Yellow Jacket"'s flirtation with race-baiting was mild stuff, and it was accompanied by more extensive claims of black equality and the injustice of slavery. "What right do we have to deprive a man of his right, on account of his colour?" he asked. "The God of Heaven has interwoven" a love of "liberty" in "their very natures—an inherent principle that they are free-born, which the hands of injustice and oppression withholds." Remarkably, "Yellow Jacket," who was clearly from a southern state, defended slaves' right to rebellion before a largely southern-born audience as he wrote in defense of southern-born Republican candidates.[38]

Just as remarkable, out of twenty Republican candidates, only two saw any need to join their calls for the exclusion of slavery with pledges to restrict the rights of free blacks or discourage free black migration to Ohio. Jacob Smith, who declared himself "against the admission of slavery into our new state," was also "against any negroes being admitted to evidence against a white person." William Craig added his wish to deny blacks the vote and the right to hold office. Both felt compelled to qualify their desire to deny Ohio blacks equal rights. Smith "wish[ed] to see their lives and properties protected to them as securely as to the whites," while Craig "believe[d] it to be their natural right to be free." The meager support voters gave to the two candidates pledged to restrict black rights—Smith received 348 votes, nearly 300 fewer than the 622 needed for election, while voters cast only 27 votes for Craig—suggests that while slavery was quite important to the voters of Ross County, white supremacy and the desire to limit the migration of free and enslaved blacks was far less important.[39]

Other Republican candidates asserted that black Ohioans deserved equal rights. Robert Finley pledged to "secure the sacred and unalienable rights of all the sons of man, who by nature stand on an equal footing." James Crawford declared it "an undeniable fact that all men should be free—a right which the Supreme being gave every species of men." Noble Crawford claimed he "always viewed" slavery "with intolerance, as an infringement on the rights of a part of our species," adding, "While we acknowledge the Africans to be a part of the human species, let us cheerfully grant them the privileges of freemen." Not all of the Ross County candidates were as "cheerful" about granting black Ohioans "the privileges of freemen" as Noble Crawford, who failed to receive enough votes for election to the convention. Edward Tiffin, president of the constitutional convention, cast the deciding vote on a measure to deny black Ohioans the right to vote. Similarly, some Ross County Republicans provided crucial votes on other measures denying equal rights to African Americans in Ohio. The former Virginia planters who won the majority of Ross County's seats in the convention apparently carried their Virginia prejudices against free blacks with them to Ohio, even though voters seemed at best undecided about the status of free blacks in Ohio.[40]

The few Federalists in Ross County tried to bolster their meager chances of election by pledging to favor slavery if elected. John Wills took out a large notice declaring "that I am in favor of the introduction of negroes as slaves, and pledge myself to support this principle" if elected to the convention. A week later, Wills and John Macan, another Federalist, printed longer essays detailing the reasons they wished to allow slavery in Ohio. But Macan's support of slavery waned in the face of popular sentiment. "If a majority of the people of this Territory should think it proper to admit slavery, I should think it right," he promised. But, "if this majority should think proper, by a legislative act, to prohibit slavery," he "should think it also right. *Let the will of the people be done,*" he concluded, wavering in the face of a growing antislavery tide.[41]

When Macan and Wills tried to turn slavery into a partisan issue, the Ross County Republicans responded with savage attacks against the "negro Feds." "Republicans, consider your dignity, as men and as citizens," wrote "Yellow Jacket." "Hold up the political ark of your freedom, resist the heralds of slavery." Duncan McArthur, who was not even a candidate, warned Republicans that "our political enemies . . . are setting up men of their party, under the pretence of advocating slavery." All good Republicans should know that "their only object is to deceive those republicans who wish for slavery and induce them to give their suffrage to the federal candidates."[42] The Ross County Federalists' offer to support the introduction of slavery failed miserably. So too did their pandering to voters and their mealymouthed promises to do the will of the majority. Voters cast only 50 and 87 votes for the two "feds," nearly 600 votes shy of the number needed for election. Ross County Republicans, all of whom pledged to oppose slavery, swept the elections. As was the case in Cincinnati, once slavery became a political issue, Ross County Republicans jumped to disassociate themselves from it. In the process, they, too, created the expectation that being both a republican and a Republican meant opposing efforts to open Ohio to slavery.[43]

IV

Outside of Hamilton and Ross counties, slavery was less of an issue and politics were far less competitive. Still, voters tended to select delegates with clear antislavery preferences. Federalists dominated Washington County, settled by New England war veterans and speculators. But to minimize Republican influence in the election, Federalists there also exploited the slavery issue. "We have hot times about slavery and Republicanism," wrote one correspondent to Return Jonathan Meigs Jr., a former Marietta Federalist who switched to the Republicans after Jefferson's election. Though Meigs's correspondent pledged to "spare no pains in detecting Federal villainy," the Federalists had a head start as they sought to discredit Meigs by associating the Republicans with slavery. In Clermont County, formed from the southwest corner of the Virginia Military District, voters selected Philip Gatch, a former Maryland slaveholder, well-known Methodist preacher, and friend of Edward Tiffin. Gatch used the influence of his pulpit to "more . . . sufficiently guard against" slavery by turning "the greater part of our people against it." In Jefferson County, the large Quaker community at Mount Pleasant elected Nathan Updegraff to serve as a convention delegate. Though a Federalist, Updegraff possessed "the Character of a Republican" and was "strongly opposed to *slavery.*"[44]

For all the noise generated during the elections, slavery stood little chance in Ohio. After the antislavery campaigns in Cincinnati and the Virginia Military District, it stood no chance at all. The campaign itself had created a clear majority of voters who stood steadfastly opposed to any form of slavery in the new state. The highly democratic world of Ohio politics forced candidates for the 1802 constitutional convention to take public stands on issues facing the state and punished those who refused to do so. Though the Ohio Enabling Act of 1802 allowed them to reject Article VI and permit slavery, Ohio's voters instead opted to preserve it.

The struggle between slavery and freedom in the Northwest had only begun, however. At the same time that Ohioans celebrated their new constitution, William Henry Harrison, governor of the Indiana Territory, was busy making plans to repeal Article VI in Indiana. This time, slaveholders and aspiring slaveholders would not make the mistake of allowing the slavery issue to become a matter of public debate.

6

Slaveholding Nationalism and Popular Antislavery Politics

Indiana and Illinois, 1801–1818

On December 14, 1810, Governor William Henry Harrison signed into law three bills relating to indentured servitude for African Americans in the Indiana Territory. The first bill repealed Indiana's indentured servant act, which had allowed slaveholders like Harrison to indenture black "servants" for periods lasting up to ninety-nine years. The second made it illegal for anyone to sell black slaves or indentured servants out of the Indiana Territory, providing $1,000 fines and disbarment from public office for offenders. The third invalidated any future indenture agreements made with black "servants" in other states. With a new round of elections looming, Harrison desperately sought to end the political turmoil over slavery that had beset the territory since 1808. The day after Harrison signed the bills into law, he announced that "an act for the introduction of negroes and mulattoes into this Territory is repealed." He then declared an end to the "party views" and "cant upon a subject finally put to rest," the future of slavery in territorial Indiana. With that, Harrison undid nearly a decade of his own efforts, for he had been at the forefront of the movement to suspend Article VI and gain congressional sanction for slavery in the Indiana Territory.[1]

Matters had not always been so bad for the cause of slavery in Indiana, nor had Harrison's political standing rested on such shaky ground. From 1802 through 1807, the Harrison-led, proslavery political leaders of the territory accomplished much on behalf of the institution in Indiana. They convinced Congress that a great majority of Indiana settlers supported slavery, even though most settlers knew nothing about their efforts, remained indifferent about slavery, or outright opposed it. Their lobbying insured that President Thomas Jefferson and other southern politicians would either support or remain indifferent to Indiana slavery. They also led three separate House committees into recommending suspension of Article VI. In Indiana itself, the proslavery political leaders instituted a series of laws allowing settlers to import black slaves as indentured servants. Harrison and the proslavery politicians also minimized the effectiveness of any antislavery sentiment in the territory by deliberately hiding their efforts to undermine Article VI from settlers in the territory itself. By 1807 the proslavery faction's control of territorial politics was unchallenged, few settlers were aware of the proslavery movement, even fewer challenged Harrison on the issue, and it seemed likely that Congress might sanction Indiana slavery by suspending Article VI. Yet by 1810 Indiana's proslavery movement was all but dead, while Harrison and slavery were the main targets of a burgeoning political opposition that threatened to undermine his influence in the territory.

Historians typically explain the rapid demise of Indiana's proslavery movement by focusing on congressional indifference to Indiana slavery, along with the sectional backgrounds and prejudices of Indiana settlers. Supposed congressional indifference allowed the Virginia-born Harrison to work with like-minded southern-born settlers to undermine Article VI and replicate their familiar system of servitude in Indiana through 1807. After 1807, an influx of antislavery northerners and non-slaveholding southerners soon outnumbered the proslavery settlers. Recognizing that these new settlers would not support their ongoing effort to overturn Article VI, and unable to compete for the attention of a Congress preoccupied with other pressing matters, Harrison and the proslavery settlers dropped the issue and it quietly disappeared.[2]

The sectional backgrounds and prejudices of settlers certainly influenced their concerns about slavery and insured its demise in Indiana. Nonetheless, local and territorial political contests, along with northern Republican congressmen's opposition to overturning Article VI, were far more important in determining slavery's fate there. Indeed, the history of Indiana slavery was quite politicized and contentious. As Harrison remarked after repealing Indiana's indentured servitude laws, he hoped to bring an end to "party views" and "cant" about slavery: party views that now threatened his political future in Indiana. As in Ohio, the slavery question became a political question intertwined with larger conflicts over what type of republican society Indianans would create. Also as in Ohio, Indiana's antislavery majority did not so much exist as it was created through political contests. The near absence of federal power in Indiana and the Illinois Country had allowed small but influential proslavery groups to evade, undermine, and challenge Article VI of the Northwest Ordinance since its passage in 1787. The same absence of federal power encouraged antislavery settlers to take it upon themselves to defeat the proslavery movement in the territory. Ultimately, competitive electoral politics in the territory, along with certain northern Republicans' opposition in Congress, stopped slavery's expansion into Indiana.

I

In January 1801 William Henry Harrison arrived in Vincennes, the capital of the newly created Indiana Territory, to assume his duties as governor.[3] The small and shabby population of the "ancient" French settlement reflected the territory's sparse population and underdevelopment. According to the official territorial census conducted in 1801, fifteen hundred or so French traders and farmers, Americans, and their slaves clustered around Vincennes. Another two thousand lived in scattered settlements along the Wabash, Ohio, and Mississippi rivers. A few thousand other settlers who illegally squatted on lands along the Ohio and Whitewater rivers eluded census officials, but rounded out Indiana's "American" population.[4]

As governor of the immense Indiana Territory (which included the future states of Indiana and Illinois), it fell on Harrison to bolster the American nation-state's presence in Indiana and the Illinois Country by making the inhabitants "happy and satisfied with their government." This would be no easy task. The United States's most notable accomplishment was to prohibit slavery, a deeply unpopular law that many inhabitants resented and evaded. Worse, the government had only the barest presence in Indiana and the Illinois Country, and had done little to address the interests or concerns of the white inhabitants. As a result, "the affairs of the whole territory" had fallen into "the greatest confusion"; the "inattention of their government" had left the people in a "state of wretchedness"; and "discord and anarchy ruled without sway." On the remote fringes of the overextended republic, Harrison found himself facing weighty concerns related to Indiana's settlement, development, and integration into the "union of interests." These concerns would profoundly affect his decision to work for suspension of Article VI.[5]

Historians recognize that Harrison's background left him predisposed to favor slavery in Indiana. The son of a prominent Virginia planter and heir to a considerable plantation, he arrived in Vincennes with a black servant in tow. Harrison often played the part of the Virginia planter on the Indiana frontier. His grand estate, Grouseland, imitated Virginia planters' great houses. He governed in the "Virginia style," forming alliances with leading men while using his prestige and patronage to influence subordinates. Harrison speculated heavily in land, a time-honored Virginia tradition and an investment sure to pay even greater dividends if Congress permitted slavery. Finally, when Congress rejected Harrison's first appeal for suspension of Article VI, he promptly instituted a set of laws allowing men like himself to hold slaves as servants, thereby replicating slavery in fact if not in name.[6]

All the same, Harrison's fixation with Indiana slavery involved much more than a desire to create a little Virginia on the banks of the Wabash, and his attachment to both Virginia localism and slavery can be overstated. Harrison lived in Virginia only until the age of seventeen, spending his formative years in Philadelphia, New Jersey, and Ohio. In 1790 he attended medical school in Philadelphia, studying medicine under Dr. Benjamin Rush, a nationalist, while residing with the financier Robert Morris, an ultra-nationalist. In 1791 he received a commission in the army, where his service during the wars against the Northwest Indian confederacy further impressed upon him the importance of federal power in securing the Northwest. Harrison resigned from the army in 1798, then entered Ohio politics with the help of his father-in-law, Federalist John Cleves Symmes, and purchased land and a home in New Jersey, where his wife and children lived. While serving as Ohio's delegate to Congress and as secretary of the territory, he gained the approval of ultra-Federalists Winthrop Sargent (whom he replaced as secretary) and Arthur St. Clair (whose son Harrison defeated to become territorial delegate).[7]

Throughout his public career Harrison remained a staunch nationalist whose outlook accorded more closely with Virginia-born nationalists such as George Washington and Henry Clay than with government minimalists like Thomas Jefferson and John Randolph. Plantation lords in the South and Southwest feared the federal government as a challenge to their own influence and local power. Conversely, Harrison's "empire for liberty" involved the use of federal power to create secure, prosperous communities in the West. While Harrison, like Clay and Washington, was a slaveholder, slavery was not central to his vision of an expanding American empire. Furthermore, Harrison's personal attachment to slavery did not run deep. In 1810, he readily dropped the slavery issue in Indiana. After the War of 1812, though he had family and land in Kentucky, he chose to resume his political career in free Ohio. By 1816, he was publicly associating with Ohio Federalists and portraying himself as an antislavery candidate for Congress. In 1840, Harrison secured the Whig nomination and the presidency, in no small part because groups as diverse as New York abolitionists and Virginia states rightists deemed him safe on the slavery question. Above all else, Harrison was a politician who used both slavery and antislavery to further his own political ends, rather than a slaveholder who used politics to protect and promote the interests of slaveholders.[8]

When Harrison arrived in Indiana in 1801, he found his nationalist and political concerns immediately focusing on slavery. Harrison was the most important American official in the Northwest borderlands once he became governor of the immense Indiana Territory and Superintendent of Indian Affairs in the Northwest. To him more than any other American fell the task of securing this remote borderland to the American Union. Slavery became important to Harrison to the degree that it furthered this goal. And though slavery was never central to Harrison's vision of an American empire in the Northwest, Article VI seemed central to his problems on the Indiana frontier.

Upon arriving in Indiana, Harrison toured the main settlements of the territory and met with leading local men from Vincennes and the Illinois Country, many of whom were French-speaking slaveholders with minimal attachment to the U.S. government. Harrison would need these notables' influence in order to govern effectively in the still intensely personal and local world of Indiana politics. These same men immediately informed Harrison that the "constitutional evils" of "the present ordinance" had thwarted settlement, depopulated the country, and left the remaining settlers deeply aggrieved. If Harrison hoped to win these men over, he had to overturn Article VI, something that they had been attempting for more than a decade, with no success.[9]

It took little to convince him that Article VI "retarded the improvement and population of this Country," in any case. National politicians had accepted Article VI's antislavery provisions in 1787, in part because they had expected free-state settlers and non-slaveholders from the South to flock to the Northwest. Though this free-labor exodus made its way to Ohio, it failed to materialize in Indiana, which remained chronically underpopulated and underdeveloped. This situation seemed unlikely to change any time soon. Unsettled lands in northern Pennsylvania, northern and western New York, and New England's northern frontier remained open to northerners, while Ohio attracted both free-state settlers and non-slaveholding southerners. Non-slaveholding settlers had little reason to hazard settlement in Indiana.[10]

To fill this void, Harrison looked to small slaveholders from the Atlantic states, Kentucky, and Tennessee who would find settlement in Indiana especially attractive, if only it would permit slavery. Though open to slavery, Kentucky and Tennessee lands remained encumbered by conflicting, overlapping claims and the resulting interminable lawsuits. In sharp contrast, Indiana lands, whether purchased from the government or from speculators, offered secure titles at low prices. Moreover, in his first years as governor Harrison had done much to put the territorial government's affairs in order: reforming the levying and collection of taxes; directing that revenue be used to finance courts, roads, and bridges; and negotiating treaties for land and salt springs with Indiana's various Indian nations. It seemed absurd to Harrison that good, loyal slaveholders from the Atlantic states—"the numerous Class of Citizens disposed to emigrate"—settled in less desirable locations only because there, "they can be permitted to enjoy their property" in slaves. Despite the clear advantages of Indiana, small slaveholders continued to bypass the territory solely because of Article VI.[11]

For Harrison, slavery became as much an instrument of nation building in the far-off Northwest as it was part of an effort to replicate Virginia in Indiana. Article VI would determine Indiana's future one way or another. It would either be "settled by emigrants from those in which slavery is tolerated, or for many years remain in its present situation": underpopulated, undeveloped, exposed to foreign and Indian attacks, and only nominally integrated into the American Union.[12]

In 1803 Congress rejected Harrison's first bid to suspend Article VI. Harrison and the three appointed judges who governed the territory then promptly adopted laws permitting settlers to turn slaves into "voluntary" indentured servants.[13] For the one hundred or so slaves who "voluntarily" agreed to indentured servitude in Indiana it made little difference if they were slaves for life or indentured servants for decades. Yet in no way did these indentured servant laws create the legal framework needed to create a secure, lasting system of slavery. Nor did the laws encourage the emergence of a true slave society, where slaveholders were the dominant class and where slave labor could become the most important form of labor. Finally, the laws failed to address Harrison's larger concerns about settlement, development, and Union.[14]

Four very different groups understood that the indentured servitude system served as a poor substitute for chattel slavery sanctioned by Congress: slaveholders from the Atlantic states and Kentucky, antislavery advocates from Ohio and Indiana, the leading proslavery men from Indiana and the Illinois Country, and indentured servants themselves. Between 1805 and 1810, slaveholders registered fewer than one hundred slaves under the territory's laws. Slaveholders understood that these agreements were of dubious legality, and servants began challenging them once the proslavery men lost their hold on power after 1810.[15] Unsurprisingly, few white settlers used the subterfuge of indentured servitude to avail themselves of slave labor in Indiana. So long as Congress refused to suspend or repeal Article VI, property in slaves remained insecure and slaveholders settled elsewhere. As critics of the indentured servitude laws charged, "the palpable unconstitutionality of the law" provided "too flimsy a security" for "the cunning slaveholder." Few if any slaveholders proved willing to "bring his horde to a country where the term of holding them [was] so precarious." Only slavery sanctioned by Congress could make Indiana "more desirable" and secure its "future prosperity."[16]

The indentured servitude laws allowed men like Harrison to realize many of the benefits of slave labor on the frontier. Yet Harrison and the proslavery men also understood that the laws failed to create even the legal framework for a slave society, let alone the real thing. Harrison did nothing to publicize the indentured servitude laws so as to attract slaveholding settlers. Indeed, except when purchasing slaves and servants, Harrison never even mentioned them in his writings. And nowhere in their correspondence did Harrison or other proslavery leaders suggest that the indentured servitude system might provide an adequate substitute for congressionally sanctioned slavery. As Harrison well understood, the "many holders of slaves" who "wish to emigrate to the territory, to advance their interest in the purchase of new lands," would arrive in serious numbers only if Congress sanctioned Indiana slavery by suspending Article VI.[17]

II

In 1802 Harrison and an influential group of politicians from Indiana and the Illinois Country began lobbying Congress and the president to open the territory to slavery. They did so without the support, let alone the knowledge, of the majority of white settlers. The sparse population, scattered settlements, and structure of the territorial government "prevented the birth of that spirit of curiosity for public affairs," which would have subjected slavery to popular political scrutiny. Territorial politics remained a closed and intensely personal affair through 1807. There were few voters and even fewer elective offices in early Indiana; in an 1804 election, only 400 voters even bothered to cast ballots. Political competition remained confined to a few leading men who competed for the allegiance of the local notables below them. That select handful often found itself involved in bitter factional disputes over office, patronage, and above all else, profit and power.[18] On one issue, however, they could unite; all agreed that slavery remained vital to unlocking the territory's potential.

Between 1802 and 1807, Harrison and his associates had a free hand to lobby for slavery. This situation permitted them to exploit the early nineteenth-century's fixation on the "people" by claiming to speak for them. During this period, Harrison presented Congress with over a dozen petitions in the name of the "people of Indiana" or their representatives. Some historians consequently assume that Indiana's mostly southern-born population supported Harrison's efforts to suspend Article VI.[19] Yet Harrison knew that no proslavery majority existed; and he had no intention of obtaining the settlers' opinions on the matter in any case.

Having learned the lesson of Ohio's defeat of slavery, Indiana's pro-slavery leaders deliberately kept their efforts out of public view. The official voting list for the 1802 election refers to "the General Convention of the Territory," but makes no reference to slavery or Article VI, even though Harrison had explicitly called the convention to meet the proslavery demands of the territory's leading men. The extant issues of the single newspaper of the territory have virtually nothing to say about slavery prior to 1808. Harrison's annual addresses and the assembly's replies, where both boasted of the reforms and improvements that would promote settlement and development, similarly made no mention of their proslavery efforts. While Harrison and the proslavery men presented their petitions to Congress in the name of the territorial legislature, they avoided recording the petitions as part of their official proceedings. The proslavery men also routinely waited for the legislature to adjourn before drafting their petitions, lest they incite the ire of any representative who might oppose slavery. Finally, Indiana's sole newspaper did not print the assembly's petitions to Congress, nor, indeed, any of the petitions calling for suspension. The only way for Indiana settlers to know of the proslavery movement was to read the *Liberty Hall and Cincinnati Mercury*, which opposed Indiana slavery.[20]

Harrison and his allies lobbied for suspension in silence, not because Indiana possessed a proslavery majority, but because they hoped to gain congressional suspension before the inhabitants became aware of their plan and tried to stop them. "The deception practised upon the public in relation to Slavery" paid off. Through 1807, there was no public discussion of slavery in the Indiana Territory and no political challenges to the Indiana proslavery party's efforts to overturn Article VI. Though few of the "people" actually knew what he was doing, and though even fewer still supported it, so long as Harrison and the proslavery faction controlled politics and public discussion of slavery, they could present their petitions to Congress as the voice of the people.[21] They did just that, claiming to speak, in various petitions, for "nine-tenths" of the people of Indiana, the "sense of the whole People by their Representatives," "the Legislative Council and House of Representatives of the said Territory," "We the People of the Indiana Territory," and "at least nine-tenths of the good citizens."[22]

After declaring themselves the voice of the people, the petitioners preyed on Congress's desire to populate the far-off Northwestern borderlands. As early as 1788 petitioners from the Illinois Country warned Congress that Article VI forced Northwest slaveholders to "remove to the Spanish dominions, where slavery is permitted." By 1800, the same group advised Congress that emigration "from sundry parts of the United States into the Spanish Province of Louisiana is immense." If not "for the absolute prohibition of Slavery or Servitude," those emigrants "would settle in this Territory." Harrison used much the same argument, informing Congress that Article VI "has prevented the Country from populating." By warning that the territory would remain sparsely settled, the petitioners implicitly exploited fears that American authority in the far-off Northwest remained weak and the region only loosely integrated into the American Union.[23]

The threats were not always so implicit. The first Vincennes petition promised to nullify Article VI if Congress refused to suspend it. "Should no law be passed by Congress for suspending the said article" by 1805, "then the Consent of the people of this Territory hereby given shall be null and void." An 1806 petition from the Illinois Country explained to Congress how suspension was in accord with the "true National policy" of the United States. "To draw a strong Cordon of regular population along the eastern bank of the Mississippi" would further bolster the American presence in "the illimitable regions of the west," where "hordes of restless adventurers . . . defy the national arm." A year later, the same group of petitioners played on fears that an impending "European peace" would permit Britain and France to further their imperial fortunes in the Mississippi Valley by exploiting Northwest settlers' alienation from the U.S. government. As another group warned, they "cannot but feel the importance of union, of energy, of population on this shore of the Mississippi." Nor could they "but shudder at the horrors which may arise from a *disaffection in the West.*"[24]

Like most early western settlers, the Illinois and Indiana petitioners expected the federal government to help them further their interests. In the Northwest this meant pacifying Indian nations and their British allies in Canada, securing markets by guaranteeing free access to the Mississippi and the port at New Orleans, and providing cheap, secure land titles. The federal government would thus gain the trust and loyalty of western settlers, who would increasingly recognize that their own personal interests were best served by a secure and stable American presence in the Northwest. Instead, the settlers found themselves "unrepresented and almost unknown in the national councils." Most had reconciled themselves to a federal government that did little if anything in the West. Yet Article VI did worse than nothing. By barring slaveholders from Indiana and Illinois, the federal government retarded the region's growth and stunted economic development. Worse still, the federal government undermined its own authority by alienating the very settlers who most mattered in determining the future of the Northwest. "From a rich and prosperous Colony," the Illinois Country had "become poor and miserable" under American rule. With the memory of the Blount Conspiracy still fresh in Congress's mind, and with the unraveling of the Burr Conspiracy in 1806, the petitioners made it clear that suspension of Article VI could painlessly check the growth of *"disaffection in the West."*[25]

It remains tempting to dismiss the Indiana proslavery movement for its unimportance, despite the threats and warnings of the proslavery petitioners. But this was no halfhearted campaign led by insignificant territorial officials and chronically complaining westerners. Harrison was a cagey politician who possessed extensive connections with influential politicians from all sections and both parties. He and other proslavery Indianans readily used their political ties to advance the cause of Indiana slavery.

Harrison's father was a prominent Virginian and signer of the Declaration of Independence, while his father-in-law, John Cleves Symmes, was a wealthy New Jersey judge who became a leader of the Ohio Federalists. Harrison used these connections to become a federal land officer, then secretary of the Northwest Territory, and in 1800 its delegate to Congress. After authoring the Harrison Land Act of 1800, he accepted President Adams's offer of the governorship of the Indiana Territory. He did so only after his Virginian and Republican connections assured him that Jefferson would retain the Federalist-appointed Harrison. In 1804 Congress and Jefferson demonstrated their confidence in Harrison by adding the temporary governorship of Upper Louisiana to his already extensive list of duties. By 1804 Harrison was the leading American official in the Northwest. His rapid rise to Superintendent of Indian Affairs for the Northwest and governor of two territories at the age of thirty provided ample testimony of lawmakers' faith in his talent, as well as his ability to use patronage and friendships to advance his interests. Harrison possessed the ability, the respect, and the connections needed to gain passage of favored legislation. The young, dashing, talented, well-connected, and undoubtedly loyal Harrison had to be taken seriously.[26] Once Harrison settled on introducing slavery to Indiana, he and the Indiana proslavery leaders worked their connections to their fullest.

After Harrison and the proslavery Indiana men held their first "convention" in 1802, Benjamin Parke, Indiana's territorial delegate to Congress, personally presented Jefferson with a copy of the petition, along with a letter from Harrison explaining its purposes. Their efforts paid off. "The president is decidedly in favor of th[e] [ar]ticle in our ordinance ag[ains]t Slavery being repealed" gushed one of the proslavery leaders.[27] Harrison and Parke also cajoled members of Congress. New Jersey Federalist Jonathan Dayton, a close friend of Harrison's and a partner in his father-in-law's land business, inquired about sending his son to Indiana. Harrison replied by lobbying for suspension of Article VI. The "limited population of this Territory"—due, of course, to Article VI—failed to "present a field sufficiently extensive" for the younger Dayton's talents. However, "if the Objects of the Memorial" on slavery should succeed, Harrison was certain that "Our Situation will be much Changed for the better in a Short time." Dayton's son would then find ample opportunity, as "wealth and population" would follow immediately in the wake of suspension.[28]

That same year, Harrison lobbied his former colleague and close friend, Ohio senator Thomas Worthington. After Parke told Harrison that Worthington would work with the Indianans "in every particular excepting that of the introduction of slaves," Harrison tried to arrange another meeting for Parke with the Ohio senator. Parke was "on his way to the seat of the Government to endeavor to effect the objects of his last years mission," and he again hoped to meet with Worthington. Harrison primed Worthington for the meeting with a discourse on the wrong-headed assumptions that underlay Worthington's opposition to suspension. Though unsuccessful with Worthington, the proslavery men from Indiana and Illinois continued to lobby other politicians, apparently with better success. "The prospect of establishing Slavery among us brightens daily," wrote John Rice Jones after receiving a favorable letter from Parke. Moreover, Parke had "no doubts of passing the H of R" after meeting with some congressmen. The "Committee to whom the memorial of the Convention was referred, were ready to report in toto in our favor." Demonstrating their clout further still, Harrison and Parke used their influence to install Parke on the next three committees charged with reporting on Article VI and Indiana slavery.[29]

Leading men from the Illinois Country also used their connections to garner congressional support. Robert Morrison, a merchant living in Kaskaskia in the Illinois Country, sought help from his brother Joseph in Philadelphia. Robert explained to his brother that the introduction of slavery was paramount "to the future prosperity of this Country," and then requested that Joseph seek assistance from his friends in Congress. Joseph's first effort failed, but later that year Robert reported that they would continue to seek suspension. Again, Robert instructed his brother "to write to your friends on this subject in Congress," and they fully expected "to get slavery."[30]

From 1803 through 1807, William Henry Harrison and his associates from Indiana and Illinois built political support in Congress and within the Jefferson administration for suspension of Article VI. They influenced committee selections and committee proceedings. They expertly framed their petitions to make it appear that their requests enjoyed the near unanimous support of the inhabitants of the territory. They addressed concerns about Indiana's settlement, development, and integration into the Union, and appealed to both racial fears and antislavery hopes by extolling diffusion. Yet for all their efforts on behalf of Indiana slavery, they had really gained little.

In January 1806 the *Liberty Hall and Cincinnati Mercury* published a letter from an Ohio congressman on Indiana slavery. "A committee had reported favourable to so much of the petition, of the members of the legislature of the Indiana Territory, as respects the introduction of slavery," reported the congressman. He remained unconcerned, however, because it "would be rejected by a large majority of the house" if it ever came up for a vote. For all their lobbying and influence, Harrison and his supporters had failed to convince a majority in Congress to support suspension of Article VI.[31]

Given the persuasive arguments of the petitioners, the unequivocal recommendations of three separate House committees, and the support of Jefferson and other southern congressmen, it is something of a mystery why Congress failed to suspend or overturn Article VI. Indeed, the Senate rejected the petitions on the one occasion when it received them. The House never considered the matter beyond committee reports that the congressmen buried as soon as they received them.[32] The question becomes more difficult to address, given historians' assumptions that southern congressmen controlled debates over slavery's expansion. The most obvious answer, and the one sometimes hinted at, is that Congress held true to its antislavery principles in the one place where slavery might not take hold.[33] Yet some historians discount this explanation. "The failure of Congress to act on these petitions was not necessarily an indication of congressional sentiment" on slavery or any desire to halt its expansion, explains Paul Finkelman. "Congress often took no action on committee reports because the press of business did not allow debates and votes on minor matters." Furthermore, as Finkelman concludes, "the status of slavery in the Indiana Territory" just did not rank among matters worth Congress's notice.[34]

This explanation proves less than satisfactory. First, it is at odds with Finkelman's larger contention that slavery was one of the more important political issues in the early republic. Second, if Indiana slavery was that unimportant, Congress would have tabled the petitions when they received them, a routine method for killing unpopular or unimportant requests. Congress instead referred them to committees on which important congressmen, like John Randolph, sat. Moreover, Congress often accepted and then passed into law other requests from Indiana that were unrelated to slavery. The House passed new laws expanding the franchise and increasing officials' salaries in Indiana, based solely on the recommendations of the committee, with Congress holding a pro forma vote on the bill. When a committee deemed a matter unworthy of Congress's attention or a diversion, committee reports and the congressional record indicated as much. A House committee rejected an Illinois request to divide the territory in April 1808, because of "the press of important business which must occupy the attention of the National Legislature." Yet Congress revisited the issue and passed the committee's proposed bill into law during the next session. In short, the House's refusal to consider the reports recommending suspension of Article VI involved more than the subject's unimportance to the House.[35]

If a majority in Congress agreed with the committee's recommendation—or merely remained indifferent—suspension would have passed with a pro forma vote, requiring little of Congress's time or attention. Instead, whenever a committee recommending suspension issued its report, the House referred it to a committee of the whole for a later date. They did this knowing full well that Congress would never take up the issue. This was a routine method for killing controversial proposals that lacked support for passage. The House's deliberate inaction was, in effect, a vote to defeat suspension.

Committed northern Republican support for upholding the antislavery provisions of Article VI best explains why Congress failed to suspend Article VI, or even vote on the issue. No bill for suspension ever made it to the House floor, because proslavery expansionists, both in Indiana and in the federal government, knew they lacked the votes needed for passage. They also knew they would face stiff opposition from northern congressmen who would strongly oppose any serious discussions about permitting slavery in the Northwest. As one of the proslavery leaders from Illinois wrote to his brother in Philadelphia, they needed him to lobby "all your friends in Congress" precisely because they expected suspension to generate considerable "apprehension." The House could appease the proslavery Indianans because it knew that suspension would never make it past a vote.[36]

Yet maintenance of the status quo—retention of Article VI, with Indiana and congressional expansionists working to undermine its antislavery provisions—presented no clear victory for supporters of Article VI either. The Louisiana debacle demonstrated what happened to unpopular bans on slavery in distant territories. This made it unlikely that Congress would reaffirm the federal government's commitment to Article VI so long as the proslavery Indianans maintained the fiction that they alone spoke for the people. Beginning in 1807, that would change, as the battle between slavery and freedom in Indiana shifted from Congress back to Indiana itself.

By January 1807 Harrison faced new pressures in the territory, having yet again failed to gain congressional sanction for Indiana slavery. Harrison knew that his system of indentured servitude remained a poor substitute for slavery sanctioned by Congress. Indentured servitude with implicit congressional sanction addressed the labor needs of wealthy landholders. But it failed to attract sufficient numbers of settlers, who remained unwilling to risk their property in slaves north of the Ohio River. It also failed to appease the Illinois men. In part because of Harrison and Parke's inability to gain suspension of Article VI, the Illinois politicians stepped up their efforts to divide the territory, hoping that they would be able to convince Congress to suspend Article VI in a separate Illinois Territory. In September 1807 a frustrated proslavery faction in the territorial legislature drafted yet another petition—their second that year—calling on Congress to permit the expansion of slavery into Indiana. This would be their last.[37]

While the proslavery faction met in Vincennes, James Beggs, an antislavery member of the assembly disgusted with the continuing proslavery intrigues, left and called for a separate antislavery convention to meet in October. The antislavery convention's petition informed Congress that "in no case has the voice of the citizens been unanimous" on slavery, despite Harrison's claims. They then detailed the long history of deceit employed by the governor and the territorial legislature in their campaign to open Indiana to slavery. The proslavery petitions would now have to compete with the voice of Indianans committed to excluding slavery and upholding Article VI.[38]

In the past, the proslavery Illinois and Indiana men successfully placed favorable congressmen on the House committees. Now, with a counterpetition claiming popular support for Article VI, northern Republicans seized the opportunity to kill the proslavery movement in Indiana. Massachusetts Republican and speaker of the house Joseph Varnum had opposed slavery in Mississippi in 1798. In 1803, he opposed even receiving the Indiana petitions for suspension of Article VI. In 1807, with antislavery petitions competing with the proslavery petitions for the first time, Varnum saw an opportunity to reaffirm Congress's commitment to a Northwest free of slavery. He referred the pro- and anti-suspension petitions to a new committee packed with northern Republicans. The first 1807 House committee, which had recommended suspension, included four southern representatives along with Benjamin Parke, but only two northern members. The second 1807 House committee, created by Varnum, contained the exact opposite. Only one southern congressman joined Parke on this committee, which included three northern Republicans and a Connecticut Federalist, and was chaired by Jacob Richards, an ardently Republican Philadelphia lawyer.[39]

According to the House committee, the antislavery petition demonstrated "that a difference of opinion exists in the territory, as to the right of holding slaves—and as to the propriety of introducing them" into Indiana. "On a subject of such magnitude," the report continued, "the voice of the citizens should be clearly ascertained." Congress was in no position to do that, but in a few years the territory would qualify for statehood. At that time "the Citizens will have a right to adopt such measures, as may comport with their wishes on the subject." Until then, Congress would uphold Article VI during the territorial phase of government.[40]

The Senate had heretofore ignored the proslavery petitions entirely, but the antislavery petition provided a new opportunity to attack the Indiana proslavery movement. This time, the Senate received the petitions and referred them to a committee unlikely to endorse suspension. The Senate committee appeared to strike a balance between the North, South, and West, but it contained three senators with proven antislavery records: Republicans Aaron Kitchell of New Jersey, Edward Tiffin of Ohio, and Jesse Franklin of North Carolina. Kitchell was a close friend of James Sloan, the New Jersey congressman who sought to prohibit slavery in the Louisiana Purchase territories in 1804. Tiffin had emancipated his slaves before resettling in Ohio, where he had presided over the 1802 convention that rejected slavery. Though a North Carolinian, Franklin had voted to prohibit the domestic slave trade to the Louisianas in 1804. The committee expressed their agreement with the antislavery petitioners and ruled that "it is not expedient at this time to suspend the sixth article of compact." And while the House and Senate had ignored the previous reports supporting slavery in Indiana, the entire Senate considered the new antislavery report and endorsed it in a resolution.[41]

The ambiguous commitment expressed in the 1807 committee reports left open the possibility that Congress might one day consent to suspension of Article VI, especially when Indiana came up for statehood. Nonetheless, Harrison, Parke, and other leading proslavery men from Indiana recognized that they had to accept the finality of Congress's decision. As Thomas Randolph, Indiana's territorial delegate, explained to the voters of Indiana in 1809, "Congress would not give its sanction to the introduction of slaves, was there a majority of the citizens of the territory in favor of it." Beyond the futility of working through Congress, the Harrison faction had bigger problems on its hands. An anti-Harrison faction had arisen in the territory and it sought to convince the expanding Indiana electorate that Harrison and his associates were little more than a group of "Virginia Aristocrats." They also insisted that "the interest of the territory, most imperiously demands a public discussion of the subject of slavery": precisely what Harrison had spent the past five years trying to avoid.[42]

III

From 1801 through 1807, the structure of the territorial government and the sparseness of the population allowed Harrison and the proslavery faction to control politics in the territory. After 1807, the population of the territory increased, the size of the legislature grew, the electorate expanded, and the inchoate opposition to Harrison and slavery began to crystallize. Through 1816 the anti-Harrison "Popular Party" developed an impressive antislavery record. They forced Harrison and the proslavery politicians to end their drive to expand slavery into Indiana. In 1810 they repealed the indentured servant laws. They also forged a popular republican ideology that was expressly and unequivocally antislavery. Their efforts ensured that when Indiana entered the Union in 1816, its constitution would forever prohibit slavery.

Cracks in the alliance between Harrison and the proslavery Illinois faction began to appear in 1804 and increased in 1805 when an Illinois leader published the *Letters of Decius* savagely attacking Harrison's governance of the territory. Agreement on the slavery issue mitigated some of the grievances, but by 1805 even the slavery issue was beginning to drive the two factions apart. In 1805 the Illinois men began presenting their own petitions to Congress calling for both suspension of Article VI and division of the territory, hoping that Congress might permit slavery in a separate Illinois Territory. In the ensuing years, the proslavery, pro-separation, anti-Harrison Illinois faction would form an important alliance with the anti-Harrison, antislavery Indiana faction.[43]

By the time the legislature met for its 1808 session, Harrison was already in trouble. His failure to satisfy the Illinois proslavery faction weakened his hold over both the governor's council and the expanded assembly. Worse still, a new group of politicians from Indiana joined James Beggs and began to attack slavery and the Harrison faction. Six talented and disaffected former associates of Harrison led the emerging antislavery opposition. From Vincennes, John Badollet, federal land officer for Indiana and close friend of treasury secretary Albert Gallatin, had long been disgusted with the movement to overturn Article VI. Joining him were his fellow land agent Nathaniel Ewing and his brother-in-law, Elias McNamee, a Quaker. Sensing the changes in territorial politics, Badollet, McNamee, and Ewing joined forces with other politicians similarly alienated by Harrison, slavery, or both. James Beggs and Jonathan Jennings, ambitious office seekers from the settlements along the Ohio River, cast their political fortunes with the anti-Harrison men from Vincennes. In the assembly, their most important ally was General Washington Johnston, who soon tried to prove that he was even more committed to republicanism and opposed to slavery than his namesake. Johnston, who was Indiana's version of Elias Langham, especially understood the importance of slavery in politics; he was himself a slaveholder and he had previously supported slavery as a member of the legislature.[44]

Prior to the meeting of the 1808 assembly, Badollet, McNamee, and other opponents of Harrison met with settlers throughout Indiana to generate opposition to both Harrison and slavery. First, they "had ascertained that the opposers of Slavery" formed a clear majority in Indiana proper. Then they circulated petitions, "Praying that no further measures be taken with the General Government for the admission of slavery into this Territory," and held their own antislavery conventions. When the assembly convened, they inundated the assembly with antislavery petitions, allowing them to force the issue in the legislature. The antislavery bloc led by Johnston and Beggs, working in conjunction with the proslavery but anti-Harrison Illinois men, then created a committee to receive the petitions and recommend appropriate action on the slavery and division questions. The Illinois men would oppose slavery in Indiana, and the antislavery Indiana men would support creating a separate Illinois Territory.[45]

When the proslavery members finally recognized what they were facing, they responded with a hasty and halfhearted petition campaign of their own. The proslavery Vincennes men presented a petition in the name of the "citizens of Knox County," in a belated effort to demonstrate popular support for slavery and against division. The Knox County petition "pray[ed] that slavery may be admitted into this Territory." This proved ineffective, as the antislavery petitions continued to arrive and outnumber the proslavery petitions. Finally, in a desperate move to kill the issue, the proslavery, pro-Harrison group introduced yet another petition, this one "praying that all the Petitions before this House against the admission of slavery into this Territory may be thrown under the Table," and thus would no longer be subject to consideration by the legislature. This failed when put to a vote, demonstrating the strength of the combined anti-Harrison factions. The legislature continued to receive both antislavery and proslavery petitions as the session continued. The antislavery faction, now backed by significant popular and legislative support, managed to refer all of the petitions to a special committee on slavery in the Indiana Territory.[46]

With each faction striving to demonstrate popular support for their position, the slavery issue, once hidden from public scrutiny, became a matter of public discussion. Even the *Western Sun*, whose pages had been closed to proslavery and antislavery pleas alike, now began printing the numerous antislavery petitions sent to the legislature. The antislavery faction had clearly benefited from both the "democratization" of politics in Indiana and the scrutiny given to slavery. During the 1808 session of the territorial legislature, the antislavery leaders held at least eleven self-styled "conventions of the people" which "prayed that slavery may not be admitted into said Territory and that the Delegate to Congress be instructed to this effect." An antislavery bloc, backed by widespread and seemingly spontaneous support from the "people," now challenged the proslavery forces for control of the territorial government.[47]

As Harrison had feared, three factions emerged in a legislature wracked by slavery and separation: the proslavery, pro-separation, anti-Harrison faction from Illinois; the anti-Harrison, antislavery faction from Indiana that remained indifferent on separation; and the proslavery, pro-Harrison, anti-separation faction from Indiana. The two anti-Harrison factions struck a bargain. The antislavery men from Indiana would support separation. The Illinois members would allow the antislavery men to attack Harrison and the proslavery "Vincennes Party." With the proslavery, pro-separation Illinois men mollified, the antislavery men sprang into action. The antislavery faction used the petitions to issue a report on slavery in the Indiana Territory, roundly condemning Harrison's "tyranny" and his gross violations of Article VI. Foreshadowing things to come, the report also warned that slavery was inseparable from aristocracy, and deemed the institution's existence morally repugnant to a free republican society.[48]

The legislative report demonstrated just how drastically politics had changed over the previous year, and the centrality of slavery to that transformation. In 1807, Harrison and the proslavery men had issued two legislative petitions calling for the suspension of Article VI. Now, barely one year later, that same legislature had issued a report denouncing Harrison and slavery. And though the antislavery faction had scored a major victory during the legislative session of 1808, much work remained to be done. Harrison was still the governor, and his connections meant that he still carried considerable weight in territorial and national politics. Moreover, the antislavery faction still lacked the numbers needed to repeal the indentured servant laws. Neither situation, however, proved all that terrible for the evolving anti-Harrison and antislavery faction.[49]

The anti-Harrison faction had already tapped the support of many settlers by sponsoring antislavery conventions during the 1808 legislative session. With elections set for 1809, they again turned to the "people." The anti-Harrison politicians understood the importance of politics in their battle against slavery; they also understood the importance of slavery in the rapidly changing world of Indiana politics. Harrison's still extensive powers and influence meant that they had to win elections if they hoped to carry any political clout in the territory. At the same time, the indentured servant laws and the Harrison faction's proslavery machinations gave them exactly the type of issue that could help win elections. If the anti-Harrison faction had their way, this election would hinge on the place of slavery in this "rising and promising portion of United America."[50]

The anti-Harrison politicians began campaigning throughout Indiana and in the pages of the *Western Sun* in November 1808, even though the elections were not scheduled until the following April. The antislavery "Popular Party" appealed to voters by fashioning an ideological creed that favored small landholders in their battle against the forces that controlled the territorial government: land speculators, office mongers, and slaveholders, all conveniently reduced to the simple epithet of "Virginia Aristocrats." They fought this campaign by appealing directly to the voters (rather than other leading men), by focusing on issues (rather than gentlemanly fitness for office), and by relentlessly identifying the "Vincennes Party" as a group of corrupt, overbearing Federalists and "Virginia Aristocrats." In doing so, they transformed territorial politics, won important electoral victories, abolished the indentured servant laws, and defined opposition to slavery as "a very important part of republicanism" in Indiana.[51]

The anti-Harrison party demonstrated a keen understanding of electoral politics. Because they lacked the wealth, prestige, and patronage that allowed Harrison and other well-connected men to control territorial politics through 1807, they organized local party structures. This allowed them both to increase interest in the election and to ensure that the anti-Harrison votes would not be scattered. As early as November 1808, they began holding local conventions "to nominate two fit persons to represent the county at the next Legislature." They also stumped for antislavery candidates at settlements throughout the territory, and circulated handbills and broadsides. Finally, they flooded the *Western Sun* with antislavery addresses and essays.[52] While it was probably not "well known" to the voters that they would "firmly divide" on the slavery issue, the antislavery politicians worked to insure that they did. In January, "A Citizen of Vincennes" proposed a "criterion, to test the principles of the several candidates" and "to prevent trimming." Each candidate should "declare unequivocally, whether they will oppose, or promote the introduction of slavery, into this Territory."[53]

Candidates responded in kind. "It has become necessary for me, as a candidate, to make a declaration of my political sentiments respecting the admission of slavery into the territory," explained one vote-seeker. John Hadden, a Harrison-backed candidate for the legislature, admitted he wished to permit "the emigration of citizens of any part of the United States, with any property they are permitted to possess," a euphemism for permitting slavery. Yet Hadden also understood the rapidly changing world of territorial politics. "A majority of the people have a right to decide, and a minority to submit, or we do not deserve the name of an elective government," the candidate explained as he wavered on the slavery issue. Likewise, another candidate declared himself "in favour of opening the door of emigration wide as well for the Eastern and the Southern states," only to equivocate. As much as he favored encouraging emigration by slaveholders, D. Sullivan would only "support such measures as a majority of my constituents will direct."[54]

Try as they might, the Harrison-backed candidates could not avoid the erupting ruckus over slavery. Nor could they escape their accountability to the people. The Harrison party tried to generate support for proslavery candidate Thomas Randolph by minimizing slavery and by extolling his relationship to Thomas Jefferson. That, they soon found, was not enough. The antislavery party's chief spokesman explained that he opposed Randolph, not "because he is the *relation* of Jefferson," but because he differed from Jefferson, whom the antislavery men considered a firm opponent of slavery. The antislavery party continued berating Randolph for his support of slavery until, finally, he relented. As much as it was "a subject I wish not revived," Randolph finally pledged that he would take no action in favor of slavery, "unless a decided majority of my constituents should particularly instruct me to do so." Such "trimming" was no match for "A Citizen of Vincennes" and Johnston's barrage of essays denouncing slavery, aristocracy, and the proslavery candidates. Indeed, Randolph was so offended by McNamee's "Citizen of Vincennes" letters, with their constant references to slaveholders as tyrants, despots, aristocrats, and anti-republicans, that Randolph finally challenged the Quaker to a duel.[55]

The antislavery party furthered their political fortunes by linking their struggle against the "Vincennes Party" to larger conflicts between Federalists and Republicans, republicans and aristocrats. And though it was doubtful that there existed any true Federalists in Indiana in 1808, the antislavery faction successfully pinned that unwelcome moniker on their opponents, while claiming the Republican banner for themselves. The antislavery candidates were true republicans and Republicans: the proslavery men, Federalists and aristocrats who sought to "tickle the fancy of John Adams." In Indiana, the one question "which necessarily separated the two parties, and called each into action" was "the introduction of slavery," wrote "A Citizen." The "Federalists with a few very honorable exceptions, were in favor, and the Republicans against it," he continued. While it was true "that many of the advocates of slavery, are violent in their profession of Republicanism, . . . this single act, speaks more loudly the contrary, than if they had written volumes in favor of aristocracy." And Indiana's slaveholding aristocrats were particularly vile. Lacking "charity, religion, and republicanism," the slaveholder "preys upon man himself, makes his person, his endless labours, his offspring his own." A "friend to slavery," then, "must not only be an aristocrat in his heart, but one of the worst kind." Nothing could "mitigate their crimes in the eyes of God, morality, or republicanism." Nor, presumably, the ballots of Indiana voters.[56]

The support of slavery and republicanism of the "Vincennes Party" provided the antislavery party rich fodder for their campaign. Randolph "professes from his earliest days to have been a republican, and at the same time; acknowledges himself a friend of slavery." But this was as impossible as was Randolph's pledge to respect the wishes of the people. "Two words more discordant" than slavery and republican "cannot be found in the English language; he must give up the one, or the other; it is impossible for him to be both." The "Vincennes Party" knew exactly how effective the antislavery party's campaign was. When recounting the causes of his defeat, Randolph wrote to the voters that "to fix upon me the political sin of aristocracy, in a country of republicans, on the eve of election, was of the first importance."[57]

The debates between the proslavery writer "Slim Simon" and General Washington Johnston illustrate just how adept the anti-Harrison politicians had become at using the slavery issue and popular appeals to rally voters. "Slim Simon" defended Indiana slavery using obtuse economic arguments delineating the relationship between free and slave labor, supply and demand. Ordinary voters who suffered through his argument undoubtedly took offense at his embrace of class differences and his assertion that only slavery could prevent the "labouring poor" from falling into "the service of the wealthy," where they would "perform all the menial offices of slaves." Continuing, "Slim" insisted that slaveholders were not the overbearing aristocrats Johnston made them out to be. They just needed "somebody to assist in the drudgery of the kitchen and the farm," hardly the kind of defense to deflect charges of aristocracy. For settlers who found it difficult to procure a freehold, let alone a slave, his flippant remarks about "50 cents a day men" only confirmed the antislavery party's warnings about the "Virginia Aristocrats."[58]

Johnston pounced on the comments "Slim Simon" made to more sharply define the differences between the two parties. In using the term "50 cents a day men," "Slim Simon" demeaned "the virtuous tho' poor citizens" of Indiana, exposing the proslavery men's aristocratic proclivities. "You advocates of slavery consider poverty a crime," and in doing so "present to the publick what they might expect, if that odious system (slavery) were once adopted." "Slim" was no match for Johnston. When "Slim" attacked him for using the term "poor men," Johnston seized the upper hand by explaining that "what I meant by 'poor men,' were those industrious citizens who earned their subsistence by the sweat of their brow." "Slim" assailed Johnston's "miraculous conversion" to the anti-slavery party. Johnston acquitted himself by attributing his conversion to the good sense "of my constituents." "Slim" objected to the antislav-ery candidates' fitness for office, because their "artifice is too clumsy to bear a moment examination." Johnston and "A Citizen of Vincennes" responded with clear, symbolically potent language, painting their op-ponents as conniving aristocrats who would trample the rights of free men as readily as they did those of slaves.[59]

The spring 1809 elections marked another important shift in Indiana politics. Running on a clear antislavery platform that asked voters "to ensure the complete triumph of the principles of universal freedom," Johnston won election from Knox County, home of Vincennes and the proslavery, pro-Harrison stronghold. In the election for territorial delegate, Jonathan Jennings, the avowed antislavery and anti-Harrison candidate, defeated Thomas Randolph. With Jennings's victory, the an-tislavery party defeated a candidate backed by all of the influence that a Harrison-backed candidate and relative of Thomas Jefferson could muster.[60]

Circumstances prevented the antislavery party from passing any laws on slavery during the 1809 "rump session" of the territorial legis-lature, which devoted its time to creating a separate Illinois Territory, redistricting Indiana, and resolving Randolph's challenge of Jennings's election.[61] Again, however, this merely allowed the antislavery party to use slavery as an issue in the 1810 election. "Now my friend," wrote Jonathan Jennings as he prepared for the upcoming elections, "I shall have printed about 1000 copies of the points upon which the election has turned as made before the committee."[62] In the 1810 elections vot-ers again selected General Washington Johnston to the lower assem-bly, along with James Beggs for the upper council. In control of both houses, the antislavery party struck down the indentured servant laws. Indiana's flirtations with repeal of Article VI were at an end.

IV

Stretching back three years to James Beggs's antislavery "convention," the antislavery, anti-Harrison "party" managed to introduce a new style of electoral politics to the territory and framed the dominant issues fac-ing white Indiana settlers in a near cosmic struggle between the forces of freedom and slavery. In the process, they made slavery a public, political issue. They also defined slavery and slaveholders as incompatible with their own evolving notions of republicanism and popular government.

The extensive and prolonged antislavery campaign made it unlikely that Indiana would permit slavery in any form when it adopted a constitution in 1816. The circumstances under which Indiana became a state lessened these chances even further. In their request for statehood, the legislature expressed their "attachment to the fundamental principles of legislation, prescribed by congress in their ordinance for the government of this territory, particularly as it respects personal freedom and involuntary servitude, and hope that they may be continued as the basis of the constitution." And while the Indiana Enabling Act made no direct mention of Article VI, it did require that the constitution "shall be republican, and not repugnant" to the Northwest Ordinance. The convention that met to frame the constitution in June 1816 put to rest any fears that they might adopt a constitution permitting slavery; it elected Jonathan Jennings president. Article VIII of the Indiana Constitution of 1816 declared that "as the holding of any part of human Creation in slavery, or involuntary servitude, can only originate in usurpation and tyranny, no alteration of this constitution shall ever take place so as to introduce slavery or involuntary servitude in this State."[63]

Two conditions proved decisive in saving Indiana from slavery. First, Congress refused to cave in to the proslavery Indianans' persistent demands to overturn Article VI. Congress placated the proslavery petitioners with committee reports suggesting suspension of Article VI, but the situation in the Northwest meant that Congress never had to consider seriously repealing the ban on slavery. Unlike Natchez or the Louisianas, the Northwest seemed comparatively stable and secure in the American Union. Greater power and authority in the Northwest allowed Congress to equivocate enough to placate the proslavery interests without ever actually giving in to their demands. By stalling, Congress inadvertently encouraged a popular antislavery movement to emerge. Ultimately, the combination of comparatively greater federal power backed by a popular antislavery party defeated Indiana's once determined proslavery movement.

The politics of slavery in Illinois followed much the same pattern as in Indiana, and the same circumstances eventually prevented Illinois from becoming a slave state, even if the results took far longer.

A majority of the white settlers and voters in Illinois continued to favor repeal of Article VI after the territory broke off from Indiana in 1809. As in Indiana, a core of proslavery politicians dominated the territorial government, the constitutional convention, and the early statehood government, largely with patronage and personal connections. Whatever the size of the antislavery population in territorial Illinois, it remained silent about the openly proslavery legislation passed and pursued by the territory's leaders. But as had happened with Indiana, Congress rebuffed the proslavery requests made by Illinois. After 1810, it became clear that Congress would never suspend Article VI while Illinois remained a territory, and the petitions ceased. Illinois politicians responded by creating an even more elaborate system of servitude, but they recognized that the subterfuge of indentured servitude was no substitute for slavery. On the whole, southern slaveholders shied away from Illinois so long as Article VI remained in effect. Even territorial governor Ninian Edwards was reluctant to risk his property in slaves in Illinois. Congressional commitment to Article VI kept Illinois a free territory even as settlers there worked to undermine it.[64]

Proslavery Illinois voters and politicians began agitating for statehood beginning in 1817, in part because they hoped that Article VI would become "a dead letter" once they became a state. While the statehood and slavery movement provoked some opposition, it was not enough to prevent a slate of proslavery politicians from dominating the constitutional convention. Ultimately, Congress and Article VI prevented Illinois from entering the Union as a slave state. The federal government had always enjoyed greater power in the Northwest than in the Southwest, and after 1815 the power, authority, and prestige of the federal government in the West was clearly expanded. Illinois politicians recognized that Congress would block admission if Illinois failed to include Article VI in its constitution, as Ohio and Indiana had.[65]

The 1818 Constitution adopted Article VI and Illinois technically prohibited slavery. It nonetheless kept intact an elaborate system of indentured servitude that had flourished in territorial Illinois, added new forms of servitude, and seemingly allowed every form of servitude short of slavery. The federal government had grown powerful enough to insist that Illinois recognize Article VI, but it was not yet powerful enough to force Illinois to abolish its extensive system of indentured servitude. Furthermore, though Congressman James Tallmadge of New

York tried to block Illinois's admission on the grounds that "the principle of slavery" was not "sufficiently prohibited" in the Constitution, a majority of northern congressmen seemed satisfied that the incorporation of Article VI in the state constitution was a sufficient safeguard against slavery in the state.[66]

Proslavery Illinois politicians opted to avoid an unnecessary quarrel with Congress over Article VI, but they also adopted Article VI because they hoped to amend the state constitution in a few years. Then, as an independent state, they could revise their constitution, eliminate Article VI, and become a full-blown slave state. In the early 1820s, proslavery Illinois politicians and land speculators sought a constitutional convention to do just that. By then, however, a committed group of antislavery leaders had begun to form around the antislavery governor of Illinois, Edward Coles. After a bitter, hard-fought, two-year campaign, Illinois voters rejected the convention, and with it any hopes that Illinois might incorporate slavery into its constitution. As in Indiana and Ohio, Illinois demonstrated that it required both the federal government and popular support to halt slavery's expansion in the West. The experiences of Ohio, Indiana, and Illinois demonstrated that no "natural" or sectional limits kept slaveholders out of any portion of the West. This lesson would not be lost on either southern or northern politicians during the Missouri Controversy, which began a mere two months after the vote on Illinois statehood.

7

Making the "Free Northwest"

Slavery and Freedom in
Ohio and Indiana, 1790–1818

"SLAVERY—An experiment is making in the west" began a remarkably frank 1816 article written in Richmond, Virginia, published in the *National Intelligencer,* and reprinted widely in the Northwest. Written in response to Indiana's recent admission to statehood with a constitution that forever prohibited slavery, the author assessed the growing divide between slavery and freedom in the West. "The Ohio River is the line," the author explained, "which exactly defines the boundaries of the experiment. To the south, are the states which permit the existence of slavery—to the north those states which forbid it." The experiment contained valuable lessons for the entire United States. It would both "assist in showing the effects of servitude upon the characters and manners of a people," and "shed light upon a much agitated question in Political Economy; how far domestic slavery retards or accelerates the advancement of a nation to wealth." The author expressed some concern that the free-labor Northwest would prove more attractive to migrants than territories and states south of the Ohio that permitted slavery. He nonetheless expected that the slaveholding West would demonstrate that the institution neither retarded economic development nor monopolized economic opportunity in the hands of planters.

Nor did it degrade the "manners of a people." The two regions would undoubtedly be different, but the free states of the Northwest would in no way be superior.[1]

Settlers in the Ohio Valley roundly disagreed. Cincinnati's great booster Dr. Daniel Drake fully expected the Northwest to demonstrate that a society free of slavery was in all ways superior; it would produce superior republican institutions, improve the morals and manners of its people, and provide greater economic opportunity and a more equal distribution of wealth and prosperity. "The prohibition of slavery has contributed greatly to the population of this state," wrote Drake in an 1815 promotional tract. When combined with "the exclusion of slavery," the Northwest's other features gave it clear advantages over states and territories in the Southwest that permitted slavery. Even Kentucky slaveholders shared Drake's convictions. After visiting Indiana, Congressman Richard Clough Anderson of Kentucky concluded that a "country populated by poor persons (divided into small tracts) & worked by freemen instead of slaves" would soon prove "more valuable than any Country settled by Virginians held in large parcels & cultivated by Slaves." Subsequent journeys through Ohio only deepened his conviction that "the rapid improvement of this Country shews the good policy of excluding slaves."[2]

Even before the Missouri Controversy forced Americans of all sections to reconsider the place of slavery in the West, many settlers in Ohio and Indiana came to believe that the absence of slavery created important—indeed, fundamental—differences between the states north and south of the Ohio River. Remarkably diverse groups of people settled in Ohio and Indiana after 1790. Religious, political, and economic differences often set them at odds with one another, as did the sectional prejudices and practices they brought with them. Nonetheless, they found common ground in their celebration of a society free from slavery.[3]

The Northwest Ordinance of 1787 did not itself produce the "free Northwest." Instead, the notion of the "free Northwest"—a region and society distinct from both the East and the Southwest, which permitted slavery—was in large part created by the people who settled there beginning in the 1790s. Settlers remained concerned that slavery would creep across the Ohio River and establish itself there, even though Article VI had declared the Northwest off-limits to slavery. With the federal

government seemingly unable or unwilling to insure slavery's permanent exclusion, settlers in Ohio and Indiana took it upon themselves to
bar slavery and prevent its future expansion across the Ohio River. By
bearing witness to the horrors of slavery, by creating free territories and
states, by participating in a host of political rituals such as constitution-
making and Fourth of July celebrations, and through the experiences of
settlement, they produced an ideal vision of a republican society composed exclusively of free people.[4]

These events and experiences, more than sectional backgrounds,
shaped their understandings of the free society they had created. The
omnipresence of slavery in the Ohio Valley forged a particular regional
identity in the Northwest that celebrated the unparalleled political and
social equality afforded to men, and the personal freedom and economic opportunity accorded to families, in a society that had self-consciously worked to exclude slavery and preserve freedom. In addition,
by defining their region as "free," settlers increasingly identified themselves not just with the West, but with the "free states" of the North as
well. The Missouri Controversy would only confirm the outcome of a
process long underway; the Northwest had become as much "North" as
it was "West."[5]

I

Knowing the sectional origins of settlers in the Northwest between 1790
and 1819 makes it tempting to attribute increased animosity toward
slavery to settlement patterns and migration trends. Migrants from
the northern states possessed their own biases against slavery. Southern migrants who crossed the Ohio River supposedly sought escape
from the detrimental effects of slavery in Kentucky and the Atlantic
slave states. Knowing that slavery cut off opportunity for many ordinary white families, these upland southerners were supposedly natural
enemies of slavery, if only because of their dislike of both blacks and
planters. Yet simple migration trends alone do not adequately explain
the Northwest's commitment to freedom over slavery as it emerged
between the 1790s and 1819. Nor does it account for the Northwest's
unique regional identity. Upland southerners, even those with few or
no slaves, proved quite enthusiastic about the prospects for farmers in
slave states like Kentucky and Missouri, as well as in southern Illinois.
Northern migrants who settled in southern states adapted quickly to

the institution. Even in Indiana and Illinois, some of the leading proslavery men hailed from Philadelphia and New Jersey.[6]

Southern and northern migrants chose settlement in the free Northwest over slave states or territories for a variety of reasons. For some, the absence of slavery was quite important. Their antislavery convictions were strengthened through settlement and the experience of living in a society struggling to exclude slavery. Others exhibited indifference about slavery as a motive for migration to the Northwest. The process of settlement and the celebration of free society helped change this: exposure to slavery for northerners, and participation in debates about slavery for northern and southern migrants, helped create the conviction that they had chosen self-consciously to live in a free society, even if they had not.

One group of southern migrants who explicitly chose to settle in the Northwest because of Article VI were antislavery evangelicals. As one explained to the residents of Virginia, it was impossible for him to remain there and support his family and ministry without "holding slaves." Many evangelicals from Virginia and the Upper South who moved west first looked to Kentucky. But Kentucky's drawbacks were obvious; "There as in Virginia, the slavery of the human race is unfortunately tolerated." Antislavery evangelicals held out hope in the 1790s that Kentucky might adopt some type of gradual abolition law, but in 1799 a Kentucky constitutional convention instead adopted even greater protections for slaveholders. Kentucky's failure made "the good land that is beyond Jordan"—that is, the Northwest—where "every trace of vassalage is rooted out and destroyed," that much more attractive to antislavery southern evangelicals. Migration to the Northwest was the only choice for those who wished to remain in "the business of agriculture," yet escape from "the present disgrace and future scourge of America." Beginning in the late 1790s, southern antislavery evangelicals poured into Ohio and Indiana.[7]

Antislavery evangelicals could hardly contain their enthusiasm upon crossing the Ohio River into free territory. "Here I felt rejoiced that I had once the privilege to set my foot on a land where hereditary slavery, the lasting and degrading curse of the eastern states should never come," wrote David Barrow after crossing into Ohio. Another southern evangelical "could but thank God, who had preserved me thro many dangers, and brought me at length to see a land where liberty prevails, and where human blood is not shed like water." A Tennessee Quaker, after taking a trip to Indiana in 1813, was similarly inspired. The trip "revived in my mind, that it would be an advantage to my sons, to remove with them over the Ohio river" and away from Tennessee and slavery. Flush from the experience of moving from a slave society to a free society, antislavery evangelicals recruited like-minded colleagues in the South to make the journey. "The Lord provided for the Virtuous sons of the Eastern States in the Liberty of the State of Ohio," wrote one Methodist. "The thing speaks for itself," he added, as he invested Article VI with providential meaning. For antislavery evangelicals who settled in the Northwest, Article VI made the Ohio River the River Jordan, Ohio and Indiana the "Land of Canaan." The decision to migrate to free territory, the experience of living in a free society, and the contrast with slavery across the river only deepened their antislavery convictions in the Northwest.[8]

Other southern migrants settled in the Northwest with more temporal objections to slavery. "The case is already decided that you must both settle on this side of the Ohio," wrote John Cleves Symmes from his home in Cincinnati to his grandsons in Kentucky. "You cannot live in Kentucky comfortably without negroes," explained this staunch Federalist from New Jersey, recoiling at the thought of his beloved grandsons growing up as Kentucky planters. But in Ohio, where the people respected labor and where prestige was not measured by the number of slaves a man owned, "you will need none." Most southern migrants to the Northwest were far less wealthy than Symmes, and their expectations of gaining honor and office far more modest. They nonetheless migrated to free soil to escape the debilitating social effects of slavery. Non-slaveholding emigrants from Kentucky, "being in modest circumstances, & owing their bread to their *own* labor," were unwilling to "brook the haughty manners of their opulent neighbors the slave-holders." While some were "opposed to slavery" in principle, others crossed the Ohio because they were "unable to purchase slaves" and thus prevented from moving into the ranks of the slaveholder class.[9]

Southern migrants of course moved to the Northwest for a variety of reasons, and the availability of cheap land with good titles was often most important. For many, the prohibition of slavery was only one of many factors, if it mattered at all in their initial decision to settle in the Northwest. In Ohio and Indiana many southern-born settlers seemed indifferent about slavery so long as the issue was not subject to public discussion. Political debates over slavery transformed that indifference. During public discussions of slavery in both Ohio and Indiana, writers, politicians, and preachers all called attention to the "great portion of the present citizens of the Territory, who removed here to avoid slavery." In their battles with proslavery politicians and boosters, antislavery advocates repeatedly appealed to southern migrants for support. Regardless of their initial attitudes about slavery, they were now christened "the votaries of *freedom* and philanthropy"; the true republicans who have "remove[d] to an asylum from the slaves states, as it were from a *Brothel* to a *Temple.*" Southern migrants could and did become the "great number" of northwesterners who "sought an asylum from the baneful influence of slavery." By 1819, an Ohio grand jury was all but certain that southern-born settlers "sought in this place a refuge from slavery," even if originally they had not.[10]

The existence of "numerous . . . persons from the Southern States who wish to fly from a system which a melancholy experience of its innumerable evils has taught them to detest" was probably never as large as antislavery advocates made it out to be. Nonetheless, pamphleteer Daniel Drake boasted that the fame of the Northwest's "prohibition of slavery" had "extended throughout the south." By 1815 Drake was all but certain that it was Article VI that had drawn southern emigrants like himself north of the Ohio River. While traveling through Ohio, an English writer met a man "who informed me he had moved from Kentucky." He "liked this country better, principally on account of the freedom from slavery, and the security of land title." In due time, southern migrants could become convinced that they had migrated to the Northwest to escape slavery, regardless of their original motives.[11]

For many northern migrants, the absence of slavery was only one of many reasons involved with their decision to settle in the Northwest. Some expressly sought to settle in states or territories where the laws prohibited slavery. As one prospective western settler who was "opposed to the south on account of the slaves" asked a friend living in Louisville, Kentucky, "Do they tolerate slavery in Indiana?" Others moved to the Northwest after a brief stay in the South. When Connecticut Republican Josiah Meigs proved too Republican to continue teaching at the Federalist bastion at Yale, he moved south to help establish the University of Georgia. He was openly contemptuous of Georgians and slavery, however, and in 1810 he left to become a surveyor in Ohio. Within three years he was openly criticizing slavery expansion in a Fourth of July toast.[12]

Regardless of northern settlers' initial preferences, countless travel and immigrant-aid guides included in their descriptions whether a particular state or territory permitted slavery. Many of the ubiquitous gazettes, geographies, immigrant-aid tracts, and newspaper accounts of the West merely acknowledged that some states and territories permitted slavery, while others excluded it.[13] Others celebrated that the absence of slavery in the Northwest promised settlers greater freedom, opportunity, and prosperity. "The State of Ohio is now in its infancy" began one tract from 1812. But because "slavery is excluded from her bosom," it would soon "rise superior to her neighbor" Kentucky. These guidebooks, published throughout the North and widely reprinted in newspapers, provided immigrants with their first glimpse of the emerging divide between slavery and freedom in the Ohio Valley.[14]

Travelers' accounts of the West also called attention to the reality of slavery in the Ohio Valley. Despite the justly celebrated bounty of Kentucky, Estwick Evans, a stout republican and Yankee traveler, expressed his utter shock at witnessing "*human beings*" forced to "toil and sweat under the lash of a task master." John Stillman Wright, another Yankee traveler who published an account of his journey to the West, told his readers he was "frequently shocked with unpleasant incidents, which naturally happen where domestic slavery is permitted." Indeed, Wright's readers could "have no conception" of "the shocking aggregate of torture and contumely, which the wretched children of Africa are doomed to undergo," unless they actually traveled to one of the western slave states. But with Wright's account of "the horrors of such a state of things," it was doubtful that many would go, instead choosing the free soil of Ohio and Indiana.[15]

Travel along the Ohio River, the preferred route for northern settlers, further impressed the distinctions between slavery and freedom upon northern migrants. At Wheeling, Virginia, northern migrants and Chesapeake slave traders met for their journeys downriver. The sight of scores of manacled slaves in Wheeling shocked a young Benjamin Lundy into embracing abolitionism. Few northern migrants who stopped in Wheeling became abolitionists like Lundy. Still, those who observed the thriving trade in human flesh flowing down the Ohio River were reminded of the growing chasm between slavery and freedom in the West. Immigrants who failed to witness the slave trade firsthand could read about it in Ohio newspapers. After reprinting accounts from eastern and southern newspapers detailing the horror of the domestic slave trade, editors added their own commentary about the evils of the slave trade in the Ohio Valley.[16]

Slaves who found themselves caught up in this trade sometimes sought freedom on their journey down the Ohio River. Two slave traders who were moving slaves from the Chesapeake to Tennessee never completed their trip. Along the Ohio, the slaves struck for their freedom, murdered the two traders, and then fanned out into the Ohio countryside. This and similar incidents sharpened the contrast between slavery and freedom on the Ohio's two banks. Cincinnati's proximity to Kentucky further exposed northern migrants to the reality of southern slavery. After recounting the wonders of Cincinnati to a friend in Massachusetts, one recent settler expressed his horror that "I often hear the Kentucky Negros yelling and singing while toiling for their unfeeling masters."[17]

Northerners were also shocked at what they saw as the debility, idleness, and contempt for honest labor that plagued the slave states on the south bank of the Ohio. In western Virginia, "every planter depends upon his NEGROES for the cultivation of his lands," wrote one traveler. "But in the State of Ohio, *where slavery is not allowed,* every farmer tills his ground HIMSELF," bringing dignity to labor. One recent settler in Ohio expressed his loathing of "the rich slaveholders in the western part of Virginia" in a letter to his brother in Massachusetts. "They do not educate their children; nor ornament their plantations; nor finish their houses genteelly; nor cultivate their own minds," he noted with disgust. It seemed that "their whole enjoyment and pride are founded upon an exemption from labor, and a never failing supply of whiskey." Another Ohioan who journeyed to Kentucky, "a slave country," was incredulous that because "almost all the labor is performed by slaves, very few of the white people, of gentility," could "wait upon themselves in the smallest matter."[18]

Disgust with the manners of westerners, along with contempt for their laziness and drunkenness, was nothing new. What was new were the sources of this contempt and its changing geographic orientation. Northern travelers in the West now celebrated the free society on the north bank of the Ohio River but derided the settlements on the south bank, attributing its degeneracy to the presence of slavery in western Virginia and Kentucky. One northern traveler in the Ohio Valley noted "a great distinction" in Louisville, Kentucky, "between the rich and the poor." The "effects of slavery are here very manifest as it is in all parts of the State of Kentucky," he continued, adding that "idleness and destitution and want of enterprise and improvement are the consequence." This stood in great contrast to free Ohio, a "fine country" that "liberally rewards the labor of the husbandman," promising to create a more free, prosperous, and moral society.[19]

For all their celebrations of living in a free society, northwesterners, whether from the North or the South, remained acutely aware of the importance of slave labor on the frontier. Personal testimonies revealed the difficulties families encountered in establishing viable farms and the ways that slaver labor expedited that process. A newly settled slaveholder in Kentucky expressed his pleasure that "my affairs are progressing as well or better than I expected." His "negroes work much more expeditiously at grubbing than could have been expected," especially "considering that they," like most settlers from the East, were "totally unused to it." Poorer families in Kentucky also sought slave labor to relieve themselves of the difficult tasks involved in clearing land and securing a freehold. The high demand for labor in Kentucky made the purchase of prime field hands prohibitively expensive for many. Some settlers instead turned to less costly alternatives, such as one settler who purchased "a negro man in middle life, and a woman rather old." Other non-slaveholding Kentuckians rented their neighbors' slaves. Kentuckian John Breckinridge regularly "hired out" slaves for periods up to a year, where they were used in a variety of tasks, from clearing land and milling corn to slaughtering and dressing meat. In Ohio, the difficulties of settlement made some southerners long for slavery. Settlers from Virginia were "so little accustomed to labor" that though they were "out of the spirit of slavery," they feared they could not do "without them in this country."[20]

Other southern migrants to the Ohio Valley were less willing to "get out of the spirit of slavery." Before Ohio even adopted its constitution, one group of settlers left for Indiana, hoping that it would permit slavery, if only for a brief period. After Ohio prohibited slavery in 1802, one settler left for Kentucky, for "he cannot do without his domesticks."

Another southern settler, who "has given up settling on that side of the Ohio" because of the prohibition on slavery, was willing to take a variety of payments for his 235 acres of land in Ohio, including "one Negro man." Westward-looking Virginians felt "prevented from purchasing" land in Ohio because of "the impossibility of carrying" their slaves "into the State of Ohio." The decision to settle in free or slave territory also caused friction in families. In 1815 Robert Henry of Georgetown, Kentucky, looked to Indiana to establish himself and further his family's fortunes. He wished that his family members would go with him, and though his father and brother declined, they nonetheless "approved of my project." The one sticking point was another brother who "unequivocally declared against an emigration; objecting the exclusion of slaves" from Indiana.[21]

Northern families who migrated to Kentucky immediately recognized the great value of slave labor in the West. John Corlis, the son of a Rhode Island merchant who settled in Bourbon County, Kentucky, in 1816 found it impossible to establish a viable homestead without resorting to slave labor. After laying out $525 to purchase a slave he considered himself "fortunate" to obtain, the younger Corlis hired nine additional free and enslaved blacks, as he tried to establish a farm for the rest of his family to settle on. Southerners who moved north of the Ohio River faced similar labor problems, which the prohibition on slavery only compounded. One Kentucky family who settled in Ohio turned to free blacks from their old state, including "a negro man of very good character," a "very industrious man about 25 years old," and "an old Negro woman with several children," to address the chronic labor shortage in the free Northwest.[22]

For gazetteers willing to overcome their predilections against slavery, the importance of slave labor—especially in the Northwest—seemed manifest. "Where slaves are numerous, one, or even two hundred acres of corn might be readily cultivated," admitted one guidebook author. The same "would be found an herculean (if not an impracticable) task" in the Northwest. Foreign travelers proved especially blunt about the benefits slave labor offered settlers. For "an Emigrant who is rich" and who "does not object to holding slaves, Kentucky offers him great advantages," wrote Englishman Elias Pym Fordham after traveling through the Ohio Valley in 1817 and 1818. In the Northwest, "there are *no* free laborers here, except a few so worthless, and yet so haughty, that an

English Gentleman can do nothing with them." Indeed, the chronic labor shortages prompted Fordham to admit that he preferred remaining in England than trying to establish a farm in the Northwest, because "if I do not have servants I cannot farm."[23]

Frontier conditions in Kentucky and western Virginia remained worlds away from the well-established markets and agricultural practices of the Chesapeake. Yet slaveholders and other migrants who settled south of the Ohio River readily forced slaves to adapt the old institution to their new environment. It was difficult to escape the great value of coerced slave labor on the frontier. As one European traveler to the Ohio Valley remarked, Kentucky was "extremely wealthy" because, "not yet having abolished slavery, it has a great advantage" over the states north of the Ohio River.[24]

Recognition of the short-term benefits of slave labor made it that much more important for northwesterners to condemn its long-term evils. To counteract the threat of slavery entering the Northwest, to compete more effectively for the thousands of easterners seeking to settle in the Ohio Valley, and to make sense of the differences between the north and south banks of the Ohio River, boosters, politicians, and others created a free-soil ideology that denounced all the evils of slavery while extolling all the virtues of free society. As they understood their own vision of the free Northwest, it would be more in accordance with the promise of the American Revolution and republican society. Free from slavery, the Northwest would allow ordinary men and women to pursue equality, propertied independence, and self-government to a degree unattainable in aristocratic slave societies composed of haughty planters, groveling free whites, and enslaved blacks.[25]

Politicians in Ohio and Indiana repeatedly pointed out that the evils of slavery were considerable. "If I have expressed an opinion upon the subject" of slavery, "it has been, that it would be a present benefit, and a future evil," proclaimed one Indiana candidate in 1812. In Ohio, antislavery candidates for the 1802 constitutional convention played directly to the fears of farmers and those struggling to secure property. "What will become of the poor farmers" should Ohio permit slavery? "Their produce will bear no price, their encouragements will cease, and in all probability they will become an easy prey to the rich and the avaricious part of the community" who owned slaves. Slavery would "destroy the present prospects of the poor man, who wishes to obtain by his labor a small portion of land, on which to support his rising family." Antislavery writers and politicians in Indiana warned of similarly dire consequences should the voters permit slavery. "The moment slavery is introduced amongst us," one writer warned, "equality of condition is done away." While it was "true that slavery will accumulate wealth in the hands" of the slaveholder, "his growth starves out all about him." Furthermore, the "scornful nabobs surrounded by their miserable slaves" would "condemn those that seek to live by their honest industry." Where slavery existed, honest families who relied on their own labor became the objects of "contempt by those that own slaves." Free non-slaveholders could simply not expect to maintain their equality, property, dignity, and independence in a society dominated by slaveholders.[26]

Condemnations of slave societies were joined by equally ardent praises for free society, along with the prosperity and equality it nurtured. The free Northwest demonstrated "that the hand of freedom can best lay the foundation to raise the fabric of public prosperity." It became a truism in the Northwest that "the industrious" of the North and the South "flock where industry is honorable and honored, . . . where equity reigns, and where no proud nabob can cast on him a look of contempt." The absence of slavery also appealed to the wealthy. "Here a man may feed and saddle his own horse without danger of losing either his bride or his election" merely because he owned no slaves. Indeed, the honorable non-slaveholder in the Northwest "may go from the bench of the supreme court to his woodpile, chop his wood and make his own fire," the kind of honest labor allegedly beneath southern slaveholders. According to Daniel Drake, in the Northwest "wealth is distributed" more equally, which was "more after the manner of the northern than southern states." Unsurprisingly, Drake attributed this to the "prohibition of slavery," which made Ohioans more "generally laborious" and more equal in their wealth.[27]

Southern evangelicals spoke of the promise of a free society in especially graphic tones. James Smith imagined a land where "the honest and industrious farmer cultivates his farm with his own hands, and eats bread of cheerfulness, and rests contented on his pillow at night." It was "no disgrace here to engage in any of the honest occupations of life." The dignity of labor crossed gender boundaries in free territory. The "ruddy damsel" north of the Ohio River "thinks it no disgrace to wash her clothes, milk her cows, or dress the food for the family." The "aged mother instructs her daughters in the useful and pleasing accomplishments" that made them "provident mothers and good housewives." The "young man" in the Northwest, rather than learning how to whip slaves with "a cowskin or some other instrument of torture," was instead taught to "follow the plow." Smith saw "genuine liberty and national happiness growing up together" in the Northwest. Free labor would transform the land north of the Ohio and prove the iniquity of slavery of any kind. "Thy unequalled soil, cultivated by the fostering hands of freemen shall e'er long display its beauties and yield an increase worthy a land of liberty."[28]

Other settlers voiced equally ardent, if less lyrical, praise of free territory. One evangelical simply expressed his great joy "to live in a Country where there is so much Equality." Another celebrated that a family which relied on slaves in Virginia could survive equally well without in Ohio, if only they were willing to "wait on themselves." Northern migrants found their own reasons to appreciate the absence of slavery in the Northwest. Ohioan Ephraim Brown's cousin in Mississippi boasted of his superior prospects "for speculation and the acquiring of property," including slaves. Brown comforted himself with the thought that "here the buying and selling of poor defenseless human beings does not form our commerce, nor the using of them like beasts our agriculture." Slaveholding offered a quicker path to riches for sure, but Brown was "willing to put up contented with what can be got from honest industry."[29]

Through 1819, the American population of Ohio and Indiana remained remarkably diverse. Those settlers possessed an equally varied set of attitudes about slavery before migrating to the Northwest. But whether settlers were upland southerners or New England Federalists, northern Quakers or southern Methodists, from the heavily enslaved Chesapeake or the slave-free Pennsylvania countryside, many came to define their common ground as a commitment to living in a society free from slavery. By debating publicly the merits and virtues of their free society, they came to identify their free-labor society as superior to slave societies wrought by inequality and degradation.

Article VI and the commitment of settlers made Ohio "an asylum to those who have foregone the temporary advantages of slavery," regardless of sectional origins. By rejecting the lure of slavery, northern and southern migrants to Ohio, "selected from all the rest of the states," had demonstrated their shared commitment to freedom over slavery. After the 1802 debates over slavery and statehood had receded into the background, Ohioans continued to celebrate that, despite their many differences and different sectional origins, they all came to Ohio because of the prohibition of slavery. As one speaker told a Cincinnati audience in 1817, Ohio's "population is an assemblage of citizens from almost every part of the globe, allured hither by the fertility of its soil, the salubrity of its climate," and last but not least, "the free principles of its constitution which forbids involuntary slavery."[30]

Indianans similarly lessened tensions within their territory by creating an antislavery past for themselves. In 1809, at the height of the political battles over slavery, antislavery politicians lauded "the peaceful citizens of this territory, who migrated and purchased land under the pledged faith of government that their rights should be protected, and slavery should never be admitted." Indiana politicians re-created this antislavery identity as they prepared for statehood in 1816. Indiana was settled by "emigrants from every part of the union, and as various in their customs and sentiments as in their persons." Yet all were united in their commitment to the "fundamental principles" of the Northwest Ordinance, "particularly as it respects personal freedom and involuntary servitude." After 1815, it seemed that Article VI would indeed fulfill the promise of a well-populated, thriving region, free of slavery. Indiana's population surpassed 25,000 in 1810, while the census recorded over 230,000 men, women, and children in Ohio. Indiana's adoption of a constitution forever barring slavery demonstrated that the Ohio River was now "the northern barrier to" the "execrable practice" of slavery.[31]

II

The Northwest's critique of slavery and praise of free society extended far beyond concerns about settlement, economic development, opportunity, and prosperity. In their denunciations of slavery and their praise for their own free society, politicians and voters defined slavery and their "principles of republicanism" as incompatible with each other. Ohio and Indiana both experienced prolonged public debates over the future of slavery in their territories, and these public debates carried over to constitutional conventions where delegates decided the institution's fate. Participation in these debates, and their continuation in rituals such as Fourth of July celebrations, political contests, and "boosterism," gave ordinary northwesterners the opportunity to define the meanings of slavery and freedom in their societies. African Americans who dashed to Ohio and Indiana for freedom provoked controversies that further fostered opposition to slavery. Religious opponents of slavery used the influence of the pulpit and of print to forge and then spread their own set of objections to slavery. At the same time, the critique of slavery challenged—and at times muted—the racism that became an increasingly important part of northern antislavery politics during the 1820s.[32]

Reflecting the immediacy of slavery's threat to the Northwest, abolitionists in Ohio and Indiana subjected the institution to stringent criticism, beginning in the early 1800s. This small group of abolitionists in Ohio and Indiana joined their deeply held religious beliefs with an equally strong commitment to the doctrine that "all men are created equally free" to condemn slavery. The direct influence of this small group of radicals probably remained limited. Nonetheless, settlers in the Northwest increasingly accepted the proposition that "the propriety of holding those in slavery whom it hath pleased the Divine Creator to create free, seems to us to be repugnant to the inestimable principles of a republican Government."[33]

Deeming slavery to be "in direct opposition to republicanism, and the whole tenor of the Gospel," the small group of antislavery radicals in Ohio and Indiana wrote several stinging critiques of slavery. Their abiding religious and political faith produced the conviction that "right and justice are the same to a black as to a white; like the God from whom they sprung they know no distinction of persons." The biblical creed that God created mankind "of one blood" complemented their faith in natural rights. "The history of the creation of man; and of the relation of our species to each other by birth," provided "the strongest argument that can be used in favor of the *original and natural equality of all mankind*," explained one antislavery writer.[34]

They easily joined their religious critique of slavery with their political convictions. "A great people flourishing under the influence of republican institutions," with "gratitude to God" for "liberty and prosperity," cannot "neglect to do justice to the Africans." One antislavery minister chided that "they cannot be republicans, they cannot be Christians," so long as they tolerated slavery. Antislavery writers also recognized the value of the antislavery creed implicit in the Declaration of

Independence. "Slavery is directly inconsistent with the declaration of American independence, which declares that *'all men are born equally free,'*" explained Alexander Mitchell. Mitchell got the precise wording of the Declaration of Independence wrong, but the message seemed clear enough. The Declaration "proved" that slavery was "in opposition to all liberal republican principles, and a violation of the unalienable rights of man." Other writers more directly worked out the implications of the Declaration. "They at the Declaration of American Independence gave us as their opinion; 'we hold these truths to be self-evident; that all men are created equal;—that they are endowed by their Creator with certain unalienable rights,'" explained one writer who elucidated the antislavery significance of the phrase "all men." Congress deliberately "include[d] the blacks as well as the whites," he explained. "They did not say 'All white men,'" instead opting for the more powerful "All men are created equal."[35]

The religious and ideological convictions that formed the core of the early abolitionists' critique came together in the Union Humane Society, formed in St. Clairsville, Ohio, in 1816. On the inside cover of their constitution and letter book they inscribed their own version of the Declaration of Independence's antislavery principles: "We hold these truths to be self-evident,—That all men are created equally free;—and are endowed by their Creator with certain inalienable rights; that among these, are life,—liberty,—and the pursuit of happiness." They then recorded the seemingly self-evident antislavery golden rule: "Whatever ye would that men should do unto you,—do ye even so unto them." These religious and political convictions formed the society's founding principle: "that all men are born equally free, that all the nations of the earth are of the same blood," and "that the universal parent of men respecteth neither the person nor colour of any." The society was created to work for the gradual abolition of slavery, and its members pledged to resist any efforts to introduce slavery into the Northwest. They also swore to vote only for politicians deemed "sincerely opposed to every species of slavery."[36]

The importance of this small group of antislavery writers and societies should not be overstated. The members of the Union Humane Society disbanded in 1819, and most were scarcely ever heard from again. Yet the Union Humane Society did have some political impact, as it counted among its members a former governor, Charles Hammond, as well as a state senator. The members of the society also remained close with James Wilson, editor of the *Western Herald and Steubenville Gazette*, which became Ohio's most vocal critic of slavery during the Missouri Controversy. Finally, the Union Humane Society bore at least one offspring, Benjamin Lundy, who launched one of the nation's first antislavery newspapers, *The Genius of Universal Emancipation*. Equally important, religious-based antislavery societies and preachers encouraged and shaped public antislavery discourse. They encouraged adherents to move their discontent with slavery from the isolated spiritual world of the church into the temporal world of politics. Finally, their astute use of the emerging print culture allowed them to take their antislavery creed to a broad, popular audience. Whatever the impact of the antislavery radicals might have been, it became an article of faith in political discourse in the Northwest that slavery was "contrary" to "republicanism" and the "immutable principle of equity, inculcated by divine authority, 'Do unto another as thou wouldst have another do unto thee.'"[37]

As early as 1799, writers in Ohio made the incompatibility of slavery and republicanism part of public discourse on the slavery question. "Is it not a fundamental principle of genuine republicanism that all men are equal?" asked one Ohioan who denounced efforts to subvert Article VI. "The holding of slaves by Americans" was "an inconsistency with their national character," and all the more reason to keep it out of the Northwest. Public debates over slavery in Ohio peaked during the campaign for statehood and the election of delegates to frame the new state's constitution. In the campaign for delegates to the constitutional convention, candidates strove to demonstrate to the voters that they were true republicans who ardently opposed slavery. As one candidate wrote to the voters: "If there is anything that is opposite to republican principles, or disgraceful to the professions of republicanism, it is the abhored system of slavery." The adoption of a constitution prohibiting slavery meant that public debates about slavery became far less frequent and intense in Ohio after 1802. Nonetheless, Ohioans continued to forge a popular ideology and political identity with opposition to slavery as a central element of that creed. The process of creating a distinct regional identity combined with events, conflicts, and celebrations to provide ample opportunity to continue the process of defining the relationship between slavery, freedom, and republican society in Ohio.[38]

John Browne, editor of the ardently Republican *Liberty Hall and Cincinnati Mercury*, delegate to the constitutional convention of 1802, and one of the leaders of the Republican corresponding societies of Cincinnati made it his personal mission to join the fight against slavery throughout the Atlantic world. Browne placed Ohio and Indiana into a worldwide struggle between the forces of republicanism and slavery, a struggle that stretched from London, Africa, and Washington to Cincinnati and Vincennes. He seemingly reprinted every article that crossed his desk detailing the horrors of slavery and the slave trade, as well as the victories of the worldwide forces opposed to slavery. Browne often added his own commentary on slavery's evils for readers who may have missed the antislavery bent of a given piece. After printing an article detailing the horrors of the domestic slave trade, the *Liberty Hall* denounced those "republicans" who "boast of their own liberty, while they, without remorse, deprive others of it." The *Liberty Hall* also encouraged its readers to pay careful attention to letters from London detailing the progress of the British abolitionists' campaign against the international slave trade. Browne deemed the reports "of considerable importance to this western country," because they provide hope that "the same spirit of wisdom, policy and equity will be encouraged in the states of America south of the Ohio."[39]

When slavery threatened to enter Indiana, Browne opened his pages to antislavery writers and warned settlers in both Ohio and Indiana of William Henry Harrison's proslavery machinations. After the *National Intelligencer* reprinted one of his articles, with further commentary on the evils of slavery in the Northwest, Browne boasted of his contributions to the battle against Indiana slavery. He backed his boast with even more antislavery pieces. In the pages of Browne's *Liberty Hall*, even disputes over public education turned into rebukes of slavery and a celebration of free society. "The lovers of oppression have often pleaded in their favor, that enslaving the poor unhappy African has been conducive to the promotion of education," explained one writer, calling for public support of education in Cincinnati. Free Ohio, blessed with "equal law and happy government," could only "depreciate and hold in utter detestation, that system of Education, which to produce a vicious learned few, will consign thousands to the shades of everlasting ignorance."[40]

Ohioans furthered their celebration of a free, republican society at Fourth of July festivities. At one such occasion in 1807, given by the "local Republicans of Sycamore Township," a toast was offered to "Liberty and equality, the rights of man." The celebrants followed up their nod to their political principles by asking for "honor to the honest—glory to the brave—and freedom to the slave." The "Mechanics of Neville, Clermont County," captured the contrast between the two banks of the Ohio River in their Fourth of July celebration ten years later. They first toasted *"The State of Ohio*—Independent and Free." In their next toast, they called on *"Our Sister States, . . .* stained with the blood of Africa," to "deal justly, love mercy, and let the oppressed go free." Similarly, "the Republicans from Whitewater and Miami Townships" called for "emancipation and competence, to every enslaved mortal who has not forfeited freedom by crimes." They then toasted that "slavery never be admitted in the state of Ohio."[41]

Not all toasts were so forthright in calling for freedom for slaves. But when Ohioans offered toasts to their state, they often named the absence of slavery as its defining feature. "The State of Ohio—Her soil is not contaminated by a single slave" went one toast at a gathering of Cincinnati's elite, where William Henry Harrison, a new convert to Ohio's version of antislavery politics, gave the main address. A decade earlier, the staunchly Republican "Apprentices of this town" offered a toast to "the state of Ohio—May it never be clouded by the demon of slavery." By toast thirteen, the celebrants had gone ever deeper into their cups. Yet another reveler asked that "slavery never disgrace our land, but the principles of Liberty and Justice be preserved continually, and transmitted generation to generation, to the end of time." Other toasts spoke for themselves. A Steubenville gathering celebrated "the state of Ohio—the most free of all the free states." In these toasts, Ohioans articulated not so much an incipient antislavery ideology (though it was at times that too), but rather a political culture that celebrated freedom from slavery as one of their society's foundational strengths.[42]

Political contests also contributed to the ongoing debate between Ohio republicanism and slavery. After the War of 1812, William Henry Harrison returned to Ohio and sought election to Congress. His prestige as the hero of Tippecanoe and the weight of his father-in-law's influence won him election to office, but his opponents denounced him as "a friend to slavery." Harrison recognized that these charges could undermine his candidacy and he responded with a slew of broadsides and newspaper columns to help establish that he was a true enemy of slavery. Ten years earlier, Harrison had led efforts to overturn Article VI in Indiana. Now Harrison bragged that he had personally "redeemed a number" of blacks from "perpetual bondage" while governor of Indiana. Earlier that year, he had volunteered a toast that "the fertile banks of the Miami be never disgraced by the cultivation of a slave or the revenue they afford go to enrich the coffers of a despot." This was quite a change of heart for a former slaveholder who had led the movement to expand the institution into Indiana. But Harrison, as adroit a politician as ever, quickly fell into line with voter sentiment, at the same time that he helped shape it.[43]

Court cases and sensationalized trials added to discussions about the meanings of slavery and freedom in Ohio. While ruling on a slander charge stemming from one man labeling another a "negro," Judge Benjamin Tappan dismissed the case along with the racial logic that underwrote it. "We live under a government which recognizes the natural equality of man," began Tappan. Ohio's constitution "hath preserved us from the dangers and the curse of slavery." As such, he would "never sanction any doctrine which directly or indirectly contravenes that principle on which our government rests, that all men are created free and equal." Scandalous trials gave Ohioans another forum for expatiating on the virtues of freedom and equality, along with the evils of slavery. In the much sensationalized 1807 Cincinnati theft trial of the white Charles Vattier, the African American Charles Britton served as the prosecution's main witness, even though Britton was implicated in the crime. The defense tried to throw out Britton's testimony on the grounds that blacks could not testify against whites. Yet the prosecutor, the judge, and the secretary of state all refused to acknowledge the law prohibiting a black's testimony. Indeed, they rejected it as "a prostitution" of the otherwise just laws and constitution of Ohio, and therefore they were not bound to observe it. Furthermore, Britton, a slave at the time of the theft, had himself participated in the crime. But as the prosecution pointed out, he had done so only on the promise of freedom: a promise that slaves like Britton, in whom "so prominent is the love of liberty," could not forgo.[44]

African Americans from Virginia and Kentucky who tested Tappan's claim that "all men are created free and equal" repeatedly reminded white Ohioans of slavery's presence just across the river. Freedom suits and allegations of interference with the recovery of runaway slaves forced the issue of slavery into Ohio's courts, the governors' office, and the press. Kentucky and Virginia slaveholders with interests in Ohio had long evaded Ohio's laws by having their slaves work in Ohio by day, only to return to Kentucky each evening. In 1817 John McLean, a future Supreme Court justice who held posts in both the Monroe and Jackson administrations, freed a Kentucky slave who had been forced to work in Ohio. The practice was "subterfuge which will not exonerate the master from the penalty of forfeiture, nor prevent the slave from demanding his liberty." This "evasion of the policy of our Constitution can never be sanctioned," explained McLean, who then ordered that "wherever the master seeks a profit, by the labor of this slave in this state, he forfeits all right to the possession and services of such slave."[45]

McLean and his two associate judges used the case to expound on the glories of Ohio's free constitution. In slave states, "a presumption may perhaps arise, that every black man is a slave unless the contrary appear." But in Ohio, "the presumption is different. Every man is supposed to be free, until his obligation to servitude be clearly shown." McLean "could not hesitate to declare, that a slave in any state or country, according to the immutable principles of natural justice, is entitled to his freedom: that that which had its origins in usurpation and fraud, can never be sanctified into a right." The much anticipated decision was reported in papers throughout Ohio. As one editor added at the end of McLean's judgment, "the above is undoubtedly a correct decision."[46]

Runaway slaves who made it to Ohio extended their own conflicts between slavery and freedom across the Ohio River. While they were not always welcome, neither were the slave catchers who followed after them. "The difficulty said to be experienced by" Kentuckians who sought their runaway slaves produced a testy exchange between the states' two governors. At the request of the legislature, Kentucky governor Gabriel Slaughter complained that Kentuckians encountered "serious obstructions to the recovery of their property" in Ohio. "Whether it is owing to a defect in your laws, or the want of promptitude and energy in those who enforce them, or the prejudices of your Citizens against slavery," they knew not. All that mattered was that Ohio take action to preserve the property rights of Kentucky slaveholders. Ohio governor Thomas Worthington shot back by indicting the sloppy work of Kentucky slave catchers. So long as "the proofs of the right of property are defective," Ohio "judges must act according to the facts" of the case and the laws of Ohio. That meant certifying alleged fugitives as free so long as Kentuckians could not satisfactorily prove ownership.[47]

Slaveholders had good reason to complain about the difficulties of recovering runaway slaves. As an English traveler commented in 1822, Ohioans "do not always show much anxiety that the owners shall recover their property." In 1816, one slaveholder tracked a fugitive to Steubenville, but the locals refused to give the slave up. Frustrated, he warned those who continued "hiring or harboring" his slave that they did so "under penalty of their lives—For I am determined to risk mine in defence of my property." He pledged serious consequences for any person who continued "to hire or harbor said fellow after this notice." The Quaker community at Mount Pleasant apparently took matters one step further. One Virginian took out a notice warning emigrants from "any of the slaveholding states" to avoid Mount Pleasant. While he traveled through the town, "a mob" swayed his slave Ben "to leave my service," after they convinced him "that he was as free as I was."[48]

Other African Americans found freedom in equally unexpected ways. After a free black man from Kentucky instituted a freedom suit for his wife and his five children in 1817, agents of the slaveholder seized the family and sent them down the Ohio River, probably for sale somewhere in the lower Mississippi Valley. The father, with assistance from an "Emancipating Society," intercepted the boat on the Ohio and forced it to stop in Cincinnati. He immediately filed a freedom suit that was heard by a local justice of the peace. The justice ruled that the mother was born in Pennsylvania in 1783, which made her, along with her children, free. After 1815, slave catchers increasingly kidnapped suspected fugitives, rather than risk losing them before unsympathetic officials in Ohio. This set off a new controversy over manstealing, reminding Ohioans that "the unjustifiable practice of slaveholding is tolerated by a people who declare 'all men are born free and equal.'" African Americans who sought greater freedom on the north bank of the Ohio—both those who secured it and those who were less fortunate—provided a constant reminder of the contrast between slavery and freedom long before Alexis de Tocqueville and Harriet Beecher Stowe immortalized those differences in *Democracy in America* and *Uncle Tom's Cabin.*[49]

Slavery also contributed heavily to debates over revising Ohio's constitution. After 1815, some politicians called for a convention to meet and revise Ohio's badly antiquated 1802 constitution. Ohio voters overwhelmingly opposed the proposal. "A fear that slavery would be introduced into the state, if any amendments were attempted, has no doubt induced many to oppose every effort to obtain such amendments," complained a supporter of constitutional revision. "The aversion to slavery" was so "deep rooted and universal" that no politician would ever so much as propose permitting slavery in Ohio, knowing that it would "forever ruin their influence," grumbled another frustrated revisionist. Though it was "impossible" that a convention would permit slavery—"neither the ordinance, nor laws permit it, and besides public opinion is every where most decisively against it"—voters continued to resist, because they "feared that slavery may be introduced."[50]

Ohio newspapers also kept a running tab of the battle over slavery in Indiana as that territory moved toward framing a constitution. "It is expected that slavery will be excluded from this new state," reported one newspaper. Two months later, the same paper gave its readers the most important news about the Indiana constitution: "Slavery prohibited, and the constitution never to be amended so as to admit of it." Another paper celebrated that "some Slave holders" would be "disappointed" by Indiana's permanent constitutional prohibition on slavery. Indiana's successful defeat of slavery gave Ohioans yet another occasion to celebrate their own free state. As Ohio governor Thomas Worthington remarked in his annual address to the legislature, he was "highly gratified" that like Ohio, Indiana had "in the most unqualified manner, prohibited slavery."[51]

Antislavery politicians in Indiana of course had their own battles to fight. Because the proslavery forces had gained so much ground in Indiana, the threat of slavery was much greater there than in Ohio. Antislavery politicians in Indiana worked extensively to create and propagate a vision of a republican society free of slavery. In Indiana, much of the debate over slavery and freedom centered on the disposition of "real republicans" toward slavery. "How preposterous must it appear to the real republicans to hear the clamorous ones, bawling out republicanism, liberty and equality, at the very moment they are exercising the uncontrolled whip of despotism, on a large portion of their fellow creatures," cried one antislavery writer. As political competition between the proslavery and antislavery politicians continued to heat up, the antislavery men insisted that "the friend of slavery cannot be a republican."[52]

"A system which has the most deleterious influence upon the morals and manners of society, which it tends to corrupt and brutalize," slavery had no place in Indianans' vision of a republican society. Slavery "converts power into right, familiarises the mind with the idea of usurpation, and thereby paves the way to despotism." As the leader of the antislavery forces in the legislature asked: "How long [could] the political institutions of a people admitting slavery . . . be expected to remain uninjured?" The answer was, "Not very long." Slave societies were simply not a "proper school for the acquirement of republican virtue," not when "usurpation is sanctioned by law," when "the commands of justice are trampled under foot," when "those claiming the right of free men are themselves the most execrable of tyrants, and where is consecrated the dangerous maxim 'that power is right.'" Slavery was "a moral and political evil, so enormous," counseled the antislavery party's chief polemicist, "that I most solemnly protest, against the patriotism of the man who wishes to extend it." Rarely did even abolitionists in the 1850s rebuke slaveholders and slave societies with such power and eloquence.[53]

Whatever Indiana settlers' disposition toward slavery might have been prior to the eruption of the slavery controversy in territorial politics—most seem to have been ambivalent—political participation invited them to identify themselves as republicans who opposed slavery. It is doubtful that the sixty-eight men who signed a petition calling for Harrison's removal in 1809 had settled in the territory because of their principled objections to slavery. By 1809, they convinced themselves that they had. "Being in principle opposed to Slavery," they explained to the Senate that they had settled in Indiana because of their "most unbounded confidence in our government that slavery in this land shall never exist."[54]

After 1810, the importance of slavery receded into the background in Indiana. Tensions between settlers and Indians led to war in 1811, followed quickly by war with Great Britain in 1812. But antislavery politics remained important through 1816, when the territory entered the Union as the nineteenth state. In the 1812 election for the territorial delegate to Congress, Waller Taylor felt compelled to explain his past support for Indiana slavery. "I am and ever have been a republican," explained Taylor, as he made amends for his past sins. Now, however, "being well assured . . . that an immense majority of the people are opposed to the measure, I here pledge myself to you not only to refrain from taking any measures myself to favor their introduction, but, to oppose it should it be brought forward by others." Harrison's replacement as governor felt similarly compelled to explain his position on slavery. Thomas Posey had received word of opposition to his appointment, on account of "the people of the Indiana Territory being principled against slavery." Though Posey was a Kentucky slaveholder who held slaves after his appointment, he nonetheless felt compelled to address Indianans' concerns. Posey asked an associate in Indiana to assure the people that "I am most opposed to slavery as any person whatever," and would "never sanction a law for slavery or any manifestation of it."[55]

In 1816 Indianans once more found themselves forced to decide the fate of slavery, when they applied for statehood. A simple question faced them: "Shall we sing 'Hail Columbia,' and boast that we have planted the tree of liberty, [while] in the same breath plant the tree of slavery?" Thanks to the efforts of Indiana's antislavery politicians, the answer could only be a resounding no.[56]

III

Prior to the Missouri Controversy, ordinary white families in Ohio and Indiana bore witness to the reality of slavery in the Ohio Valley, and to wide-ranging public debates centering on the relationship between slavery, freedom, and republican society. These debates produced a popular ideology that celebrated the virtues of free society while denouncing slavery and all the vices of slave societies in the strongest terms. Before the Missouri Controversy made slavery and expansion an issue of national importance, many white northwesterners had already become convinced that the absence of slavery elevated them and their society. "As moral and political light increases, the principles of slavery, with other superstitions, must vanish before it," wrote one northwesterner, as he looked to the future with both confidence and trepidation.[57]

Ohio, Indiana, and, in 1818, Illinois all incorporated the antislavery provisions of Article VI into their constitutions. Yet the future of slavery and freedom in the West remained unresolved. The writer from the *Richmond Compiler* expected that when "the Michigan and Missouri Territories fall into the ranks of American States, an eternal prohibition will be raised by their constitution to the introduction of involuntary slaves." Ohioans were less certain of freedom's prospects. At a Fourth of

July celebration in Cincinnati in 1813, Republican Josiah Meigs offered his toast to "The Mississippi, father of rivers: may the rains and dews of Heaven, never fertilize the fields which he drains, if they are occupied by slaves." As Meigs sensed, American expansion into the trans-Mississippi West invited a replay of the struggles between slavery and freedom in the Ohio Valley. Little did he know the prescience of his toast.[58]

8

"The States or Territories Which May Hereafter Be Admitted into the Union"

The Missouri Crisis and the West

In the late 1850s Abraham Lincoln recognized that Stephen Douglas's principle of popular sovereignty proved most dangerous to the cause of freedom. Popular sovereignty, which allowed settlers in a given territory to accept or reject slavery, turned a principled question of national importance into a local question decided on the basis of interest and preference. Lincoln also recognized that allowing Congress to address the problem on a case-by-case basis as it arose with the creation of new territories would prove equally inadequate. The decision would become a mere matter of policy, decided on the basis of sectional and partisan political power in Congress. Both situations pitted freedom against slavery; the history of expansion revealed that freedom rarely prevailed. For Lincoln, a Union dedicated to the cause of liberty could not afford to stand on such shaky ground. Slavery's expansion could be halted and the institution placed on the road to gradual extinction only if the nation as a whole adopted the principle that slavery was a moral and political evil that would not be permitted to expand.[1]

Lincoln's position was not at all new; during the Missouri Crisis, northern restrictionists in general, and northern Republicans in particular, came to understand the problem of slavery's expansion in much the same way.[2] As Congress prepared to take up the Missouri question for the second time, in December 1819, the *Saratoga Sentinel* confidently predicted that "No state or territory . . . will ever again be admitted to the union, with the privilege of exercising a prerogative so illy comporting with our republican form of government, and so obnoxious to the principles of a great proportion of the people." Though his expectations were great, the editor's confidence was not entirely misplaced.[3]

The Missouri Controversy raised fundamental questions about the past, present, and future of slavery in a Union poised to expand across the continent. It irrevocably changed the orientation of the slavery expansion quandary. What was once a problem of the West was now a crisis that defined and divided a free North from a slave South. Northerners convinced themselves that the fate of slavery in Missouri would determine the future of the American empire in the West. Recognizing the importance of the issue, people and politicians from across the North insisted that Congress forever stop slavery's expansion by prohibiting slavery, not just in Missouri, but "in all new states and territories to be formed and admitted into the Union." According to northern restrictionists, precedent, the nation's founding principles, and the Constitution all created a potent antislavery past which demanded that Congress work to halt slavery's expansion as an important step toward gradually abolishing the institution. Like Lincoln would in 1860, they also sought a definitive solution to the problem of slavery's expansion.[4]

Southern politicians especially understood just how far northern proposals went. They responded by creating their own pro-expansionist past, denying that the federal government possessed any authority to restrict expansion into western territories. They also demanded that the federal government protect slavery in the southern states by permitting—indeed, even encouraging—its expansion. Southern defenses of slavery, whether on principled or expedient grounds, increasingly accepted slavery as a permanent, ineradicable institution. Indefinite and unrestricted expansion became the best way to soften slavery's excesses in the South, not a means for gradually abolishing the institution. Missouri was a battle they could not afford to lose, "no matter what the northern people may say."[5]

I

Since the 1790s, northern Republicans and select Federalists had tried
to force Congress to confront the problem of slavery expansion. Furthermore, northern Republicans had long demonstrated an interest in
limiting slavery in Upper Louisiana and then Missouri. On three separate occasions, dating back to 1804, northern Republicans had sought
to place restrictions on slavery in what became Missouri. Obstinate
western slaveholders and problems of Union in the farthest West insured the defeat of these proposals. After 1815, however, the emergence
of "a more connected union of the different and distant sections of this
great republic" removed one persistent obstacle to slavery restriction
in the West. Though western slaveholders remained obstinate, the federal government now possessed power that matched its authority in the
West, the type of power necessary to enforce unpopular but important
restrictions on western slavery.[6]

The nation's survival through the trials of the War of 1812 stood as
testimony to the strength of the Union and its ability to unite an extended republic, even in time of crisis. Prior to the war, the West had
always appeared to be but an incident away from crisis and possible
disunion. Yet western Americans had acquitted themselves especially
well during the war; disunionist threats emanated from Hartford and
New England, not St. Louis, New Orleans, or the Mississippi Valley.
In addition, peace in Europe and Andrew Jackson's smashing defeat of
the British at New Orleans destroyed European imperial ambitions for
western America. The West now seemed unquestionably secure. The
postwar years, marked by an ambitious program of economic development and internal improvements designed to strengthen connections
between the East and the West, promised to complete the process of
integrating the West more fully into the Union.[7]

The years between 1815 and 1819 were also marked by both expansion and consolidation in the West. By late 1818 Congress had admitted
Indiana, Illinois, and Mississippi to the Union; Alabama and Missouri
stood ready for statehood; and the United States was poised to continue
its rapid expansion to the south and the west. In 1818 Britain acknowledged some American claims to the Oregon Country on the Pacific
Coast. Spain would cede Florida in 1819, and many politicians believed
the United States possessed legitimate claims to Texas. To many contemporaries, it seemed clear by early 1819 that the United States had

secured the Union and was on the verge of creating a continental republic.[8]

The "Era of Good Feelings" also saw a renewed interest in slavery, especially in the North. British authors penned a host of widely read narratives detailing their travels in the United States. Most were critical of slavery, setting off an embarrassing trans-Atlantic debate about American slavery. In the Middle Atlantic states, antislavery groups like the Pennsylvania Abolition Society stepped up their attacks on the slave trade and increased efforts to secure freedom for both free and fugitive African Americans. A long-simmering dispute over fugitive slaves in the Ohio Valley and Pennsylvania led southern congressmen to call for a new, more comprehensive fugitive slave law. The surge in kidnappings of free and enslaved blacks from the North, the glaring inhumanity of the domestic slave trade, and the continuation of the international slave trade through Amelia Island off the Georgia coast produced outrage in both the North and South. The North also produced a plethora of antislavery literature after the war, from Captain James Riley's narrative of his captivity in Africa, to *Niles' Weekly Register*'s periodic essays on gradual emancipation, to the even more aggressive stance against slavery taken by Philadelphia Republican William Duane's *Aurora and General Advertiser*.[9]

The rapid admission of western states also renewed interest in slavery's expansion. In April 1818, New Hampshire Republican Arthur Livermore proposed a constitutional amendment prohibiting slavery "in any State hereafter admitted into the Union," though the House immediately voted down his proposal. Six months later, New York Republican James Tallmadge again raised the issue of western slavery, when he tried blocking Illinois statehood on the grounds that their constitution failed to guard sufficiently against "the principle of slavery."[10]

None of these developments—the emergence of a more secure Union, new and old concerns about slavery, or the prospect of a continental republic—prefigured the Missouri Controversy. Indeed, no one anticipated the fury unleashed by the proposed restrictions on Missouri slavery. Nonetheless, the changes that occurred after 1815, coupled with past failures to stop slavery expansion in the trans-Mississippi West, made it all the more likely that northern Republicans would lead and support any practical attempt to curb slavery's growth. Given southern politicians' past objections to restrictions because of the weakness of the Union in the West, and given their own criticisms of slavery's excesses after 1815, it seemed likely that they too would support restrictions.

II

On February 13, 1819, James Tallmadge of New York brought the so-called Era of Good Feelings to an end when he introduced two amendments to the Missouri Enabling Bill before the House.[11] Tallmadge's most reasonable proposal would prohibit the further introduction of slaves into Missouri and provide for the eventual emancipation of all slaves born in the new state. The Tallmadge restrictions set off a firestorm of debate over slavery, sectional interest, and the meaning of republicanism in a nation committed to western expansion. With the Tallmadge restrictions passing the House by narrow majorities, only to meet defeat in the Senate, these debates consumed parts of two congressional sessions, along with the recess between them. Increased public interest in national political issues and the prolonged debate created in the North new concerns about the relationship between slavery, expansion, the West, and the nation.[12]

As northern restrictionists grappled with the past, present, and future of slavery's expansion, they worked out the fuller implications of what they termed "republican principles" to create an antislavery past profoundly hostile toward slavery and its expansion. They then tried, just as Lincoln would do in the late 1850s, to turn that antislavery heritage into a set of binding principles which promised that slavery would not expand along with the nation. As the Missouri Controversy wore on, northern restrictionists aligned themselves with an antislavery founding generation, claimed the Revolutionary heritage for themselves, and charged that it was their opponents who had broken violently with the nation's rich antislavery past. According to northern restrictionists, there was little new or radical in the Tallmadge restrictions. They merely insisted that the federal government use its limited but proper constitutional powers to restrict slavery expansion now that more favorable circumstances allowed for the greater use of federal power in the West.

Northerners sensed immediately that Tallmadge's plan involved much more than the future of Missouri slavery. In 1811, Louisiana sought admission to the Union with a constitution protecting slavery, but the already large slave population and mounting concerns about the West on the eve of the War of 1812 made it impossible to do anything about slavery in Louisiana. By 1819, however, the changed situation in the West permitted the use of federal power. More importantly, Missouri would set a precedent for the remainder of the vast Louisiana Purchase. Adding to the urgency about Missouri, developments in the Old Northwest—the continuing flirtations in Illinois with slavery and fears that slaveholders were secretly plotting to overturn Ohio's constitutional ban on slavery—demonstrated just how precarious freedom was in the West. Warnings that Missouri would determine the fate of slavery in the entire West abounded in northern speeches and newspaper columns; at issue was whether the United States would become an "empire for liberty" or an "empire for slavery."[13]

"The question has fairly met us, whether freedom or slavery is to be the lot of the regions beyond the Mississippi," explained Pennsylvania Republican Jonathan Roberts to his colleagues in the Senate. Northern restrictionists shared Roberts's fear that unrestricted slavery in Missouri would set a precedent for the entire trans-Mississippi West. Soon enough, "other states and territories will spring up; the same privilege of slavery will be required," and "the authority of precedent" would then justify an uncontrollable expansion of slavery across the West. The current crisis threatened "to extend this cursed blot on our country over the immense regions west of the Mississippi." This tragedy could be prevented only by insisting on restrictions on slavery in Missouri and the rest of the West.[14]

The Missouri Controversy infused the North with a new appreciation of the fundamental conflict between freedom and slavery that had been playing out in the West. For a brief but intense moment, northern "republicans and friends of freedom" insisted that Congress halt slavery's expansion and lay the groundwork for "the emancipation of the blacks and the restriction of slavery in those territories which are about to unfold the American banner as stars in our republican constellation." Checking slavery in Missouri would be the first step toward a more general abolition or prohibition of slavery in America's western territories, laying the groundwork for the expansion of freedom. As one northern Republican newspaper explained, "If the extension of slavery is ever to be prohibited, if the truth promulgated in the Constitution of the U. States, that 'all men are born equal,' is ever to be enforced, [then] now is the moment in which the ax ought to be laid at the root of the tree."[15]

Northern commitment to restrictions was fueled by new debates over the meaning of republicanism and its applicability to slavery. Since the 1790s, northerners had listened to southern contrarians complain that the North had strayed from the principles of republicanism that stood at the heart of the American Revolution and founding. Postwar debates over federal funding for internal improvements and other projects increased southern criticism that the North was somehow less republican than the South. With southerners defending slavery during the Missouri Controversy, northerners embraced the opportunity to become the new devotees of true republicanism. "We could not conceive that a republican majority in Congress would sanction the principle of perpetuating slavery," explained a group of Ohioans, who defined the Missouri Controversy as a conflict between the "principles of republicanism" and the "principles of slavery." The *Aurora* deemed it "a detestable paradox" to claim to be both *"a republican,* and an enemy to the *restriction of slavery."* According to Massachusetts Republican Timothy Fuller, the "predominant principles" for which Northern restrictionists fought was "that all men are free, and have an equal right to liberty"—in a word, "republicanism." With "public opinion" now "awake to the great importance of the question," northern restrictionists freely indulged their animus against the "anti-republican principles" of slavery.[16]

For all their rhetoric, northern restrictionists recognized that their speeches and writings amounted to little so long as Congress failed to implement policy that could effectively halt slavery's expansion. The current crisis, along with past failures, demonstrated that popular sovereignty alone could never address the problem of slavery expansion. According to southern expansionists, the fate of slavery in the West was "one of those questions on which those interested, whether States or Territories, ought to have the exclusive right to decide." For northern restrictionists, that was precisely the problem; slaveholders, especially in the West, would never give up the institution on their own.[17]

At its worst, popular sovereignty made the interests of the nation "subordinate to fifty thousand in the Territory of Missouri." Experience demonstrated that those "fifty thousand" could not be counted on to give up slavery without prodding from the federal government. The "general habit of slave-holding has never produced and never will produce, in individuals, the disposition to forsake the practice." When the federal government allowed popular sovereignty alone to decide the institution's fate, human nature and the demands of western settlement dictated that western territories would choose slavery over freedom. The Missouri Controversy only confirmed a fact long known: popular sovereignty and nonintervention failed completely and utterly. No natural, sectional, or geographical limits confined slavery's expansion. Popular sovereignty insured that Missouri would remain a slave state. Should it be applied to the rest of the West, slavery would soon extend "in all its horrors over a vast and boundless tract of country."[18]

Allowing Congress to decide the place of slavery in the West on a case-by-case basis as new territories and states were formed seemed equally inadequate. James Tallmadge proposed his restrictions in February 1819, and Congress spent the better part of the next two months debating his proposal. While the House continued to pass the Tallmadge restrictions by narrow majorities, the Senate continued to vote them down. When Congress picked up the question the following year, it found itself locked in the same pattern. Here was sectional politics at its worst. The present and future of slavery's expansion was of interest to the nation as a whole. Yet the debate had quickly degenerated into a sectional struggle, with both sides unwilling to budge. By turning a principled question into a matter of sectional and political conflict, Congress had set "all morals at defiance," leaving them to debate the issue "as a matter of mere personal interest" that would be decided—not on the basis of right—but on sectional political strength. Congress had to rise above sectional bickering and self-interest to put the question of expansion to rest by adopting a uniform policy that would cover Missouri and the entire trans-Mississippi West. Otherwise, the problem would revisit Congress again. Deep sectional divisions would rive Congress, and slavery would prevail over freedom.[19]

The failure of popular sovereignty to restrict slavery in Missouri created a new appreciation for the Northwest Ordinance and the role of the federal government in restricting slavery in the West. The exclusion of slavery from Ohio, Indiana, and Illinois demonstrated that the most effective course for arresting western slavery involved both the federal government and the people of a territory. Slaveholders had tested and evaded Article VI in all three states. But prodded by the promise of freedom enshrined in Article VI, Congress and the people had committed themselves to the Northwest Ordinance and managed to prevent the institution from taking root in those territories. Experience demonstrated that slavery could be effectively shut out of Missouri and future territories only if the federal government established a new antislavery ordinance that would guide future settlers in the West, just as Article VI had inspired the Old Northwest to reject slavery. This required northerners to defend against the southern assault on Article VI and the Northwest Ordinance. Southern politicians denounced the Northwest Ordinance as "an usurpation" and "an act of illegitimate power," then denied that it could offer any guidance or precedent. But southern denunciations of the Northwest Ordinance only strengthened northern arguments that the federal government had to take the lead in restricting slavery expansion.[20]

Senator Benjamin Ruggles of Ohio especially took exception to southern attacks on the Northwest Ordinance. Ruggles understood that the ordinance had become much more than a requirement imposed by the federal government. Article VI and the Northwest Ordinance were "adopted under the influence of those great principles of liberty and the rights of man," the same principles that had inspired the Declaration of Independence and the Constitution. In the intervening thirty years, the Northwest Ordinance had become a biblical "'cloud by day and a pillar of fire by night,'" directing settlers in the Northwest as surely as God had once guided the Israelites to the promised land. Indeed, according to Ruggles, "the Israelites of old could not have been more prosperous in settling their favorite Canaan, under the immediate government of God himself," than the people who settled the Northwest under the Ordinance of 1787. Now, Congress could extend the same providential designs to Missouri and the West.[21]

As northern restrictionists came to understand the problem facing Congress, it seemed increasingly akin to the problem solved by the Continental Congress in the 1780s, a problem that in retrospect they defined as the incompatibility of slavery and republicanism. The founding generation, "so anxious . . . to confine human bondage," wisely included Article VI in the Northwest Ordinance. Republican government and society had subsequently flourished in the Northwest and slavery failed to take hold. The challenge facing the present generation was in essence the same. The nation now had to lay the groundwork for republican society in the trans-Mississippi West. Congress could put an end to slavery's expansion by creating a new "'cloud by day and a pillar of fire by night'" for Missouri and the trans-Mississippi West. In short, Congress had to "prohibit slavery in all those States that may hereafter become members of the American confederacy" by creating a new Northwest Ordinance for the trans-Mississippi West.[22]

For the Northwest Ordinance to provide a useful precedent, restrictionists had to explain why slavery expansion had been permitted everywhere else. Past congressional actions had left a mixed precedent, as slavery had been permitted in Kentucky, Tennessee, Alabama, Mississippi, and Louisiana. Still, restrictionists proved unwilling to yield the past to southern expansionists, and with it valuable precedent. Robert Walsh's widely read *Free Remarks on the Spirit of the Federal Constitution* and Rufus King's widely circulated speech before the Senate both claimed that the United States possessed an antislavery and anti-expansionist past. In congressional speeches, newspapers, state houses, and mass rallies against extension, northerners echoed their sentiments.[23]

According to restrictionists, the anti-expansionist past was neither haphazard nor accidental, but by design. The antislavery provisions of Article VI set the standard for the expansion of republican states and territories, unblemished by slavery, across the West. "In their first instance in which a portion of the American territory was subjected to their jurisdiction," Congress "recognized the principle of *universal emancipation*" in Article VI. In doing so, they "prohibited *slavery* for ever" and "stigmatized it as repugnant to the noble ends" of the American Revolution. Despite this antislavery standard, Congress permitted slavery in Kentucky, the Southwest, Mississippi, and Louisiana territories from what all parties had recognized as "uncontrollable necessity." Because these examples were special exemptions based on necessity, slavery's past expansion did nothing "to invalidate the force of precedent" established by the Northwest Ordinance. In no way did slavery's previous expansion justify its expansion in Missouri or elsewhere. Indeed, restrictionists confidently claimed that "it was *always* intended" that the federal government prohibit slavery in western territories, despite the failed efforts to do so in the past. For northern restrictionists, the history of expansion—which seemingly favored expansion—now amounted to a broad precedent favoring restriction in Missouri and the entire trans-Mississippi West.[24]

Northerners strengthened their case for an anti-restrictionist heritage by grounding it in a broader antislavery past that they traced back to the Declaration of Independence and the Constitution of 1787. Slavery was plainly in "hostility to the first principles of our Government, and certainly so with its first official act—the Declaration of Independence." The guiding principle of the Declaration, "that all men are created equal," demanded that Congress act "always to control this evil" when it possessed the authority and power to do so, as they did with Missouri. The same antislavery principles infused the Constitution, which contained "general principles" favoring freedom and the "exceptions." The right "to keep slaves" in the states where slavery existed was merely "an exception to the general principles of the Constitution," which favored freedom over slavery. Whatever special rights slaveholders enjoyed in the original states, those rights did not necessarily extend to the West. In short, *"slavery could find no shelter under the constitution."* Intended to be "highly propitious to universal abolition," the Constitution not only justified action against slavery in the West, it demanded it.[25]

This antislavery reading of the Constitution and Declaration of Independence applied directly to the problem at hand. The Pennsylvania legislature could only "deprecate any departure from the humane and enlightened policy pursued" by the "illustrious congress of 1787" and their successors, "without exception." The newfound antislavery past infused speeches in Congress. According to James Tallmadge, "it is an old principle, adopted by" the founders, that "whenever the United States have had the right and power, they have heretofore prevented the extension of slavery." Benjamin Ruggles deemed "manifest" the "intention of those who made the Constitution, to confine slavery to the States then existing, and forever to prohibit it" elsewhere. Not only did Congress possess the power to restrict slavery expansion, it was obligated to use it. Bolstered by their antislavery reading of the past and their construction of an anti-expansionist constitution, northern restrictionists called on Congress to take far-reaching action against slavery's expansion in Missouri and the remainder of the West. That demanded nothing less than "the Abolition of Slavery in the states or territories which may hereafter be admitted into the Union."[26]

In January 1820 a "very large meeting of the people of New Castle County" was held in Wilmington, Delaware. The meeting, where longtime Jeffersonian Republican Caesar Rodney spoke, unanimously passed a resolution "that it was constitutional and highly expedient to prohibit the further extension of slavery" into new states and territories, including Missouri. Shortly after the Wilmington meeting, the Delaware legislature adopted a resolution calling for a complete prohibition "on the future introduction of slaves into the territories of the United States, and into such new states as may be hereafter admitted into the union." Both resolutions were symptomatic of a larger commitment to block slavery from Missouri and to take on slavery in all territories—to rectify past failures and irrevocably place the West on the path to freedom.[27]

As Congress met to decide the Missouri question, in December 1819, public meetings and state legislatures throughout the North flooded Congress and newspapers with resolutions. People from northern villages, towns, and cities spoke to Congress in the same broad terms as the Wilmington meeting and the Delaware legislature had. All stated their conviction that Congress should "prohibit the introduction of slavery into any of the new states or territories," as well as Missouri. The founding generation knew that slavery "could not be eradicated at once." They nonetheless believed that "it could be circumscribed and restrained, and time would pave the way for the introduction of more powerful and controlling laws."[28]

That time had arrived. In April 1818, Arthur Livermore of New Hampshire had proposed amending the Constitution to prohibit slavery "in any State hereafter admitted into the Union." The House quickly dismissed his proposal without debate. Less than two years later, "every dog-hole town and blacksmith's village in the northern states" called on Congress to end slavery's expansion forever.[29]

III

Southern politicians and slaveholders could not afford to ignore what the North had to say—not when northern restrictionists made "the prohibition of slavery in new states" their "professed object." During the Missouri Controversy, southern politicians found themselves on the defensive as never before. The "grossest" slanders heaped on slavery left one Virginian "abused," worried, and "deeply aggrieved." And what northerners had to say, along with the measures they now called for, deeply disturbed southern whites. Southern politicians fully recognized that the Missouri Controversy opened the way for the use of national power to hem in slavery. More menacing, they saw a widespread popular mandate in the North to do so. Unlike in the North, the white population of the South remained silent during the Missouri Controversy. Nonetheless, southern politicians' speeches, essays, and threats more than made up for the silence of the public.[30]

In true Jeffersonian fashion, southern politicians continued to allow that slavery was an evil. Yet in a marked divergence from the past they now deemed slavery and republican government compatible, made slaveholding an inalienable right, claimed that slavery was permanent, and insisted that the federal government possessed no authority to block its expansion. Equally important, previous congressional attempts to limit western slavery had been blocked by disunion-threatening western slaveholders. Now, slaveholding politicians from the Atlantic states warned that restrictions on slavery in the West might just break apart the Union between the North and the South. Restrictions on Missouri slavery menaced the South as much as they promised to eradicate slavery from the West. Consequently, southern politicians took up the cause of Missouri as their own. In doing so, they redefined the problem of slavery in the West. What was once a conflict between eastern and western interests now became a battle between the free North and the slave South.

The northern case for restriction rested on the argument that slavery perverted the normal workings of republican government and that the Constitution expressly permitted action against slavery outside the states where it existed. These charges led southern politicians to codify already changing beliefs about the relationship between slavery, republicanism, the Constitution, and the federal government.[31] "Whatever may be the sentiment of the moralist or of the divine, it does not appear that *slavery* can be regarded, in any degree, as a *political evil*," wrote the essayist "Cato." Southern politicians agreed. Nowhere in the United States did there exist a "greater devotion to the true principles of liberty" than in the slave states. Indeed, "in no part" of the United States "have the pure principles of democracy been so cherished, as among the inhabitants of the slaveholding States."[32]

Above all else, the Constitution itself illustrated the sublime bonds between slavery and republican government. "Slavery was recognized in the formation of this government, as not *inconsistent with republican institutions*." Under a federal constitution expressly protecting slavery, the slave states had made the United States the "greatest republic in the world." Quite simply, the Constitution "admits that slavery and a republican form of government are not incongruous. It associates and binds" slavery together, thus repudiating the North's "wild" claim that the Constitution contained an antislavery bent. Not only were slavery and republican government compatible, the Constitution recognized as much. Individual states and the people of a given territory could of course exclude slavery from their borders, but the federal government could prohibit slavery in the West only with the express consent of the people, something that was not forthcoming from Missouri. Like their counterparts in Missouri, southern politicians had turned the United States into a slaveholders' republic.[33]

This slaveholders' republic was explicitly charged with protecting slaveholders' rights to "our part" of the West, which now meant any part of the West that southern slaveholders deemed their own. The Constitution recognized slaveholders' "local rights" as sacred throughout the Union. The right to carry slaves to federal territories was not just an indulgence extended to slaveholders in limited cases, as northerners contended and as precedent suggested. It was instead one of "the rights, privileges, and immunities of citizens of the United States." Past Congresses had, "in the most explicit manner," protected slaveholders' property rights in western territories. Those same protections had to be extended to slaveholders who wished to migrate to Missouri or other parts of the West, for the federal government had no more authority to interfere with slaveholders' rights in western territories than in South Carolina or Virginia.[34]

That southern politicians had acknowledged federal power in the past proved no obstacle to aggressive southern expansionists. Even the Jefferson-inspired Northwest Ordinance was open to attack. James Barbour of Virginia denounced the "Ordinance itself," because its passage by the old Continental Congress "was founded in usurpation" and thus "not entitled to the least weight as precedent." In other cases, expansionists turned the Northwest Ordinance into the exception and expansion into the rule. Expansionists could "stand together upon the basis of precedent" because whenever Congress had created new territories, "the operation of the 6th article has been suspended or destroyed." The Constitution also stood on their side. "On the question of slavery, Congress have no right to restrict even the territorial government." The territorial clause of the Constitution meant only "that Congress may sell and manage their own property, but not the property of the people." When it came to slavery, there was simply "no power in the General Government to touch it in any way," not even in federal territories.[35]

Their construction of a proslavery past undergirded claims that slavery was inseparable from southern expansion. Slave labor was "peculiarly necessary" for southern expansion. The "manners, customs, and habits" of southern whites had long been "familiarized to the toleration of slavery." The "convenience" of slaveholding had "become somewhat necessary" for southerners in the West, "where much labor was necessary." Consequently, any laws restricting slavery in Missouri would "be tantamount to a prohibition of the emigration of the Southern people." The same principle applied to the remainder of the West. If Congress could prohibit slavery in Missouri, then it could bar the institution from "the whole tract of country" lying west of the Mississippi. Such restrictions would "entirely shut out the Southern people" from the West.[36]

Here was something new from southern politicians. Southern slaveholders had traditionally protected slavery from federal interference by claiming that it was exclusively a state institution. Northern and southern politicians generally agreed that the federal government lacked the authority to interfere with slavery in the states where it existed. But at the same time, southerners had yielded to the federal government authority to place restrictions on slavery when it involved the interests of the nation as a whole, as it did with the international slave trade and slavery in federal territories. Prior to the Missouri Controversy, most southern politicians who opposed restrictions insisted that nonintervention reflected immediate circumstances that made it impossible for the United States to enforce limits on western slavery. Rather than denying that Congress could restrict slavery in the West, they cautioned that the unsettled situation there made it dangerous to exercise that power. Now, in their zeal to defeat northern efforts to prohibit slavery in the rest of the West, southerners stripped the federal government of its authority to restrict slavery's expansion and threatened disunion should the government exercise it. To do so was all the more important, as southern politicians drew new connections between the future of slavery in the Atlantic states and its continued expansion in the West.

In previous conflicts over slavery expansion, southern politicians drew mainly cursory associations between slavery in the East and the West. At most, some argued that because slaveholders were shut out of the Northwest, fairness dictated that parts of the Southwest should remain open to southern migrants. But the Missouri Controversy both reflected and caused significant changes in southern-white thinking about the future of slavery. Southern politicians now linked the well-being of slavery in the Atlantic states—even its very survival—with its indefinite and uncontrolled expansion into the West. During the Missouri Controversy, a few southerners, such as Thomas Jefferson, still held hope that expansion and diffusion might lead to gradual emancipation. Yet Jefferson proved to be nearly alone in his near obsession with diffusion leading to abolition.[37]

Instead, southern defenders of expansion steered clear of even suggesting that expansion might lead to "some safe and practicable mode" for the "gradual reduction" of slavery. Those who did quickly wrapped themselves in the Constitution and states' rights, reflexively buried the suggestion under a heap of qualifications, or mused on the impossibilities of emancipation no matter how gradual or far off. Most simply dropped the suggestion as soon as they mentioned it. Expansionists eagerly pointed out that to permit slaves "to spread over an extensive country" in the West would both "diffuse" and "ameliorate" the institution. Despite the incredibly harsh realties that slaves forced to migrate to the West faced, southern politicians maintained that the bounties of the West would "ameliorate" the harsh conditions under which slaves lived in the Atlantic states. At the same time, it would "diffuse" and thin out the growing population of slaves in the Atlantic states, which by 1819 slaveholders were likening to a powder keg ready to explode. Thus "diffused" and "ameliorated," the South's enslaved African Americans would be far less likely to rebel. Expansion thus benefited slave and slaveholder alike. But self-preservation and humanitarian gestures aside, southern politicians recognized that expansion and diffusion provided no remedy for ending slavery. Instead, expansion was now the best means for the "proper and effectual management" of the South's enslaved masses.[38]

If southern politicians allowed that slavery was an evil, it was now both a necessary and permanent one. Furthermore, though politicians remained reluctant to defend slavery on principled grounds, they were no less insistent that slavery was a permanent institution that had to expand, lest it destroy itself in the conflagration of rebellion in the Atlantic states. Speeches in Congress and articles in such bellwethers of southern opinion as the *Richmond Enquirer* and the *National Intelligencer* reveal a slaveholding South that looked to expansion—not to terminate slavery, as Jefferson had once hoped—but to mitigate the excesses of an institution they now accepted as permanent. When added to other southern concerns about the growing power of the federal government, there was simply no way that southern politicians would allow any federally imposed restrictions on Missouri slavery.[39]

IV

Northern restrictionists fully understood that the southern position called for nothing less than the indefinite and uncontrolled expansion of slavery. What remained so disconcerting for many northerners was the South's insistence that the nation could do nothing about slavery but manage it properly through permanent expansion and diffusion. "Let me ask gentlemen where this diffusion is to end," demanded John Sergeant of Pennsylvania. "If circumstances require it at present, will not the same circumstances demand it hereafter? Will they not, at some future time, become straitened in their new limits, however large? And what will you do then? Diffuse again—and what then? Even this diffusion will have its limits, and when they are reached, the case is without remedy and without hope." As Sergeant recognized, southern politicians had begun codifying the rationale for an empire for slavery.[40]

Despite restrictionists' insistence that Congress accept the Tallmadge restrictions and forge a comprehensive ban on slavery in the West, by January 1820 it became increasingly clear that southern obstinacy would prevail, "no matter what the northern people may say." Some northern restrictionists wished to ride the question out, hoping that the South or Missouri would acquiesce to restrictions, but there were too many obstacles to overcome. Southern politicians refused to accept any restrictions on Missouri slavery, and they fortified their position by promising disunion if Congress insisted on them as a condition of Missouri statehood. Northern congressmen knew they could ignore Missouri's hollow threats of disunion; they could not disregard the South's promise to do the same. Furthermore, with pressing business concerning land, commerce, money, and manufacturing stalled by the Missouri question, with much of the nation tiring over the crisis, and with expansionists holding Maine's statehood hostage, some northern and southern politicians began to look for a way out. Ultimately, it took all the talents of Henry Clay and intense presidential pressure on a select group of northern congressmen to work out a compromise. In March 1820, in a series of narrow votes, Congress admitted Missouri without restrictions and closed off the remainder of the Louisiana Purchase north of latitude 36°30' to slavery.[41]

Some expansionists expressed anger at even the notion of a settlement; having expended so much energy and doctrine proving that the government could not restrict expansion, they were not about to yield now. Most, however, understood just how little the slave South had yielded. While slavery was "forever prohibited" from the lands north of the 36°30' line, southerners doubted that Congress would actually impose the restriction when the region was organized into territories. They still denied that Congress possessed the authority to do so, and they insisted that the restrictions were not binding on any states formed out of the region now declared off-limits to slaveholders. When a northern congressman asked his southern colleagues if they were "conceding the point that Congress has the power to make that restriction or territorial prohibition perpetual and binding," William Lowndes merely "smiled and shook his head" no. Furthermore, on at least three separate occasions, John Taylor of New York prodded Congress "to inquire into the expediency of prohibiting by law the introduction of slaves into the territories of the United States west of the Mississippi." While this would have blanketed the entire trans-Mississippi West, as well as any territory acquired in the future with an Article VI–like prohibition on slavery, the final compromise limited itself to the remaining unorganized territory in the northern parts of the Louisiana Purchase.[42]

Northern restrictionists had demanded that Congress prohibit slavery in all states or territories "hereafter admitted to the Union," halting the United States's march toward becoming an empire for slavery. Instead, they received a prohibition on slavery in the northern plains of the West. Even this would prove insufficient to stop slavery's expansion there, as the Kansas fiasco of the 1850s made plain. But Congress's failure to solve the problem of expansion during the Missouri Controversy created more immediate problems. As Congress put the final touches on the compromise, Thomas Ritchie's *Richmond Enquirer* complained that, being "cooped up on the north," slaveholders must have "elbow room to the west." Indeed, southerners "owe it to themselves," claimed Ritchie, "to keep their eye firmly fixed on Texas." Little did Ritchie know, and perhaps even less would he have cared, but the gross intransigence and proslavery polemics that filled his newspaper columns all but insured that the United States would never peaceably halt slavery's expansion.[43]

Epilogue

Empire for Slavery, Empire for Freedom

By default more than by design, by 1820 the United States was on the verge of becoming a slaveholders' republic, and the West a vast empire for slavery's expansion. The prospects for freedom had not looked so dim in 1790 when the first federal Congress had exempted the Southwest Territory from Article VI; they had seemed brighter still in 1787 when the Confederation Congress had accepted the Northwest Ordinance with Article VI. The history of slavery in the West, however, followed the same tragic trajectory as slavery in the nation. As the historian Don Fehrenbacher has argued, though the United States was not founded as a slaveholders' republic, it nonetheless became one in practice. Similarly, even though the purpose of the Union was to construct an "empire for liberty," it instead created an "empire for slavery."[1]

The concept of a lasting federal Union required an expansive course of acquisition and incorporation in the trans-Appalachian West and the lower Mississippi Valley. Reinforcing conditions persistently encouraged the sanction of western slavery. First and foremost, the United States remained far too weak to enforce unpopular restrictions on slavery in the West. Except in the Northwest—and even there, federal power remained somewhat limited—the federal government simply lacked the coercive means that would have been necessary to pass and uphold unpopular restrictions on slavery, or to quell the popular protests they provoked. Slavery could be stopped only with the consent of the white inhabitants. Other than in the Northwest, that consent would not be forthcoming. Even then, the failures in Kentucky, and even the ultimate successes in the Northwest, demonstrated just how difficult it was to generate popular political opposition to slavery in a labor-starved West. In the early American West, slavery was already too entrenched, its potential uses far too valuable, for slaveholders to accept any meaningful restrictions on their right to "an unlimited slavery."

At the same time, by sanctioning slavery the United States could demonstrate to white westerners that the American Union would protect and promote local interests, including slavery. As Winthrop Sargent explained in his inaugural address as governor of the Mississippi Territory, slavery was permitted "in special indulgence to the people of this territory." Similarly, as an official in Louisiana explained, repeal of the 1804 slavery restrictions "would go farther with them, and better reconcile them to the Government of the United States, than any other privilege."[2] Whether it involved permitting North Carolinians to carry their slaves to the Southwest Territory, protecting the interests of slaveholders in Natchez, or granting American slaveholders access to the Louisiana Purchase, sanction for slavery became a cheap, effective means of securing the American empire in the West. Practical and ideological considerations meant that Jefferson's "empire for liberty" had to be grounded to a great degree on consent, not coercion and violence. As western whites repeatedly made clear, consent was contingent on protection of their interests, especially their interests in slaves. They would join the empire for liberty only if it became an empire for slavery; they would give their consent only if the government backed the coercion and violence used to keep African Americans in slavery.[3]

In and of itself, the emerging western empire for slavery neither made the outcome of the Missouri Controversy predictable nor foreordained that the United States would stop slavery expansion only by civil war. The post-1815 prospects for permanent union between the East and the West made disunionist saber-rattling from the West far less effective than it had once been. On their own, Missourians could never have forced Congress to admit their state without restrictions on slavery. They did not have to; by then, southern whites had shaken off any lingering antislavery scruples left over from the Revolution. In its stead came a new acceptance of slavery's permanency, a new appreciation for the value of slave labor, and a new set of concerns centering on its proper management and long-term preservation. It was this proslavery militancy, derived from the experiences of western settlement, internal changes in the Atlantic slave states, and the steady stream of slaveholders moving from the East to the West which insured that Missourians would find committed, like-minded allies to take up their cause in 1819.

The 1789 re-passage of the Northwest Ordinance and the 1790 passage of the Southwest Ordinance had made freedom the national norm in the West, slavery the exception. The wording of subsequent territorial acts specifically exempting slave territories from "the sixth article of compact" or omitting references to slavery altogether only reaffirmed that freedom remained the national standard, slavery the exception. The practice of establishing slaveholding territories in the West challenged the precedents of 1787 through 1790, but it had not undermined it in a sustained and systematic way until the Missouri Controversy. The consolidation of the union between East and West after 1815 made possible northern Republicans' attempt to reassert the precedent of the Northwest Ordinance in Missouri and the remainder of the American West. Yet that consolidation had in part been made possible by the government's willingness to sanction slavery in the Southwest while overlooking evasions of Article VI in the Northwest. Sanction for slavery in western territories was the price of Union. But that meant that by 1820 slaveholders could maintain that the West was part of a slave South instead of a larger Union where freedom was the norm and slavery the exception.

Consequently, southern and western slaveholders created a coherent and contrary vision of an empire for slavery in the West: an empire that would be integrated into a vast slaveholders' republic stretching from Virginia to Georgia to Mississippi to Missouri. By the early 1830s, Texas was next on the slaveholding expansionists' list, ultimately leading to a war that brought even more territory into the slaveholders' orbit. In the Compromise of 1850 slaveholding expansionists were unwilling to forego the desert Southwest and California in either practice or principle. Southern politicians refused to allow Congress to set another precedent by prohibiting slavery in the Utah and New Mexico territories; popular sovereignty would determine slavery's future there. And though California was admitted as a free state in 1848, as early as 1850 southern slaveholders were plotting to break California into two, with southern California entering the Union as a separate slave state. While some slaveholders looked to the Far West for slavery's expansion, others looked to the Caribbean and the "Golden Circle"—the fantastically lucrative tropical lands that stretched from Mexico into Central America, around the northern coast of South America, northward to the Caribbean's many small sugar islands, and ended at the crown jewel of Cuba, which included 500,000 slaves. As De Bow's Review boasted in 1850, "We have a destiny to perform, a 'manifest destiny' over all Mexico, over South America, over the West Indies."[4]

While some slaveholders in the 1850s looked to expand the empire for slavery southward, others sought its consolidation at home. With Bleeding Kansas and the Dred Scott decision, southern politicians achieved the constitutional sanction for slavery expansion that their predecessors had sought in the Missouri Controversy. The Kansas–Nebraska Act and Bleeding Kansas demonstrated that even a clear antislavery majority was insufficient to stop aggressive southern expansion backed by the federal government. The Dred Scott decision promised southern expansionists that they would no longer have to suffer the subterfuge of popular sovereignty when the Supreme Court ruled that neither Congress nor the people of a territory could ban slavery. According to the court, all federal territories were now slave territories. By 1860, southerners demanded a federal slave code to protect their property in the territories, completing the constitutional and legal framework for their empire for slavery. In the slaveholders' vision of an empire for slavery, enlarged with each expansion crisis, slavery was now the national norm, freedom the exception. It would take a civil war before freedom would finally prevail.

NOTES

Abbreviations Used in the Notes

AEP	Andrew Ellicott Papers
ASP	Arthur St. Clair Papers
BFP	Breckinridge Family Papers
CHS	Cincinnati Historical Society
FHS	Filson Historical Society, Louisville, Kentucky
HSP/LCP	Historical Society of Pennsylvania holdings at the Library Company of Philadelphia
IHS	Indiana Historical Society, Indianapolis
ISL	Indiana State Library, Indianapolis
KHS	Kentucky Historical Society, Frankfort
LCP	Library Company of Philadelphia
LOC	Library of Congress, Manuscript Division, Washington, D.C.
LVA	Library of Virginia, Richmond
MHS	Missouri Historical Society, St. Louis
OHS	Ohio Historical Society, Columbus
PAG	Papers of Albert Gallatin
RFP	Rochester Family Papers, 1774–1836
TJP	Thomas Jefferson Papers, Series 1, General Correspondence
TPP	Timothy Pickering Papers
TWP	Thomas Worthington Papers
UKSC	University of Kentucky, Special Collections, Margaret I. King Library, Lexington
WHH	William Henry Harrison Papers, 1800–1815
WSP	Winthrop Sargent Papers

Introduction

1. Howard A. Ohline, "Slavery, Economics, and Congressional Politics, 1790," *Journal of Southern History* 46 (August 1980): 335–59; William C. diGiacomantonio, "'For the Gratification of a Volunteering Society': Antislavery and Pressure Group Politics in the First Federal Congress," *Journal of the Early Republic* 15 (Summer 1995): 169–97; Richard S. Newman, "Prelude to

the Gag Rule: Southern Reaction to Antislavery Petitions in the First Federal Congress," *Journal of the Early Republic* 16 (Winter 1996): 571–99.

2. *Annals of the Congress of the United States, 1789–1824* [hereafter cited as *Annals of Congress*], 1st Cong., 1st sess., 52, 56; *Senate Journal*, 1st Cong., 1st sess., 56. For the North Carolina Cession Act of 1789 and the Southwest Ordinance of 1790, see Clarence E. Carter, ed., *The Territorial Papers of the United States*, 28 vols. (Washington, DC, 1934–1975), 4:3–19, quote at 7; *Annals of Congress*, 1st Cong., 2nd sess., 988; *House Journal*, 1st Cong., 2nd sess., 188.

3. *American State Papers: Miscellaneous*, 1:12; *Annals of Congress*, 1st Cong., 2nd sess., 1465–66; William Wiecek, *The Sources of Antislavery Constitutionalism in America, 1760–1848* (Ithaca, NY, 1977), 16. The territorial clause is Article IV, section 3 of the Constitution. For its origins and ambiguities, see Don Fehrenbacher, *The Dred Scott Case: Its Significance in American Law and Politics* (New York, 1978), 82–84; and Don Fehrenbacher, *The Slaveholding Republic: An Account of the United States Government's Relations to Slavery* (New York, 2001), 28–47. Fred Anderson and Andrew Cayton have rightly deemed the Northwest Ordinance "the single most important element of the Revolutionary Settlement" after the Constitution and the Bill of Rights; see Fred Anderson and Andrew Cayton, *The Dominion of War: Empire and Liberty in North America, 1500–2000* (New York, 2005), 190.

4. The best overviews of the American Revolution's effects on slavery are David Brion Davis, *The Problem of Slavery in the Age of Revolution, 1770–1823* (Ithaca, NY, 1975); Matthew Mason, *Slavery and Politics in the Early American Republic* (Chapel Hill, NC, 2006), 9–41; Ira Berlin, *Many Thousands Gone: The First Two Centuries of Slavery in North America* (Cambridge, MA, 1998), 217–356; and Ira Berlin, *Generations of Captivity: A History of African-American Slaves* (Cambridge, MA, 2003).

5. The synopsis here of the political causes of expansion is derived from Fehrenbacher, *Dred Scott Case*, 74–100; Fehrenbacher, *Slaveholding Republic*, 253–63, quote at 263; William W. Freehling, "The Founding Fathers and Conditional Antislavery," in *The Reintegration of American History: Slavery and the Civil War* (New York, 1994); William W. Freehling, *The Road to Disunion*, Vol. 1, *Secessionists at Bay, 1776–1854* (New York, 1990), 138–43; Paul Finkelman, *Slavery and the Founders: Race and Liberty in the Age of Jefferson*, 2nd ed.(Armonk, NY, 2001); Adam Rothman, *Slave Country: American Expansion and the Origins of the Deep South* (Cambridge, MA, 2005), 18–34; Mason, *Slavery and Politics*, 24–26, 145–50; Douglas R. Egerton, "The Empire of Liberty Reconsidered," in *The Revolution of 1800: Democracy, Race, and the New Republic*, ed. James Horn, Jan Ellen Lewis, and Peter S. Onuf (Charlottesville, VA, 2002), 309–30; Berlin, *Generations of Captivity*, 161–68; Leonard L. Richards, *The Slave Power: The Free North and Southern Domination, 1780–1860* (Baton Rouge, 2000), 43; Roger G. Kennedy, *Mr. Jefferson's Lost Cause: Land, Farmers, and the Louisiana Purchase* (New York, 2003); Garry Wills, *"Negro President": Jefferson and the Slave Power* (Boston, 2003); Donald Robinson,

Slavery in the Structure of American Politics, 1765–1820 (New York, 1971), 378–400; Gary Nash, *Race and Revolution* (Madison, WI, 1990), 25–55; Duncan MacLeod, *Slavery, Race, and the American Revolution* (New York, 1974), 47–61; and Linda K. Kerber, *Federalists in Dissent: Imagery and Ideology in Jeffersonian America* (New York, 1970), 43.

6. Freehling, "Founding Fathers and Conditional Antislavery," 12; Freehling, *Road to Disunion*, 138–43; Fehrenbacher, *Dred Scott Case*, 90; Fehrenbacher, *Slaveholding Republic*, 261; Finkelman, *Slavery and the Founders*, 58–80.

7. Historians typically assume, because northern Republicans refused to clash with the southern wing of their party, that New England Federalists rather than northern Republicans led efforts to reign in slavery expansion. Finkelman especially stresses New England Federalist opposition to slavery for partisan, humanitarian, and cultural reasons, along with northern Republicans' aversion to challenging their southern colleagues on slavery (see "The Problem of Slavery in the Age of Federalism," in *Slavery and the Founders*, 105–28). For similar assumptions, see Fehrenbacher, *Dred Scott Case*, 89–97; Fehrenbacher, *Slaveholding Republic*, 260; Rothman, *Slave Country*, 18–34; Egerton, "Empire of Liberty Reconsidered"; Kennedy, *Mr. Jefferson's Lost Cause*; Wills, *"Negro President"*; Richards, *Slave Power*, 43; and Kerber, *Federalists in Dissent*, 43. Recently, historians have challenged the dichotomy of antislavery New England Federalists and functionally proslavery northern Republicans; see Jonathan H. Earle, *Jacksonian Antislavery and the Politics of Free Soil, 1824–1854* (Chapel Hill, NC, 2004); Sean Wilentz, *The Rise of American Democracy: Jefferson to Lincoln* (New York, 2005); and Mason, *Slavery and Politics*.

8. "A firebell in the night" was Thomas Jefferson's description of the unexpected and terrifying emergence of the slavery question with the Missouri Controversy (Jefferson to John Holmes, April 22, 1820, TJP, LOC).

9. For the phrase "power politics of territorial hegemony" and the ways this increased the power of residents of "borderlands," see Jeremy Adelman and Stephen Aron, "From Borderlands to Borders: Empires, Nation-States, and the Peoples In Between in North American History," *American Historical Review* 104 (June 1999): 814–41. For the problem of incorporating the West into the American Union, see Drew R. McCoy, "James Madison and Visions of American Nationality in the Confederation Period: A Regional Perspective," in *Beyond Confederation: Origins of the Constitution and American National Identity*, ed. Richard Beeman, Stephen Botein, and Edward C. Carter II (Chapel Hill, NC, 1987), 226–58; Peter S. Onuf, "The Expanding Union," in *Devising Liberty: Preserving and Creating Freedom in the New American Republic*, ed. David T. Konig (Stanford, CA, 1995), 50–80; James E. Lewis Jr., *The American Union and the Problem of Neighborhood: The United States and the Collapse of the Spanish Empire, 1783–1829* (Chapel Hill, NC, 1998); Peter J. Kastor, "'Motives of Peculiar Urgency': Local Diplomacy in Louisiana, 1803–1821," *William and Mary Quarterly* 58 (October 2001): 819–48; Peter J. Kastor, *The Nation's Crucible: The Louisiana Purchase and the Creation of America* (New Haven,

CT, 2004); Andrew R. L. Cayton, "'When Shall We Cease to Have Judases?' The Blount Conspiracy and the Limits of the Extended Republic," in *Launching the "Extended Republic": The Federalist Era,* ed. Ronald J. Hoffman and Peter J. Albert (Charlottesville, VA, 1996), 156–89; and Andrew R. L. Cayton, "'Separate Interests' and the Nation-State: The Washington Administration and the Origins of Regionalism in the Trans-Appalachian West," *Journal of American History* 79 (June 1992): 39–67.

10. "Resolutions of the Pennsylvania Legislature," *Niles' Weekly Register* (Baltimore), January 1, 1820; see also 233n27.

11. "From the Rhode Island American," *Niles' Weekly Register,* December 20, 1819.

1. Ordinances, Limits, and Precedents, 1784–1796

1. For the various proposals to prohibit slavery in the West, which culminated in the Northwest Ordinance of 1787, see Peter S. Onuf, *Statehood and Union: A History of the Northwest Ordinance* (Bloomington, IN, 1987); Don Fehrenbacher, *The Dred Scott Case: Its Significance in American Law and Politics* (New York, 1978), 74–82; Don Fehrenbacher, *The Slaveholding Republic: An Account of the United States Government's Relations to Slavery* (New York, 2001), 253–56; and Paul Finkelman, *Slavery and the Founders: Race and Liberty in the Age of Jefferson,* 2nd ed. (Armonk, NY, 2001), 37–57. Suggestions that the passage and re-passage of the Northwest Ordinance and Article VI were part of a grand compromise to prohibit slavery north of the Ohio River but permit it to the south are thoroughly discredited in Fehrenbacher, *Dred Scott Case,* 80–81.

2. Clarence E. Carter, ed., *The Territorial Papers of the United States,* 28 vols. (Washington, DC, 1934–1975), 4:3–19, quote at 7; John R. Finger, *Tennessee Frontiers: Three Regions in Transition* (Bloomington, IN, 2001), 99–131; Fehrenbacher, *Dred Scott Case,* 86–87.

3. Finger, *Tennessee Frontiers,* 99–131. Blount would, of course, later be involved with plots to bring Kentucky and Tennessee into the Spanish empire. For the Southwest's grievances with the federal government, centering mainly on its weaknesses and ineffectiveness, see Andrew R. L. Cayton, "'When Shall We Cease to Have Judases?' The Blount Conspiracy and the Limits of the Extended Republic," in *Launching the "Extended Republic": The Federalist Era,* ed. Ronald J. Hoffman and Peter J. Albert (Charlottesville, VA, 1996), 156–89; and Andrew R. L. Cayton, "'Separate Interests' and the Nation-State: The Washington Administration and the Origins of Regionalism in the Trans-Appalachian West," *Journal of American History* 79 (June 1992): 39–67. As Cayton points out, though later generations of western planters were concerned that a powerful federal government challenged planters' local interests and power, in the late 1780s and early 1790s western planters wanted a more powerful

government that could provide security for land titles, financing for improvements such as roads, guaranteed access to the Mississippi River and New Orleans, and protection from foreign powers and Indian nations.

4. "An Act for the Government of the Territory South of the Ohio River," in Carter, *Territorial Papers*, 4:17; *Annals of Congress*, 1st Cong., 2nd sess., 988; *House Journal*, 1st Cong., 2nd sess., 188.

5. Jeremy Adelman and Stephen Aron, "From Borderlands to Borders: Empires, Nation-States, and the Peoples In Between in North American History," *American Historical Review* 104 (June 1999): 814–41.

6. Stephen Aron, *How the West Was Lost: The Transformation of Kentucky from Daniel Boone to Henry Clay* (Baltimore, 1996), 89–95; Harold Tallant, *Evil Necessity: Slavery and Political Culture in Antebellum Kentucky* (Lexington, 2003); Andrew Lee Feight, "James Blythe and the Slavery Controversy in the Presbyterian Churches of Kentucky, 1791–1802," *Register of the Kentucky Historical Society* 102 (Winter 2004): 13–38.

7. *Annals of Congress*, 4th Cong., 1st sess., 1299–1328.

2. "That Species of Property Already Exists"

1. *Annals of Congress*, 5th Cong., 2nd sess., 1306–12; *Message from the President of the United States, accompanying a report to him from the Secretary of State, and Sundry Documents relative to the Affairs of the United States on the Mississippi . . . January 23, 1798* (Philadelphia, 1798); *American State Papers: Foreign Relations*, 2:78–82. In 1796 most of the Southwest Territory entered the Union as the state of Tennessee. In 1798 Congress created the Mississippi Territory, which included the remainder of the Southwest Territory and all the land between Georgia's western boundary, the Mississippi River, and the 31st parallel. This corresponded to the limits of present-day Alabama and Mississippi, less their Gulf Coast lands, which remained part of Spanish West Florida until 1819.

2. Don Fehrenbacher, *The Slaveholding Republic: An Account of the United States Government's Relations to Slavery* (New York, 2001), 258; Don Fehrenbacher, *The Dred Scott Case: Its Significance in American Law and Politics* (New York, 1978), 87–89; Adam Rothman, *Slave Country: American Expansion and the Origins of the Deep South* (Cambridge, MA, 2005), 24–26; Matthew Mason, *Slavery and Politics in the Early American Republic* (Chapel Hill, NC, 2006), 24–25; Donald Robinson, *Slavery in the Structure of American Politics, 1765–1820* (New York, 1971), 386–91; Duncan MacLeod, *Slavery, Race, and the American Revolution* (New York, 1974), 56.

3. *Annals of Congress*, 5th Cong., 2nd sess., 1310. Though Thatcher was a persistent opponent of slavery while serving as a representative in the first five federal Congresses, historians have produced regrettably little work on him. For Thatcher and slavery in the first federal Congress, see Howard A. Ohline,

"Slavery, Economics, and Congressional Politics, 1790," *Journal of Southern History* 46 (August 1980): 355–59, esp. 355. For more on Thatcher's proposal in 1800 that the House consider a compensated emancipation program, see Betty L. Fladeland, "Compensated Emancipation: A Rejected Alternative," *Journal of Southern History* 42 (May 1976): 169–93.

4. Andrew Ellicott to Sarah Ellicott, February 17, 1799, AEP, LOC. James E. Lewis Jr. makes this point particularly well for the federal government's policy toward the crumbling Spanish empire; see James E. Lewis Jr., *The American Union and the Problem of Neighborhood: The United States and the Collapse of the Spanish Empire, 1783–1829* (Chapel Hill, NC, 1998). For more general concerns about extending the American Union south and west, see Peter S. Onuf, "The Expanding Union," in *Devising Liberty: Preserving and Creating Freedom in the New American Republic*, ed. David T. Konig (Stanford, CA, 1995), 50–80. For the need to placate leading men in the Southwest, see Andrew R. L. Cayton, "'When Shall We Cease to Have Judases?' The Blount Conspiracy and the Limits of the Extended Republic," in *Launching the "Extended Republic": The Federalist Era*, ed. Ronald J. Hoffman and Peter J. Albert (Charlottesville, VA, 1996), 156–89; and Andrew R. L. Cayton, "'Separate Interests' and the Nation-State: The Washington Administration and the Origins of Regionalism in the Trans-Appalachian West," *Journal of American History* 79 (June 1992): 39–67. For the role of American officials in reconciling white settlers in the lower Mississippi Valley to American rule, see Peter J. Kastor, "'Motives of Peculiar Urgency': Local Diplomacy in Louisiana, 1803–1821," *William and Mary Quarterly* 58 (October 2001): 819–48.

5. Lewis, *American Union and the Problem of Neighborhood*, 25; Samuel Flagg Bemis, *Pinckney's Treaty: A Study of America's Advantage from Europe's Distress, 1783–1800* (New York, 1926); Jon Kukla, *A Wilderness So Immense: The Louisiana Purchase and the Destiny of America* (New York, 2003), 179–94.

6. Andrew Ellicott to Sarah Ellicott, February 17, 1799, AEP, LOC; Andrew Ellicott, *The Journal of Andrew Ellicott, Late Commissioner on Behalf of the United States . . . for Determining the Boundary between the United States and the Possessions of His Catholic Majesty* (Philadelphia, 1803; rpt., Chicago, 1962), 139, 41–117. For settlement in and around Natchez, see D. Clayton James, *Antebellum Natchez* (Baton Rouge, 1968); David J. Libby, *Slavery and Frontier Mississippi, 1720–1835* (Jackson, MS, 2004), 30–36; and Daniel H. Usner Jr., "American Indians on the Cotton Frontier: Changing Economic Relations with Citizens and Slaves in the Mississippi Territory," *Journal of American History* 72 (September 1985): 297–317.

7. Ellicott, *Journal of Andrew Ellicott*, 40–140. For Spanish interest, see *Journal of Andrew Ellicott*, 203. For British interest, see Timothy Pickering to Andrew Ellicott, July 28, 1797, AEP, LOC; and Ellicott to Pickering, November 14, 1797, TPP, microfilm edition, Boston, 1966. For French interest, see Timothy Pickering to Andrew Ellicott, April 1, 1798, in Clarence E. Carter, *The Terri-*

torial Papers of the United States, 28 vols. (Washington, DC, 1934–1975), 5:17. For concerns that Spanish officials, who retained close ties with the Indian nations, were attempting to incite the Choctaws and Chickasaws to undermine American influence even further, see "Extract of a letter from Andrew Ellicott, . . . May 10, 1797," and "Report of the Secretary of State to the President of the United States . . . , January 23, 1797," in *American State Papers: Foreign Relations,* 2:67, 78–79; and Ellicott, *Journal of Andrew Ellicott,* 85, 181. For the effects of the Southwest Indian nations on American objectives in the region, see Cayton, "'When Shall We Cease to Have Judases?'"; and Usner, "American Indians on the Cotton Frontier." For the problems created by conflicting land titles and engrossment, see Daniel Dupre, *Transforming the Cotton Frontier: Madison County, Alabama, 1800–1840* (Baton Rouge, 1997), 10–25. For concerns about slaves, see Daniel Clark Sr. to Andrew Ellicott, March 18, 1798, AEP, LOC; and "Memorial to Congress By Permanent Committee of the Natchez District," October 23, 1797, in Carter, *Territorial Papers,* 5:9–11.

8. Daniel H. Usner Jr., *Indians, Settlers, and Slaves in a Frontier Exchange Economy: The Lower Mississippi Valley before 1783* (Chapel Hill, NC, 1992); James, *Antebellum Natchez,* 3–53; Libby, *Slavery and Frontier Mississippi,* 3–32. For the generally uneven development of slavery in the lower Mississippi Valley, see Ira Berlin, *Many Thousands Gone: The First Two Centuries of Slavery in North America* (Cambridge, MA, 1998), 195–215.

9. "Proclamation of the Spanish Governor of Louisiana and West Florida," [September 1789], and Arthur St. Clair to the Secretary for Foreign Affairs, December 13, 1788, in Carter, *Territorial Papers,* 2:214, 168–69; "Miro's Offer to Western Americans, April 20, 1789," in *Spain in the Mississippi Valley, 1765–1794: Translations of Materials from the Spanish Archives in the Bancroft Library, Annual Report of the American Historical Association for the Year 1945,* ed. Lawrence Kinnaird (Washington, DC, 1946), 2:269–71; Arthur St. Clair to George Washington, August 1789, in Carter, *Territorial Papers,* 2:210. For settlers leaving the Northwest Territory to gain greater protection for their property in slaves in Spanish possessions, see, e.g., Barthelemi Tardiveau to Arthur St. Clair, June 30, 1789, ASP, OHS; and Arthur St. Clair to Thomas Jefferson, February 10, 1791, in Carter, *Territorial Papers,* 3:23–37. For Spanish immigration policy, see Gilbert C. Din, "Spain's Immigration Policy in Louisiana and the American Penetration, 1792–1803," *Southwestern Historical Quarterly* 76 (January 1973): 255–76. For Spanish reforms in the lower Mississippi Valley, including the appointment of an English-speaking governor to the Natchez District, see David J. Weber, *The Spanish Frontier in North America* (New Haven, CT, 1992), 279–82; and Libby, *Slavery and Frontier Mississippi,* 32–36.

10. William S. Coker, "The Bruins and Spanish Immigration Policy in the Old Southwest, 1787–1788," in *The Spanish in the Mississippi Valley, 1762–1804,* ed. John Francis McDermott (Urbana, IL, 1976), 61–71; "Report of Americans Arriving at Natchez, July 5, 1788," in Kinnaird, ed., *Spain in the Mississippi Valley,* 2:237; Manuel Gayoso to Carondelet, Natchez, April 17, 1792, in "Pa-

pers from the Spanish Archives Relating to Tennessee and the Old Southwest, 1783–1800," *East Tennessee Historical Society Publications* 27 (1955): 82; William Lytle to John Breckinridge, January 10, 1797, BFP, LOC.

11. St. Clair to Washington, August 1789, in Carter, *Territorial Papers,* 2:210–11; William Lytle to John Breckinridge, January 10, 1797, BFP, LOC. American officials recognized that American settlers had few quarrels with Spanish rule; see Arthur St. Clair to the Secretary for Foreign Affairs, December 13, 1788, and St. Clair to Washington, month of August 1789, in Carter, *Territorial Papers,* 2:168–69, 210–11; Ellicott, *Journal of Andrew Ellicott,* 155–56; and Andrew Ellicott to Timothy Pickering, September 24, 1797, in Carter, *Territorial Papers,* 5:5. For the difficulties families faced in acquiring land in Tennessee and Kentucky because of speculation, see John R. Finger, *Tennessee Frontiers: Three Regions in Transition* (Bloomington, IN, 2001); and Stephen Aron, *How the West Was Lost: The Transformation of Kentucky from Daniel Boone to Henry Clay* (Baltimore, 1996). For Anglo-American settlers' general contentedness with Spanish rule in West Florida, see Andrew McMichael, "The Kemper 'Rebellion,' Filibustering and Resident Anglo American Loyalty in Spanish West Florida," *Louisiana History* 43 (Spring 2002): 133–65; and Weber, *Spanish Frontier in North America,* 279–82.

12. James, *Antebellum Natchez,* 31–53; Usner, "American Indians on the Cotton Frontier." For Spanish deregulation of the international slave trade, see Paul F. Lachance, "The Politics of Fear: French Louisianans and the Slave Trade, 1786–1809," *Plantation Society* 1 (1979): 162–97; Libby, *Slavery and Frontier Mississippi,* 32–36. Ira Berlin's *Many Thousands Gone* is indispensable for understanding the local, regional, and trans-Atlantic forces that fed the "plantation revolution" in the lower Mississippi Valley (see esp. 195–215, 325–57). I borrow the distinction between "societies with slaves" and "slave societies" from Ira Berlin, who defines a "society with slaves" as one in which "slaves were marginal to the central economic processes" and "slavery was just one form of labor among many." In a slave society, "slavery stood at the center of economic production, and the master-slave relationship provided the model for all social relations" (Berlin, *Generations of Captivity: A History of African-American Slaves* [Cambridge, MA, 2003], 8–9).

13. James, *Antebellum Natchez,* 45, 52; Usner, "American Indians on the Cotton Frontier." According to James, the 2,500 bales of cotton produced on Stephen Minor's plantations were worth an astounding $52,100 at the prevailing rate in New Orleans.

14. Louis Anatasius Tarascon, Diary, November 15, 1799, translation and typescript by Jane F. Kauffman, FHS.

15. Daniel Clark Sr. to Andrew Ellicott, March 18, 1798, AEP, LOC; Ellicott, *Journal of Andrew Ellicott,* 152–53.

16. Ellicott, *Journal of Andrew Ellicott,* 15–42; Manuel Gayoso to Andrew Ellicott, February 17, 1797, and Ellicott to Pickering, April 15, 1797, AEP. LOC; John C. Van Horne, "Andrew Ellicott's Mission to Natchez, 1796–1798," *Jour-*

nal of Mississippi History 45 (Fall 1983): 160–85; Arthur Whitaker, *The Mississippi Question, 1795–1803: A Study in Trade, Politics, and Diplomacy* (New York, 1934), 58.

17. Ellicott, *Journal of Andrew Ellicott*, 44, 138–41; Andrew Ellicott to Sarah Ellicott, April 8, 1797, and Ellicott to Pickering, April 15, 1797, AEP, LOC; "Extract of a Letter from Mr. Pickering, Secretary of State, to Mr. Ellicott, . . . August 30, 1797," and "Report of the Secretary of State to the President of the United States, Communicated to Congress, January 23, 1797," in *American State Papers: Foreign Relations*, 2:102, 78–79.

18. Ellicott, *Journal of Andrew Ellicott*, 139, 162, 177; Resolution of the Permanent Committee, August 29, 1797, and Permanent Committee to Ellicott, September 12, 1797, AEP, LOC.

19. Ellicott, *Journal of Andrew Ellicott*, 148, 152–53, 96; Ellicott to Pickering, September 12, 1797, AEP, LOC. For alleged Spanish, British, and French plans for "detaching the western country from the union," see Ellicott to Pickering, November 14, 1797, TPP, microfilm edition, Boston, 1966; Ellicott to Pickering, June 5, 1797, Pickering to Ellicott, July 28, 1797, Ellicott to Thomas Jefferson, September 25, 1797, Circular Letter to a Member of Congress, September 25, 1797, and Ellicott to Senator James Ross, September 24, 1797, AEP, LOC. For the warnings that Hutchins was planning something, see William Dunbar to Ellicott, August 27, 1797, Peter Bruin to Ellicott, September 3, 1797, and George Cochran to Ellicott, September 20, 1797, AEP, LOC.

20. Ellicott, *Journal of Andrew Ellicott*, 152–53, 156–57; Circular Letter to the Inhabitants of the Natchez District, October 13, 1797, AEP, LOC. Because so many white inhabitants possessed inflated, dubious land claims, Hutchins also claimed that the United States would challenge the land grants.

21. Ellicott, *Journal of Andrew Ellicott*, 152–57; Circular Letter to the Inhabitants of the Natchez District, October 13, 1797, Ellicott to Captain Green, October 19, 1797, and Daniel Clark to Ellicott, March 18, 1798, AEP, LOC; Ellicott to Pickering, September 24, 1797, in Carter, *Territorial Papers*, 5:5.

22. Libby, *Slavery and Frontier Mississippi*, xv; Ellicott, *Journal of Andrew Ellicott*, 152–57; Circular Letter to the Inhabitants of the Natchez District, October 13, 1797, AEP, LOC.

23. Ellicott to Pickering, September 24, 1797, in Carter, *Territorial Papers*, 5:5; Ellicott to the Permanent Committee, September 26, 1797, and Ellicott to Pickering, September 26, 1797, AEP, LOC.

24. "Memorial to Congress By Permanent Committee of the Natchez District," October 23, 1797, in Carter, *Territorial Papers*, 5:9–11; Ellicott to the Permanent Committee, September 26, 1797, and Ellicott to Pickering, September 26, 1797, AEP, LOC. For American officials' conviction that they had to address the interests of leading men in the West, see Cayton, "'When Shall We Cease to Have Judases?'"

25. *American State Papers: Foreign Relations*, 2:78–82; *Message from the President of the United States . . . relative to the Affairs of the United States on*

the Mississippi . . . January 23, 1798; Pickering to Ellicott, February 12, 1798, AEP, LOC. For Pickering's dislike of slavery and planters, which is somewhat overstated, see Douglas R. Egerton, "The Empire of Liberty Reconsidered," in *The Revolution of 1800: Democracy, Race, and the New Republic,* ed. James Horn, Jan Ellen Lewis, and Peter S. Onuf (Charlottesville, VA, 2002), 309–30; Kevin M. Gannon, "Escaping 'Mr. Jefferson's Plan of Destruction': New England Federalists and the Idea of a Northern Confederacy, 1803–1804," *Journal of the Early Republic* 21 (Fall 2001): 413–43; and Garry Wills, "*Negro President*": Jefferson and the Slave Power (Boston, 2003).

26. For concerns about the ability of the United States to secure the lower Mississippi Valley, see, in addition to Pickering's correspondence with Congress, Andrew Ellicott to Thomas Jefferson, September 25, 1797, Circular Letter to a Member of Congress, September 25, 1797, and Ellicott to Senator James Ross, September 24, 1797, AEP, LOC; and Thomas Jefferson to James Madison, January 25, 1798, TJP, LOC. For "the extraordinary [political] climate of the spring and summer of 1798," see Stanley Elkins and Eric McKitrick, *The Age of Federalism: The Early American Republic, 1788–1800* (New York, 1993), 595. Between late 1797 and March 1798, Congress had gone through the Blount impeachment trial, where the Tennessee senator stood trial for plotting with the British to seize Florida and Louisiana; twice debated antislavery petitions from Quakers and free blacks (which Thatcher defended); debated commercial and diplomatic relations with Toussaint Louverture, leader of the rebellious slaves who would soon form the nation of Haiti; and received word that France and the United States were on the verge of war. For the Blount Conspiracy, see Cayton, "'When Shall We Cease to Have Judases?'" For the Quaker and free-black petitions, see *Annals of Congress,* 5th Cong., 2nd sess., 665–70, 1030, 132–33. For Haiti, see Egerton, "Empire of Liberty Reconsidered." For relations with France, see *Annals of Congress,* 5th Cong., 2nd sess., 1201.

27. *Annals of Congress,* 5th Cong., 2nd sess., 1306.

28. *Annals of Congress,* 5th Cong., 2nd sess., 1307–8.

29. *Annals of Congress,* 5th Cong., 2nd sess., 1308. Otis consistently championed the rights of slaveholders during his long political career; see James M. Banner, *To The Hartford Convention: The Federalists and the Origins of Party Politics in Massachusetts, 1789–1815* (New York, 1970), 107. Otis actually voted in favor of slavery for the Missouri Territory in 1819 on the first vote. For the important alliance between South Carolina Federalists and some Massachusetts Federalists, which partly explains Otis's defense of slaveholders, see Banner, "The Problem of South Carolina," in *The Hofstadter Aegis: A Memorial,* ed. Stanley Elkins and Eric McKitrick (New York, 1974), 60–93. For American understandings of the Haitian Rebellion, see Alfred N. Hunt, *Haiti's Influence on Antebellum America: Slumbering Volcano in the Caribbean* (Baton Rouge, 1988).

30. *Annals of Congress,* 5th Cong., 2nd sess., 1309. For Hartley's involve-

ment in the 1790 debates over slavery, see Ohline, "Slavery, Economics, and Congressional Politics, 1790"; and William C. diGiacomantonio, "'For the Gratification of a Volunteering Society': Antislavery and Pressure Group Politics in the First Federal Congress," *Journal of the Early Republic* 15 (Summer 1995): 169–97. For Hartley's work with the Pennsylvania Abolition Society, see Richard S. Newman, *The Transformation of American Abolitionism: Fighting Slavery in the Early Republic* (Chapel Hill, NC, 2002), 42.

31. *Annals of Congress,* 5th Cong., 2nd sess., 1307, 1309.

32. *Annals of Congress,* 5th Cong., 2nd sess., 1311. The *Annals of Congress* do not contain a breakdown of who voted for the amendment.

33. *Annals of Congress,* 5th Cong., 2nd sess., 1313.

34. "An Act for the Government of the Mississippi Territory," March 26, 1798, in Carter, *Territorial Papers,* 5:20.

35. Pickering to Ellicott, March 27, 1798, in Carter, *Territorial Papers,* 5:16.

36. Pickering to Ellicott, April 1, 1798, in Carter, *Territorial Papers,* 5:17–18; Pickering to Winthrop Sargent, May 4, 1798, WSP, OHS.

37. "Governor Sargent's Address to the Inhabitants of this Territory," August 18, 1798, in Dunbar Rowland, ed., *Mississippi Territorial Archives, 1798–1819* (Nashville, TN, 1905), 1:26; Sargent to Pickering, May 29, 1798, WSP, OHS; Van Horne, "Andrew Ellicott's Mission to Natchez."

38. Benjamin Hawkins to James Madison, November 27, 1801, in *The Papers of James Madison: Secretary of State Series* (Charlottesville, VA, 1993), 2:275; Governor W. C. C. Claiborne to Madison, December 20, 1801, January 23, 1802, in Rowland, *Mississippi Territorial Archives,* 1:363–64, 374; Winthrop Sargent, Proclamation, Grove Plantation, Mississippi Territory, November 16, 1800, WSP, OHS; Abyal Hunt (Natchez) to John Wesley Hunt (Lexington, Kentucky), November 9, 1798, John Wesley Hunt Papers, Special Collections, Transylvania University. For the subsequent development of the cotton frontier in the Mississippi Territory, see Rothman, *Slave Country,* 37–70; and Libby, *Slavery and Frontier Mississippi,* 37–78.

39. William Claiborne to Thomas Jefferson, January 20, 1802, in Dunbar Rowland, ed., *Official Letter Books of W. C. C. Claiborne, 1801–1816* (Jackson, Miss., 1917), 1:36.

3. "Grant Us to Make Slaves of Others"

1. "Remonstrance and Petition of the Representatives elected by the Freemen of their Respective Districts in the District of Louisiana," *American State Papers: Miscellaneous,* 1:401. In 1804 Congress created two territories in the Louisiana Purchase. Orleans Territory, or Lower Louisiana, encompassed the present-day state of Louisiana, minus the Florida parishes. Upper Louisiana encompassed the remainder of the territory, including the main settlements in present-day Missouri, and was referred to as the District of Louisiana.

2. Historians tend to assume that southern Republican pressure and northern Republican acquiescence assured that the United States would permit slavery expansion in the Louisiana Purchase, and that the federal government supposedly did "nothing about slavery" (William W. Freehling, "The Founding Fathers and Conditional Antislavery," in *The Reintegration of American History: Slavery and the Civil War* [New York, 1994], 12–33, quote at 12). When historians do acknowledge political resistance to permitting slavery in the Louisiana Purchase, they tend to underestimate the depth of congressional support for restricting expansion and incorrectly attribute it to New England Federalists; see Adam Rothman, *Slave Country: American Expansion and the Origins of the Deep South* (Cambridge, MA, 2005), 24–34; Matthew Mason, *Slavery and Politics in the Early American Republic* (Chapel Hill, NC, 2006), 24–26; William W. Freehling, *The Road to Disunion*, Vol. 1, *Secessionists at Bay, 1776–1854* (New York, 1990), 138–43; Don Fehrenbacher, *The Dred Scott Case: Its Significance in American Law and Politics* (New York, 1978), 74–100; Don Fehrenbacher, *The Slaveholding Republic: An Account of the United States Government's Relations to Slavery* (New York, 2001), 253–63; Paul Finkelman, *Slavery and the Founders: Race and Liberty in the Age of Jefferson,* 2nd ed. (Armonk, NY, 2001); Douglas R. Egerton, "The Empire of Liberty Reconsidered," in *The Revolution of 1800: Democracy, Race, and the New Republic,* ed. James Horn, Jan Ellen Lewis, and Peter S. Onuf (Charlottesville, VA, 2002), 309–30; Leonard L. Richards, *The Slave Power: The Free North and Southern Domination, 1780–1860* (Baton Rouge, 2000), 43; Linda K. Kerber, *Federalists in Dissent: Imagery and Ideology in Jeffersonian America* (New York, 1970), 43; Stephen Deyle, "The Irony of Liberty: Origins of the Domestic Slave Trade," *Journal of the Early Republic* 12 (Spring 1992): 37–62; and Donald Robinson, *Slavery in the Structure of American Politics, 1765–1820* (New York, 1971), 378–400.

3. "An Act for the Organization of Orleans Territory and the Louisiana District," March 26, 1804, in Clarence E. Carter, ed., *The Territorial Papers of the United States,* 28 vols. (Washington, DC, 1934–1975), 9:202–13, quote at 209.

4. "Remonstrance of the People of Louisiana against the Political System Adopted by Congress for Them," *American State Papers: Miscellaneous,* 1:399; *National Intelligencer* (Washington, DC), September 4, 1804.

5. "Extracts from a letter from a gentleman . . . relating to Louisiana," *Aurora and General Advertiser,* October 21 and November 23, 1803. For other suggestions that the United States could settle and develop the Louisianas without slave labor, see, e.g., "Columbus," *Aurora,* August 8, 1803; Allan Magruder, *Political, Commercial, and Moral Reflections, on the Late Cession of Louisiana, to the United States* (Lexington, KY, 1803), 112–13; and Thomas Paine to Thomas Jefferson, January 25, 1805, TJP, LOC.

6. For brief accounts of slavery prior to American possession, see William E. Foley, *The Genesis of Missouri: From Wilderness Outpost to Statehood* (Columbia, MO, 1989); John Mack Faragher, "'More Motley than Mackinaw':

From Ethnic Mixing to Ethnic Cleansing on the Frontier of the Lower Missouri, 1783–1833," in *Contact Points: American Frontiers from the Mohawk Valley to the Mississippi, 1750–1830,* ed. Andrew R. L. Cayton and Fredrika J. Teute (Chapel Hill, NC, 1998), 304–26; and Stephen Aron, *American Confluence: The Missouri Frontier from Borderland to Border State* (Bloomington, IN, 2006), 78–79, 84.

7. "Memorial of Barthelemi Tardiveau, July 8, 1788," in Clarence W. Alvord, ed., *Kaskaskia Records, 1778–1790* (Springfield, IL, 1909), 488; Meriwether Lewis to Thomas Jefferson, December 28, 1803, in Donald Jackson, ed., *Letters of the Lewis and Clark Expedition with Related Documents, 1783–1854* (Urbana, IL, 1962), 148–53; Thomas Jefferson, "Queries on Louisiana, 1803," and Benjamin Stoddert, Notes on Louisiana, June 3, 1803, TJP, LOC; "Description of Louisiana," *Annals of Congress,* 8th Cong., 2nd sess., Appendix: 1576. For Spanish efforts to lure settlers from the American side of the Mississippi into Spanish Upper Louisiana, see Aron, *American Confluence,* 97–99.

8. Thomas T. Davis to Thomas Jefferson, November 5, 1803, and John Edgar to [Kentucky representative] John Fowler, September 25, 1803, in Carter, *Territorial Papers,* 13:7–8, 5–7; Thomas T. Davis to [Kentucky senator] John Breckinridge, October 17, 1803, in Carter, *Territorial Papers,* 7:124; Lewis to Jefferson, December 28, 1803, in Jackson, ed., *Letters of the Lewis and Clark Expedition,* 153.

9. Davis to Jefferson, November 5, 1803, and Edgar to Fowler, September 25, 1803, in Carter, *Territorial Papers,* 13:7–8, 5–7; Davis to Breckinridge, October 17, 1803, in Carter, *Territorial Papers,* 7:124; Lewis to Jefferson, December 28, 1803, in Jackson, *Letters of the Lewis and Clark Expedition,* 153. These concerns were exacerbated by fears that American officials might invalidate the land grants covering 1.4 million acres of land that Spanish officials had fraudulently issued to themselves and many inhabitants after they received word of the Spanish cession of Upper Louisiana to France and then the United States; see Aron, *American Confluence,* 111–20.

10. Ira Berlin, *Many Thousands Gone: The First Two Centuries of Slavery in North America* (Cambridge, MA, 1998), 77–90, 325–40, quote at 90; Thomas N. Ingersoll, *Mammon and Manon in Early New Orleans: The First Slave Society in the Deep South, 1718–1819* (Knoxville, TN, 1999), 3–144; Daniel H. Usner Jr., *Indians, Settlers, and Slaves in a Frontier Exchange Economy: The Lower Mississippi Valley before 1783* (Chapel Hill, NC, 1992), 122–30; Paul F. Lachance, "The Politics of Fear: French Louisianans and the Slave Trade, 1786–1809," *Plantation Society* 1 (1979): 162–97.

11. Berlin, *Many Thousands Gone,* 325–40; Lachance, "Politics of Fear"; Ingersoll, *Mammon and Manon,* 147–239; Rothman, *Slave Country,* 74–77.

12. Diary Entry, November 28, 1799, New Orleans, Louis Anatasius Tarascon, Diary, 1799, translation and typescript by Jane F. Kauffman, FHS; "Journal of John Sibley, July–October 1802," *Louisiana Historical Quarterly* 10 (October 1927): 474–95, quotes at 480, 483.

13. C. C. Robin, *Voyage to Louisiana, 1803–1805*, trans. Stuart O. Landry (1806; rpt., New Orleans, 1966), 53–54; François Marie Perrin du Lac, *Travels through the two Louisianas and among the savage nations of the Missouri; also, in the United States, along the Ohio, and the adjacent provinces, in 1801, 1802, & 1803* (London, 1807), 94.

14. Daniel Clark to James Madison, September 8, 1803, in Carter, *Territorial Papers*, 9:33–44; "Description of Louisiana," *Annals of Congress*, 8th Cong., 2nd sess., Appendix: 1498–1576, quotes at 1524, 1515. For additional letters detailing the importance of slave-produced staples, see, e.g., Timothy Pickering to Caleb Strong, November 22, 1803, TPP, microfilm edition, Boston, 1966; Andrew Ellicott, *The Journal of Andrew Ellicott, Late Commissioner on Behalf of the United States . . . for Determining the Boundary between the United States and the Possessions of His Catholic Majesty* (Philadelphia, 1803; rpt., Chicago, 1962), 134; Thomas Rodney to Caesar Augustus Rodney, December 5 and December 23, 1803, "Thomas Rodney," in Simon Gratz, ed., *Pennsylvania Magazine of History and Biography* 43 (1919): 210, 221; and Petition of Alexander Baudin to Governor Claiborne and the President and Congress of the United States, February 14, 1804, in Carter, *Territorial Papers*, 9:187–88. For Jefferson's interest in the extent of sugar production and slavery in Lower Louisiana, see "Queries on Louisiana, 1803," TJP, LOC. The federal government published the "Description" as *An Account of Louisiana, Being an Abstract of Documents in the Offices of the Department of State and of the Treasury* (Philadelphia, 1803), and printers circulated it widely in newspapers and as a pamphlet; see, e.g., *Aurora*, December 23, 1803, and *Western Spy and Hamilton Gazette* (Cincinnati), issues for December 1803.

15. "Livingston's Memorial," *Balance and Columbian Repository* (Albany, NY), July 19, 1803; *Columbian Centinel* (Boston), July 2, 1803; *Courier* (Charleston, SC), July 18, 1803; "Louisiana," *Connecticut Courant* (Hartford), August 24, 1803. For Federalist commentary on Livingston's memorial, see also "Calculator VI," *Balance and Columbian Repository*, September 20, 1803; *Alexandria (Va.) Daily Advertiser*, September 29, 1803; and *Repertory* (Boston), June 15, 1804. For additional accounts of Louisiana, see, e.g., "Calculator VI," *Balance and Columbian Repository*, September 20, 1803; "A Letter from Dr. John Sibley, . . . August 15, 1803," *National Intelligencer*, January 13 and January 16, 1804; "Extract of a letter from a respectable merchant at New Orleans," *Aurora*, October 21, 1803; *Aurora*, November 23, 1803; "Columbus," *Aurora*, August 8, 1808; "From the N.Y. Daily Advertiser," *Aurora*, August 1, 1803; and Magruder, *Political, Commercial, and Moral Reflections*, 112–20.

16. Adams spent his evening studying "the eleventh book of Raynal," which contained "an account of the slave trade, and closes with the articles cultivated in the West Indies by slaves—cotton, coffee, sugar, and arnotto" (John Quincy Adams, Diary Entry of January 24, 1804, in Charles Francis Adams, ed., *Memoirs of John Quincy Adams: Comprising Portions of His Diary from 1795 to 1848*, 12 vols. [Philadelphia, 1874–1877], 1:292).

17. For diffusion, expansion, and the domestic slave trade, see Freehling, *Road to Disunion*, 121–43; Peter Onuf, "'To Declare Them a Free and Independent People': Race, Slavery, and National Identity in Jefferson's Thought," *Journal of the Early Republic* 18 (Spring 1998): 1–46; Peter Onuf, *Jefferson's Empire: The Language of American Nationhood* (Charlottesville, VA, 2000), 185–87; Rothman, *Slave Country,* 19–31; and Deyle, "Irony of Liberty."

18. Notes on Administration of Louisiana Territory, 1803; Jefferson to Albert Gallatin, October 29 and November 9, 1803, TJP, LOC; James E. Scanlon, "A Sudden Conceit: Jefferson and the Louisiana Government Bill of 1804," *Louisiana History* 9 (Spring 1968): 152–55; Samuel Maclay, February 17, 1804, in Everett S. Brown, ed., "The Senate Debate on the Breckinridge Bill for the Government of Louisiana, 1804," *American Historical Review* 22 (January 1917): 340–64, quote at 361.

19. *Annals of Congress,* 8th Cong., 2nd sess., 238, Appendix: 1596–97; *American State Papers: Miscellaneous,* 1:386.

20. Brown, "Senate Debate on the Breckinridge Bill," 345–51. Brown's edited account is drawn from New Hampshire senator William Plumer's journal, which is reprinted in its entirety in Brown, ed., *William Plumer's Memorandum of Proceedings in the United States Senate, 1803–1807* (Ann Arbor, 1923). The *Annals of Congress* for this period records primarily motions and role calls in the Senate, but little in the way of debate.

21. Brown, "Senate Debate on the Breckinridge Bill," 348, 347. For concerns about a Haitian-style slave revolt in Louisiana should Congress permit the international slave trade, see the speeches of John Smith, James Hillhouse, Jesse Franklin, and Samuel White, in Brown, "Senate Debate on the Breckinridge Bill," 345–50.

22. Brown, "Senate Debate on the Breckinridge Bill," 352; *Annals of Congress,* 8th Cong., 1st sess., 242. Congress failed to reenact this law in the 1805 Territorial Bill, which retained the prohibition on the international slave trade. Consequently, Charleston slave traders exploited it by sending slave ships to Louisiana after touching port in Charleston. For South Carolina's reopening of the international slave trade in response to the Louisiana Purchase, see Jed Handelsman Shugerman, "The Louisiana Purchase and South Carolina's Reopening of the Slave Trade in 1803," *Journal of the Early Republic* 22 (Summer 2002): 263–90.

23. *Annals of Congress,* 8th Cong., 1st sess., 244. The amendment passed by a vote of 18 to 11. For the importance of Caribbean planters in fostering the transition to a full-scale plantation economy in Lower Louisiana, see Berlin, *Many Thousands Gone,* 325–57; and Lachance, "Politics of Fear." At the behest of white Louisianans, in 1809 American officials permitted a group of Saint Domingue refugees to settle with their slaves in Louisiana in 1809; see Paul F. Lachance, "The 1809 Immigration of Saint-Domingue Refugees to New Orleans: Reception, Integration and Impact," *Louisiana History* 29 (Winter 1988): 109–41.

24. For the importance of the international slave trade in providing slaves for Louisiana from the 1780s through 1818, see Berlin, *Many Thousands Gone*, 338–57; Fehrenbacher, *Slaveholding Republic*, 150–52; Shugerman "Louisiana Purchase and South Carolina's Reopening of the Slave Trade"; and Rothman, *Slave Country*, 83–95. From 1805 through 1808, Louisianans relied on the international slave trade through Charleston, South Carolina, along with smuggling from Spanish West Florida and Texas. After 1808 they increasingly turned to the illegal trade operating out of Spanish Texas, Mexico, and Central America through smuggler bases on Galveston Island. It was only after 1815 that the domestic slave trade could adequately meet the demands of Louisiana planters.

25. Brown, "Senate Debate on the Breckinridge Bill," 351; *Annals of Congress*, 8th Cong., 1st sess., 242. Six of ten northern Republicans favored emancipation, along with four of seven northern Federalists. John Brown from Kentucky, a former Virginian and a cousin of Breckinridge, was the only southern Republican to support the measure.

26. *Annals of Congress*, 8th Cong., 1st sess., 1186; *National Intelligencer*, March 16, 1804. Neither the *Annals of Congress* nor the *National Intelligencer* recorded debates or a roll call on Sloan's proposal. For the motions and votes on the House bill, see *Annals of Congress*, 8th Cong., 1st sess., 256, 290, 1186, 1196–99, 1206–8, 1229–30, 1293–1300. For South Carolina's reopening of the international slave trade, see *Annals of Congress*, 8th Cong., 1st sess., 991–1020.

27. For the importance of the lower Mississippi Valley in securing the trans-Appalachian West, see James E. Lewis Jr., *The American Union and the Problem of Neighborhood: The United States and the Collapse of the Spanish Empire, 1783–1829* (Chapel Hill, NC, 1998), 24–32. For the ways in which American policymakers tried to "cultivate the attachment of white Louisianans" to the United States, see Peter J. Kastor, "'Motives of Peculiar Urgency': Local Diplomacy in Louisiana, 1803–1821," *William and Mary Quarterly* 58 (October 2001): 819–48, quote at 831; and Peter J. Kastor, *The Nation's Crucible: The Louisiana Purchase and the Creation of America* (New Haven, CT, 2004), 1–75. For the crisis of Union produced by French possession of Louisiana, see Peter S. Onuf, "The Expanding Union," in *Devising Liberty: Preserving and Creating Freedom in the New American Republic*, ed. David T. Konig (Stanford, CA, 1995), 50–80. For the diplomatic concerns involved with the Louisiana Purchase, see Robert W. Tucker and David C. Hendrickson, *Empire For Liberty: The Statecraft of Thomas Jefferson* (New York, 1990).

28. Gallatin to Jefferson, August 20, 1804, PAG, microfilm ed., Philadelphia, 1970 (originals, Massachusetts Historical Society, Boston); "Looker-On," *Indiana Gazette*, August 28, 1804; Samuel Smith of Maryland and Israel Smith of Vermont, in Brown, "Senate Debate on the Breckinridge Bill," 344, 349–50; *Port Folio*, September 3, 1803; Abraham Ellery to Alexander Hamilton, October 25, 1803, in Harold C. Syrett and Jacob E. Cooke, eds., *The Papers of*

Alexander Hamilton (New York, 1978), 26:166–67. For the problems of union and disunion associated with incorporating the "marginal settlements and foreigners" of the Louisiana Purchase into contested nationalist identities, see David Waldstreicher, *In the Midst of Perpetual Fetes: The Making of American Nationalism, 1776–1820* (Chapel Hill, NC, 1997), 274–87; and Kastor, *Nation's Crucible*, 41–52.

29. "A Letter from Dr. John Sibley, . . . August 15, 1803," *National Intelligencer,* January 13, 1804; Daniel Clark to James Madison, April 27, 1803, in "Despatches from the United States Consul in New Orleans, 1801–1803," Part 2, *American Historical Review* 33 (January 1928): 331–59, quote at 340; Daniel Clark to William Claiborne, November 28, 1803, in Carter, *Territorial Papers,* 9:114. For an extended account on Americans and foreigners plotting western rebellion and disunion, see Ellicott, *Journal of Andrew Ellicott.* Onuf provides a wealth of primary sources expressing fears for continued union between East and West in light of French possession and interest in Louisiana ("Expanding Union," 50–56). See also Lewis, *American Union and the Problem of Neighborhood,* 25–31.

30. Henry Marie Brackenridge, *Views of Louisiana, Together with a Journal of a Voyage up the Missouri River, in 1811* (Pittsburgh, 1812; rpt., Chicago, 1962), 145; *Port Folio* (Philadelphia), September 3, 1803; Thomas Rodney to Caesar A. Rodney, December 5, 1803, February 8, April 4, and March 21, 1804, "Rodney Letters," in Gratz, ed., *Pennsylvania Magazine of History and Biography,* 211, 333, 353, 346, 333; John Watkins to John Graham, September 6, 1805, in Carter, *Territorial Papers,* 9:504; John Breckinridge to Jefferson, September 10, 1803, TJP, LOC.

31. Gallatin to Isaac Briggs, May 8, 1806, PAG, microfilm ed., Philadelphia, 1970 (originals, Massachusetts Historical Society, Boston); Brown, *Plumer's Memorandum,* 474; *Annals of Congress,* 9th. Cong., 1st sess., 164; Jefferson to Henry Dearborn, Albert Gallatin, and James Madison, February 28, 1806, TJP, LOC. For concerns that white Louisianans might rebel against American authority in hopes of reuniting with Spain, which helped shape Gallatin's land policies, see John Brown to Gallatin, August 24, 1805, and Brown to Gallatin, January 7, 1806, PAG, microfilm ed., Philadelphia, 1970 (originals, Massachusetts Historical Society, Boston); and Benedict Van Pradelles to Gallatin, June 11, 1808, in Carter, *Territorial Papers,* 9:792. Federal officials also bent Indian policy to strengthen American authority in Upper Louisiana; see Andrew C. Isenberg, "The Market Revolution in the Borderlands: George Champlin Sibley in Missouri and New Mexico, 1808–1826," *Journal of the Early Republic* 21 (Autumn 2001): 445–65.

32. "Petition of the Vincennes Convention," December 28, 1802, in Jacob Piatt Dunn, ed., "Slavery Petitions and Papers," *Indiana Historical Society Publications* (Indianapolis, 1894), 2:462; *Annals of Congress,* 8th Cong., 1st sess., 779, 1023–24; William Henry Harrison to Jonathan Dayton, January 12, 1803, WHH Papers, IHS. The Indiana petitions are examined in chapter 6.

33. Brown, "Senate Debate on the Breckinridge Bill," 354, 351; *Annals of Congress,* 8th Cong., 2nd sess., 242. For Breckinridge's expectation that Americans had to settle Louisiana, see Breckinridge to Jefferson, September 10, 1803, TJP, LOC. For the supposed importance of "leading men" in cultivating the attachments of ordinary settlers, see, e.g., Clark to Madison, October 28, 1803, in "Despatches," 346–50. This point is well developed in Andrew R. L. Cayton, "Radicals in the 'Western World': The Federalist Conquest of Trans-Appalachian North America," in *Federalists Reconsidered,* ed. Doron Ben-Atar and Barbara B. Oberg (Charlottesville, VA, 1998), 77–96.

34. *Annals of Congress,* 8th Cong., 1st sess., 243–44; Brown, "Senate Debate on the Breckinridge Bill," 361; "An Act for the Organization of Orleans Territory and the Louisiana District," March 26, 1804, in Carter, *Territorial Papers,* 9:209.

35. Brown, "Senate Debate on the Breckinridge Bill," 361, 345; *Annals of Congress,* 8th Cong., 1st sess., 243–44. The vote to prohibit the domestic slave trade was preceded by a motion to change the bill, by having illegally imported slaves forfeited and then sold. The motion to change the penalty from freedom to forfeiture was defeated, 15 to 13. Five senators who voted for forfeiture over freedom nonetheless supported the final version, which provided for immediate freedom. For the proposed change and the roll call, see *Annals of Congress,* 8th Cong., 1st sess., 243–44. The debate over freeing illegally imported slaves was minimal compared to the debates it would provoke in 1807, when Congress was formulating a national law to prohibit the international trade; see Matthew E. Mason, "Slavery Overshadowed: Congress Debates the Atlantic Slave Trade to the United States, 1806–1807," *Journal of the Early Republic* 20 (Spring 2000): 59–81.

36. *Annals of Congress,* 8th Cong., 1st sess., 244; Brown, "Senate Debate on the Breckinridge Bill," 350. For Pickering's concerns about a French Louisiana, see Pickering to Caleb Strong, November 22, 1803, TPP, microfilm edition, Boston, 1966. For Pickering, slavery, and the South, see Kevin M. Gannon, "Escaping 'Mr. Jefferson's Plan of Destruction': New England Federalists and the Idea of a Northern Confederacy, 1803–1804," *Journal of the Early Republic* 21 (Fall 2001): 413–43; Robert H. Abzug, *Cosmos Crumbling: American Reform and the Religious Imagination* (New York, 1994), 136–37; and Egerton, "Empire of Liberty Reconsidered." Given Pickering's actions as secretary of state and senator, Garry Wills's attempt to make Pickering into an antislavery arch foe of racist, proslavery Republicans is somewhat absurd; see Garry Wills, *"Negro President:" Jefferson and the Slave Power* (Boston, 2003).

37. Brown, "Senate Debate on the Breckinridge Bill," 361, 345; *Annals of Congress,* 8th Cong., 1st sess., 243–44. Of the two northern Republicans who opposed, one, John Smith of Ohio, spent the better part of the debates warning that without diffusion a slave rebellion on the order of Haiti's would surely strike the Atlantic states. The other, Christopher Ellerly of Rhode Island, was suspected of involvement in the international slave trade. These votes, of

course, challenge historians' assumptions that northern Federalists opposed slavery expansion, whereas northern Republicans supported it; see Finkelman, *Slavery and the Founders*, 105–28; Rothman, *Slave Country*, 24–34; Fehrenbacher, *Dred Scott Case*, 74–100; Fehrenbacher, *Slaveholding Republic*, 253–63; Egerton, "Empire of Liberty Reconsidered"; Robinson, *Slavery in the Structure of American Politics*, 378–400; Richards, *Slave Power*, 43; and Kerber, *Federalists in Dissent*, 43.

38. Brown, "Senate Debate on the Breckinridge Bill," 349, 354. For the votes, see *Annals of Congress*, 8th Cong., 1st sess., 244. The other southern Republicans to vote for the bona fide settler restriction were Brown of Kentucky and Cocke of Tennessee.

39. "An Act for the Organization of Orleans Territory and the Louisiana District," March 26, 1804, in Carter, *Territorial Papers*, 9:209. There is no evidence that the prohibition on the domestic slave trade was ever enforced; see Fehrenbacher, *Slaveholding Republic*, 260. There is, however, evidence that it caused concern; see James Brown [U.S. District Attorney for the Territory of Orleans] to Albert Gallatin, December 11, 1805, in Carter, *Territorial Papers*, 9:548. Brown informed Gallatin that he interpreted the 1805 Ordinance to mean that "our citizens" now "possess the right of importing into this Country any Slaves already legally introduced into any of the States," which was prohibited by the 1804 Territorial Ordinance (Carter, *Territorial Papers*, 9:548).

40. Governor W. C. C. Claiborne to James Madison, March 10, 1804, in Dunbar Rowland, ed., *Official Letter Books of W. C. C. Claiborne, 1801–1816* (Jackson, MS, 1917), 2:25; Pierre Clement de Laussat to Denis Decres, April 7, 1804, in James A. Robertson, *Louisiana under the Rule of Spain, France, and the United States* (Cleveland, 1911), 2:51–59.

41. "Police of Slaves," in "Description of Louisiana," *Annals of Congress*, 8th Cong., 2nd sess., Appendix: 1567.

42. For Louisianans' contention that the 1804 Orleans Territorial Act seemed a prelude to extending the Northwest Ordinance's prohibitions on slavery to Louisiana, see "Petition of the Agents of the inhabitants of Louisiana," *Annals of Congress*, 8th Cong., 2nd sess., 1017–19. For the increased number of African-born slaves beginning in the 1780s and the fears of rebellion it generated, see Berlin, *Many Thousands Gone*, 344–45; and Lachance, "Politics of Fear." For greater restrictions on free and enslaved blacks prior to American possession, see Gwendolyn Midlo Hall, *Africans in Colonial Louisiana: The Development of Afro-Creole Culture in the Eighteenth Century* (Baton Rouge, 1992), 376–80; Kastor, *Nation's Crucible*, 81–84; Gilbert Din, *Spaniards, Planters, and Slaves: The Spanish Regulation of Slavery in Louisiana, 1763–1803* (College Station, TX, 1999); and Ingersoll, *Mammon and Manon*, 181–237. For white Louisianans' fears that the United States might upset the region's delicate and changing racial hierarchy, see Lachance, "Politics of Fear"; Judith Kelleher Schafer, *Slavery, the Civil Law, and the Supreme Court of Louisiana* (Baton Rouge, 1994), 3–8; Sarah Russell, "Ethnicity, Commerce, and Commu-

nity on Lower Louisiana's Plantation Frontier, 1803–1828," *Louisiana History* 40 (Fall 1999): 389–405; Thomas N. Ingersoll, "Free Blacks in a Slave Society: New Orleans, 1718–1812," *William and Mary Quarterly* 48 (April 1991): 173–200; and Andrew F. McMichael, "Reluctant Revolutionaries: The West Florida Borderlands, 1785–1810" (Ph.D. diss., Vanderbilt University, 2000).

43. "Address . . . of the free people of colour of New Orleans," *National Intelligencer,* March 16, 1804, and Carter, *Territorial Papers,* 9:174; Claiborne to General James Wilkinson, April 18, 1804, in Rowland, ed., *Letter Books,* 2:104; James Wilkinson to Henry Dearborn, January 11, 1804, in Carter, *Territorial Papers,* 9:159–60; Thomas Paine, "To the French Inhabitants of Louisiana," in Philip S. Foner, ed., *The Complete Writings of Thomas Paine* (New York, 1945), 2:963–68, originally published in the *Louisiana Gazette* (New Orleans), November 2, 1804.

44. Entry of February 18, 1804, Notes of Cabinet Meetings, May 7, 1803–November 19, 1805, Thomas Jefferson, Notes on Louisiana Territory, October 29, 1803, TJP, LOC. For American officials working to insure greater free and enslaved black subordination, see Kastor, *Nation's Crucible,* 62–66, 80–85, 107. For the lessening of tensions between white Louisianans and the United States, see Kastor, *Nation's Crucible;* Kastor "'Motives of Peculiar Urgency'"; and Ingersoll, *Mammon and Manon,* 243–82.

45. "Remonstrance of the People of Louisiana against the Political System Adopted by Congress for Them," *American State Papers: Miscellaneous,* 1:396–99; *Annals of Congress,* 8th Cong., 2nd sess., 727–28. Lower Louisianans printed English and French versions of the petition and hired three agents to present the petition to Congress. For the publication of the memorial, see *Mémoire présenté au Congres des Etats-Unis d'Amérique par les habitants de la Louisiane* (New Orleans, 1804); *Memorial Presented by the Inhabitants of Louisiana to the Congress of the United States* (Washington, DC, 1804); *National Intelligencer,* September 4, 1804; and Louisiana Citizens' Memorial to Thomas Jefferson, October 1, 1804, TJP, LOC. For white Louisianans' other concerns with the territorial government and American rule, see Kastor, *Nation's Crucible,* 55–75.

46. Governor Claiborne to Madison, October 3, November 22, and November 5, 1804, and Claiborne to Jefferson, January 25, 1805, in Carter, *Territorial Papers,* 9:305, 312, 320, 338; Claiborne to Madison, March 10, 1804, in Rowland, *Letter Books,* 2:26. For reference to "the Farmers," and slavery, see Claiborne to Jefferson, June 3, 1804, in Rowland, *Letter Books,* 2:187; and Claiborne to Madison, March 10, 1804, in Robertson, *Louisiana,* 2:258–59. For other references to "the people generally," see Claiborne to Madison, March 1, 1804, in Rowland, *Letter Books,* 2:13–14. Claiborne mentioned discontent over slavery in most of his correspondence during the summer of 1804; see, e.g., Claiborne to Jefferson, May 29, 1804, and Claiborne to Madison, June 22, July 1, July 12, and July 26, 1804, in Rowland, *Letter Books,* 2:174–75, 187, 216–17, 233, 244–45, 269–72. Except for the preference for enslaved Africans over

indentured Europeans, the mania for unfree labor in Louisiana in 1804 was quite similar to that described by Edmund Morgan in tobacco-boom Virginia beginning in the 1620s; see Edmund S. Morgan, *American Slavery, American Freedom: The Ordeal of Colonial Virginia* (New York, 1975), 108–30.

47. Claiborne to Madison, March 10, 1804, in Rowland, *Letter Books*, 2:26; Claiborne to Madison, October 3, 1804, in Carter, *Territorial Papers*, 9:305; "Extract of a letter from Natchez dated August 23," *Western Spy*, October 10, 1804; "Extract from a letter to the editor from Natchez, from a Lexington, KY paper," *Western Spy*, December 12, 1804; "A Kentucky Farmer at New York," *Western Spy*, August 22, 1804; "Looker-On," *Indiana Gazette*, August 28, 1804; John Sibley to Thomas Jefferson, September 2, 1804, TJP, LOC. For the "Remonstrance," see, e.g., *National Intelligencer*, September 4, 1804; and *Columbian Centinel*, September 5, 1804. For further reports of trouble in Louisiana, see, e.g., "DISCONTENT IN LOUISIANA," *National Intelligencer*, August 24, 1804; and "Of New Orleans, . . . to the editor of the Philadelphia Gazette," *Western Spy*, September 12, 1804.

48. John W. Gurley to the Postmaster General [forwarded to Jefferson], July 14, 1804, and Claiborne to Madison, October 10, 1804, in Carter, *Territorial Papers*, 9:262, 305; John Watkins to Claiborne, February 2, 1804, in Rowland, *Letter Books*, 2:10. As Peter Kastor points out, white Louisianans' threats were aimed not so much toward actual disunion itself, but were instead part of a strategy to force the United States to take their demands seriously (*Nation's Crucible*, 56–67). The threats nonetheless seemed menacing to officials in Washington, who remained concerned about securing the entire trans-Appalachian West in the Union.

49. "The Louisiana Memorial Abridged," unsigned poem, September 4, 1804, TJP, LOC.

50. "Committee Report," *Annals of Congress*, 8th Cong., 2nd sess., 1014–17; "An Act for the Government of Orleans Territory," in Carter, *Territorial Papers*, 9:405–7. The rather murky legislative history of the 1805 bills is covered in Fehrenbacher, *Dred Scott Case*, 97–98. No records other than roll calls (and these are incomplete) remain from the 1805 debates. For Quaker petitions calling on Congress to uphold the ban on the slave trade, see Brown, *Plumer's Memorandum*, 250–51; and Adams, *Memoirs*, 1:336–37. For the agents and their meetings with congressmen and American officials, see Everett S. Brown, "The Orleans Territory Memorialists to Congress, 1804," *Louisiana Historical Quarterly* 1 (January 1917): 99–104; Brown, *Plumer's Memorandum*, 222–24; Adams, *Memoirs*, 1:320–21; and Kastor, *Nation's Crucible*, 58–61. For the committee report and the Louisiana agents' arguments against prohibiting slavery, see *Annals of Congress*, 8th Cong., 2nd sess., 727–28, 1017–19. In early 1805 Congress was largely occupied by the bitter impeachment trial of Judge Samuel Chase.

51. Rothman, *Slave Country*, 27–34; Freehling, *Road to Disunion*, 141; Fehrenbacher, *Dred Scott Case*, 89–97; Robinson, *Slavery and the Structure*

of American Politics, 397–400; Finkelman, *Slavery and the Founders*, 151. For three especially critical indictments of Jeffersonian Republican responsibility for Louisiana slavery, all of which assume that a Federalist administration might have acquired Louisiana's "under free-soil conditions," see Egerton, "Empire of Liberty Reconsidered," quote at 309; Wills, *"Negro President"*; and Roger G. Kennedy, *Mr. Jefferson's Lost Cause: Land, Farmers, and the Louisiana Purchase* (New York, 2003), 208–13.

52. "The Louisiana Memorial Abridged," unsigned poem, September 4, 1804, TJP, LOC. For the ways that "intense imperial rivalries" allowed the inhabitants of "borderlands" to negotiate from a position of strength during the "transition from borderlands to borders," a situation especially applicable to the transfer of Louisiana to the United States, see Jeremy Adelman and Stephen Aron, "From Borderlands to Borders: Empires, Nation-States, and the Peoples In Between in North America History," *American Historical Review* 104 (June 1999): 814–41. For the expansion of slavery in Louisiana after 1805, see Rothman, *Slave Country*, 73–117.

53. Freehling, *Road to Disunion*, 141–42; Fehrenbacher, *Dred Scott Case*, 96–99; Fehrenbacher, *Slaveholding Republic*, 260–61; Finkelman, *Slavery and the Founders*, 151.

54. "Memorial of Barthelemi Tardiveau, July 8, 1788," in Alvord, *Kaskaskia Records*, 488; Meriwether Lewis to Thomas Jefferson, December 28, 1803, in Jackson, *Letters of the Lewis and Clark Expedition*, 148–53; Benjamin Stoddert, Notes on Louisiana, June 3, 1803, TJP, LOC; "Description of Louisiana," *Annals of Congress*, 8th Cong., 2nd sess., Appendix: 1576; Thomas T. Davis to Thomas Jefferson, November 5, 1803, and John Edgar to John Fowler, September 25, 1803, in Carter, *Territorial Papers*, 13:7–8, 5–7; Thomas T. Davis to [Kentucky senator] John Breckinridge, October 17, 1803, in Carter, *Territorial Papers*, 7:124.

55. "Remonstrance and Petition of the Representatives elected by the Freemen of their Respective Districts in the District of Louisiana," *American State Papers: Miscellaneous*, 1:401–4. They might have been correct. Plumer's notes have little to say about slavery in Upper Louisiana. However, Samuel Smith's comment that he favored joining the two territories, because "I know that it will estop [sic] slavery there, and to that I agree," suggests that senators were at least aware that this feature of the territorial bill could be interpreted as portending future abolition (Brown, "Senate Debate on the Breckinridge Bill," 360).

56. William C. Carr to John Breckinridge, July 4, 1804, in Carter, *Territorial Papers*, 13:29–30; "Remonstrance and Petition of the Representatives elected by the Freemen of their Respective Districts in the District of Louisiana," *American State Papers: Miscellaneous*, 1:401–4.

57. "Remonstrance of the Representatives elected by the Freemen of their Respective Districts in the District of Louisiana," *American State Papers: Miscellaneous*, 1:401–4. For concerns about British interest in the Missouri Coun-

try, see Albert Gallatin to Thomas Jefferson, April 13, 1803, TJP, LOC. For the situation in Upper Louisiana in 1804, see William Henry Harrison to Jefferson, June 24 and November 6, 1804, Harrison to Auguste Chouteau, December 21, 1804, and Harrison to Thomas Worthington, December 24, 1804, WHH Papers, IHS; and Rufus Easton to Jefferson, January 17, 1805, TJP, LOC. Harrison and Easton reported a more favorable disposition among the white settlers in Upper Louisiana, attributing the discord to "some few designing Men" who "have taken advantage of this circumstance to make the people believe that the government of the U.S. was not well disposed towards them" (Harrison to Jonathan Dayton, October 29, 1804, WHH Papers, IHS). It is doubtful that these letters reached Congress in time to affect their decision.

58. "An Act for the Government of Louisiana Territory," March 3, 1805, in Carter, *Territorial Papers*, 13:92–95. It is unclear if Congress purposely omitted any reference to slavery or Article VI. However, an earlier version of the bill would have indirectly acknowledged slavery by creating "a government in all respects similar to that now exercised in the Mississippi Territory" ("A Bill for the Government of the Territory of Louisiana," February 7, 1805, in Carter, *Territorial Papers*, 13:87–89). Some contemporaries claimed that this omission was deliberate and would allow Congress to prohibit slavery in Upper Louisiana when circumstances proved more favorable; see Amos Stoddard, *Sketches, Historical and Descriptive, of Louisiana* (Philadelphia, 1812), HSP/ LCP; A Citizen of Ohio [Alexander Mitchell], *An Address to the Inhabitants of the Indiana Territory, on the Subject of Slavery* (Hamilton, OH, 1816), OHS; and [Robert Walsh], *Free Remarks on the Spirit of the Federal Constitution, the Practice of the Federal Government, and the Obligations of the Union, Respecting the Exclusion of Slavery from the Territories and New States* (Philadelphia, 1819).

59. Freehling, *Road to Disunion*, 141–42; Finkelman, *Slavery and the Founders*, 151. For similar overemphasis on Jefferson, see also Fehrenbacher, *Slaveholding Republic*, 259–60; Fehrenbacher, *Dred Scott Case*, 89–91; and Kennedy, *Jefferson's Lost Cause*, 208–10. Freehling notes that Congress's failure to prohibit slavery in Upper Louisiana "invited slaveholders to flow into the midwestern area of Missouri rather than into the neighboring area of Illinois. The result by 1820: Missouri's 10,222 slaves constituted 15.8% of its population" (*Road to Disunion*, 142). However, in 1803 the percentage of slaves in Missouri was actually greater than it was in 1820, standing at 18.6 percent in 1803. If the five settlements containing fewer than three slaves are excluded, the proportion of slaves in white settlements rises to almost 25 percent. For a breakdown of population in Upper Louisiana, see "Description of Louisiana," *Annals of Congress*, 8th Cong., 2nd sess., Appendix: 1576. These figures probably underestimate the number of slaves in Upper Louisiana, because slaveholders in the Northwest Territory had been migrating across the Mississippi River, fearing the security of their property in slaves; see chapter 6. William Foley estimates that blacks accounted for 18 percent of the non-Indian popula-

tion of Upper Louisiana in 1800, and places the black populations of St. Louis and St. Genevieve, the two largest non-Indian settlements in the territory, at approximately one-third of the total population (*Genesis of Missouri*, 114). In short, slaves accounted for a greater percentage of Upper Louisiana's population before American possession than in 1819, when Missouri's application for statehood provoked the Missouri Crisis.

4. Slaveholders' Democracy, the Union, and the Nation

1. *Missouri Intelligencer* (Franklin), June 4, 1819.

2. *St. Louis Enquirer*, November 10, 1816.

3. "A Bill for the Government of the Territory of Louisiana," February 7, 1805, and "An Act for the Government of Louisiana Territory," March 3, 1805, in Clarence E. Carter, ed., *The Territorial Papers of the United States*, 28 vols. (Washington, DC, 1934–1975), 13:87–89, 92–95. At least some contemporaries claimed that Congress's failure to explicitly sanction slavery left open the possibility of action against the institution in Missouri; see Amos Stoddard, *Sketches, Historical and Descriptive, of Louisiana* (Philadelphia, 1812), HSP/LCP; A Citizen of Ohio [Alexander Mitchell], *An Address to the Inhabitants of the Indiana Territory, on the Subject of Slavery* (Hamilton, OH, 1816), OHS; and [Robert Walsh], *Free Remarks on the Spirit of the Federal Constitution, the Practice of the Federal Government, and the Obligations of the union, Respecting the Exclusion of Slavery from the Territories and New States* (Philadelphia, 1819).

4. *Annals of Congress*, 12th Cong., 1st sess., 1248; *Annals of Congress*, 16th Cong., 1st sess., 336–37; Carter, *Territorial Papers*, 14:552–59. In 1812, Orleans Territory became the state of Louisiana and the Louisiana Territory became the Missouri Territory.

5. For "silent sanction," see Don Fehrenbacher, *The Dred Scott Case: Its Significance in American Law and Politics* (New York, 1978), 89–91; Don Fehrenbacher, *The Slaveholding Republic: An Account of the United States Government's Relations to Slavery* (New York, 2001), 259–60; William W. Freehling, *Road to Disunion*, Vol. 1, *Secessionists at Bay, 1776–1854* (New York, 1990), 141–42; Paul Finkelman, *Slavery and the Founders: Race and Liberty in the Age of Jefferson*, 2nd ed. (Armonk, NY, 2001), 151; and Roger G. Kennedy, *Mr. Jefferson's Lost Cause: Land, Farmers, and the Louisiana Purchase* (New York, 2003), 208–10.

6. Stephen Aron, *How the West Was Lost: The Transformation of Kentucky from Daniel Boone to Henry Clay* (Baltimore, 1996), 58–81; David Hackett Fischer and James C. Kelly, *Bound Away: Virginia and the Westward Movement* (Charlottesville, VA, 2000); Philip J. Schwarz, *Migrants against Slavery: Virginians and the Nation* (Charlottesville, VA, 2001). For a more general overview of social, economic, and political conflicts between planters, small slave-

holders, and non-slaveholders in the Upper and Deep South, see Freehling, *Road to Disunion,* 39–58, 98–196; Lacy K. Ford Jr., "Making the 'White Man's Country' White: Race, Slavery, and State-Building in the Jacksonian South," *Journal of the Early Republic* 19 (Winter 1999): 713–37; Ford, "Popular Ideology of the Old South's Plain Folk: The Limits of Egalitarianism in a Slaveholding Society," in *Plain Folk of the South Revisited,* ed. Samuel C. Hyde Jr. (Baton Rouge, 1997), 205–27; and Harry L. Watson, "Conflict and Collaboration: Yeomen, Slaveholders and Politics in the Antebellum South," *Social History* 10 (1985): 277–85. For the relationship between race, class, gender, and political power, see Stephanie McCurry, *Masters of Small Worlds: Yeoman Households, Gender Relations, and the Political Culture of the Antebellum South Carolina Low Country* (New York, 1995). For the changes that expansion produced in the lives of slaves, see Ira Berlin, *Generations of Captivity: A History of African-American Slaves* (Cambridge, MA, 2003), 159–244.

7. George Sibley to Samuel H. Sibley, September 25, 1813, Sibley Papers, MHS. For Sibley, see Andrew C. Isenberg, "The Market Revolution in the Borderlands: George Champlin Sibley in Missouri and New Mexico, 1808–1826," *Journal of the Early Republic* 21 (Autumn 2001): 445–65. For settlement and the experiences of slaves, see Stephen Aron, *American Confluence: The Missouri Frontier from Borderland to Border State* (Bloomington, IN, 2006), 173–77. For an excellent account of white settlement in territorial Missouri, which unfortunately has little to say about slavery, see William E. Foley, *The Genesis of Missouri: From Wilderness Outpost to Statehood* (Columbia, MO, 1989), 131–46, 238–68.

8. Thomas Maitland Marshall, ed., *The Life and Papers of Frederick Bates,* 2 vols. (St. Louis, 1926; rpt., New York, 1975), 1:5–25.

9. Frederick Bates to John Michie, August 22, 1810, in Marshall, *Papers of Frederick Bates,* 2:154–56. Slaves also served as a form of liquid capital for their owners, which proved especially important in Missouri's cash-strapped economy; see, e.g., William C. Carr to Charles Carr, August 25, 1809, William C. Carr Papers, MHS. Carr purchased a slave for $333, but then immediately traded his slave for 320 acres of land valued at $2 per acre.

10. Bates to Michie, July 23, 1811, and Confirmation of Sale of Slaves, June 26, 1812, in Marshall, *Papers of Frederick Bates,* 2:185–87, 225–26.

11. Confirmation of Sale of Slaves, June 26, 1812, Frederick Bates to Mrs. Caroline M. Bates, July 19, 1812, Bates to William Carr, July 31, 1812, and Edward Bates to Frederick Bates, August 18, 1818, in Marshall, *Papers of Frederick Bates,* 2:225–26, 228–29, 229–31, 306. For the difficulty of purchasing slaves, because of cost and scarcity, see William C. Carr to Charles Carr, July 3 and September 8, 1807, and August 25, 1809, William C. Carr Papers, MHS.

12. Judge Alexander Stuart to the Secretary of State, February 13, 1813, in Carter, *Territorial Papers,* 14:298–99; Justus Post to John Post, October 17, 1817, Justus Post Papers, 1807–1821, MHS. For other federal officials who sought a transfer from the Northwest Territory to Missouri so that they could

better profit from their slaves, see Matthew Lyon to President James Madison, January 26, 1810, in Carter, *Territorial Papers,* 14:364–65.

13. Henry Marie Brackenridge, *Views of Louisiana, Together with a Journal of a Voyage up the Missouri River, in 1811* (Pittsburgh, 1812; rpt., 1962), 116; Timothy Flint, *Recollections of the Last Ten Years, Passed in Occasional Residences and Journeyings in the Valley of the Mississippi* (Boston, 1826; rpt., New York, 1968), 197–98, 211; Stoddard, *Sketches, Historical and Descriptive,* 226–27.

14. For a brief but excellent account of the postwar boom stimulated by paper money and the opening of additional public lands in the West, see Charles Sellers, *The Market Revolution: Jacksonian America, 1815–1846* (New York, 1991), 131–36. The cessation of the War of 1812 also removed the British–Indian threat on Missouri's northern and western borders, further encouraging American settlement; see Foley, *Genesis of Missouri,* 215–37.

15. Samuel R. Brown, *The Western Gazetteer; or, Emigrant's Directory, Containing a Geographical Description of the Western States and Territories* (Auburn, NY, 1817), 194–95, 216, UKSC; D. T. Madox, *Late Account of the Missouri Territory* (Paris, KY, 1817), 46–47, UKSC; William Doswell to Thomas W. Claybrooke, June 17, 1817, Claybrooke-Doswell Family Papers, 1804–1833, LVA; Diary entries of Richard Clough Anderson, August 26 and October 11, 1817, in Alfred Tischendorf and E. Taylor Parks, eds., *The Diary and Journal of Richard Clough Anderson, Jr., 1814–1825* (Durham, NC, 1964), 61, 63; *Missouri Gazette and Illinois Advertiser,* October 26, 1816; Philip Hamilton, *The Making and Unmaking of a Revolutionary Family: The Tuckers of Virginia, 1752–1830* (Charlottesville, VA, 2003), 183–85. For the great rush of Kentuckians to Missouri, see also Justus Post to John Post, November 20, 1816, Justus Post Papers, 1807–1821, MHS. For Kentucky's land claim mess and the great out-migration (much of it to Missouri) that it prompted, see Aron, *How the West Was Lost.*

16. Flint, *Recollections,* 198–201, 204–6. For federal land policies, see Malcolm J. Rohrbough, *The Land Office Business: The Settlement and Administration of American Public Lands, 1789–1837* (New York, 1968). For the prevalence of purchasing land, improving it, and then selling it, see Walter A. Schroeder, "Spread of Settlement in Howard County, Missouri, 1810–1859," *Missouri Historical Review* 63 (October 1968): 1–37, which unfortunately has nothing to say about slave labor. For land values, see Foley, *Genesis of Missouri,* 253.

17. Charles Sellers's seminal *Market Revolution* overstates the degree to which rural families sought to remove themselves from the market. For a corrective which argues that ordinary farming families sought greater access to the market to satisfy other, nonmarket aspirations such as land ownership, see Richard L. Bushman, "Markets and Farms in Early America," *William and Mary Quarterly* 55 (July 1998): 351–74.

18. William C. Carr to Charles Carr, August 25, 1809, William C. Carr Papers, MHS; Stoddard, *Sketches, Historical and Descriptive,* 226–27. For the importance of selling goods to newly arrived settlers, see Frederick Bates to

Mrs. Caroline M. Bates, July 19, 1812, and Bates to William Carr, July 31, 1812, in Marshall, *Papers of Frederick Bates*, 2:228–29, 229–23.

19. Charles Carroll to Nathaniel Rochester, December 15, 1818, and Carroll to Rochester, April 15, 1819, RFP, LVA.

20. Charles Carroll to Nathaniel Rochester, December 15, 1818, February 22 and April 15, 1819, February 21, May 10, and August 8, 1820, John Rochester to Nathaniel Rochester, January 2, 1819, RFP, LVA.

21. An exhaustive and detailed account of the drive for statehood within Missouri is F. C. Shoemaker, *Missouri's Struggle, 1804–1821* (New York, 1943), 37–55. For brief accounts, see Foley, *Genesis of Missouri*, 292–94; and Aron, *American Confluence*, 178–79.

22. [Nathaniel Beverley Tucker], "From Missouri, Extract of a Late letter from this interesting country to a Virginian," *Richmond Enquirer*, December 11, 1819.

23. *St. Louis Enquirer*, April 14, 1819; *Missouri Intelligencer*, July 30, 1819; Charles Carroll to Nathaniel Rochester, April 15, 1819, RFP, LVA. See also the *St. Louis Enquirer* for May 12, 1819; and the *Missouri Intelligencer* for April 23, June 25, and August 20, 1819. Resolutions from public meetings were often sent to the most important national papers, including *Niles' Weekly Register* (Baltimore), the *National Intelligencer* (Washington, DC), and the *Richmond Enquirer*. See, e.g., the instructions to publish resolutions in a host of national papers, contained in the *Missouri Gazette and Public Advertiser* (St. Louis) for August 4, 1819. Missourians also boasted that their anti-restriction resolutions were adopted "WITHOUT A DISSENTING VOICE" (*Missouri Intelligencer*, July 9, 1819).

24. *Annals of Congress*, 15th Cong., 2nd sess., 1170–79, 1202; *St. Louis Enquirer*, March 31 and May 12, 1819; *Missouri Intelligencer*, July 9, 1819. See also the *Missouri Intelligencer* for May 9, 1819, and January 28, 1820.

25. *St. Louis Enquirer*, July 14, 1819; *Missouri Intelligencer*, May 9 and July 16, 1819.

26. *Missouri Intelligencer*, July 16, 1819; *Missouri Gazette*, May 12, 1819.

27. "To the Editor, Letters from St. Louis," *Richmond Enquirer*, May 14 and May 21, 1819.

28. *Missouri Gazette*, April 28, 1819; *St. Louis Enquirer*, June 30 and October 30, 1819, reprinted in *Niles' Weekly Register*, December 25, 1819; "Letter from St. Louis," *Richmond Enquirer*, May 21, 1819.

29. *Richmond Enquirer*, May 14, 1819; *Missouri Intelligencer*, March 24, 1819, April 29, 1820; *Missouri Gazette*, April 28, 1819 (also in *St. Louis Enquirer*, April 28, 1819). For similar claims, see *Missouri Gazette*, August 11, 1819; and *St. Louis Enquirer*, April 29, 1819. For an especially strident defense of the slaveholders' constitution, see "Petition of the Mount Pleasant Baptist Association, to the senate and house of representatives of the United States of America, in congress assembled," *Niles' Weekly Register*, November 27, 1819, also published in the *Missouri Intelligencer*, October 1, 1819, which is examined below.

30. [Nathaniel Beverley Tucker], "From Missouri, Extract of a Late letter from this interesting country to a Virginian," *Richmond Enquirer,* December 11, 1819. For Tucker's authorship of this letter, see Robert J. Brugger, *Beverley Tucker: Heart over Head in the Old South* (Baltimore, 1978), 58–59. For Tucker in Missouri, see Hamilton, *Making and Unmaking of a Revolutionary Family,* 185–89. For similar sentiments, including "Our fine country here is becoming a New Virginia," see Thomas Hart Benton to Governor James Preston of Virginia, November 14, 1819, in William M. Meigs, *The Life of Thomas Hart Benton* (Philadelphia, 1904), 102–3. For toasts calling on "The Citizens of our Mother States" to settle in "this land of Liberty and plenty," see, e.g., *St. Louis Enquirer,* July 14, 1819.

31. Charles Carroll to Nathaniel Rochester, December 15, 1818, RFP, LVA; James Devore to John Cabell Breckinridge, December 23, 1820, BFP, LOC; the *Missouri Gazette* for April 7, April 14, and May 12, 1819; *St. Louis Enquirer,* April 21, 1819.

32. *Missouri Intelligencer,* August 6 and August 20, 1819.

33. *Edwardsville (Ill.) Spectator,* in *Richmond Enquirer,* October 8, 1819; *Missouri Intelligencer,* September 24, 1819; *St. Louis Enquirer,* April 3, April 15, April 19, and April 29, 1820. For warnings that northern "emancipationists" might arm slaves and thus must be driven out, see the *St. Louis Enquirer* for March 25, 1820. For the importance of mobbing as a means of silencing dissent against slavery, see David Grimsted, *American Mobbing, 1828–1861: Toward Civil War* (New York, 1998).

34. "Petition of the Mount Pleasant Baptist Association," *Niles' Weekly Register,* November 27, 1819, also published in *Missouri Intelligencer,* October 1, 1819.

35. *Niles' Weekly Register,* November 27, 1819; *St. Louis Enquirer,* July 28, 1819; *Missouri Gazette,* August 4, 1819. For other pieces on diffusion that extolled "amelioration" but condemned the Tallmadge restrictions, see, e.g., "One of the People of Missouri," *National Intelligencer,* August 25, 1819; and the *Missouri Intelligencer* for July 16 and August 20, 1819, February 18 and April 15, 1820; *St. Louis Enquirer,* April 21, 1819, and April 29, 1820. For protests reconciling slavery and republican government, see, e.g., *Niles' Weekly Register,* October 2, 1819. For claims that slaves were nothing other than property, see, e.g., the *Missouri Gazette* for August 11, 1819; and the *St. Louis Enquirer* for April 29, 1819.

36. Charles Carroll to Nathaniel Rochester, April 15, 1819, RFP, LVA. Some national and northern papers, badly overestimating the strength of the restrictionists in Missouri, believed that the Missouri Convention might voluntarily adopt restrictions on slavery; see *Niles' Weekly Register,* May 13, 1820.

37. *Missouri Gazette,* April 12 and May 3, 1820. The *Gazette* was the only Missouri paper willing to print antislavery articles.

38. *Missouri Gazette,* April 12 and May 3, 1820. See also Lucas to John Quincy Adams, December 1, 1820, in Carter, *Territorial Papers,* 15:679–80.

Even Benjamin Lundy, who moved to Missouri in 1820 in hopes of furthering the cause of restriction among white Missourians, only called for a prohibition on the introduction of additional slaves with no provision for emancipation. For two antislavery pieces that Lundy probably authored, see Merton L. Dillon, *Benjamin Lundy and the Struggle for Negro Freedom* (Urbana, IL, 1966), 37–39.

39. Geo. Tompkins to George C. Sibley, July 30, 1819, Sibley Papers, MHS; John B. C. Lucas to Robert Moore, October 27, 1820, John Lucas to Mahlon Dickerson, January 12, 1821, in John B. C. Lucas, ed., *Letters of Hon. J. B. C. Lucas, from 1815 to 1836* (St. Louis, 1905), 29–30, 40; Lucas to John Quincy Adams, December 1, 1820, in Carter, *Territorial Papers*, 15:679–80; Timothy Flint, *Recollections*, 214. For charges that proslavery candidates were insufficiently proslavery and that Independent tickets were secretly antislavery, see, e.g., the *St. Louis Enquirer* for April 15, 1820; the *Missouri Intelligencer* for April 22, 1820; and the *St. Louis Enquirer* for April 3, 1820.

40. The voting records from the 1820 contest are incomplete, but for an analysis, see Shoemaker, *Missouri's Struggle*, 129–31. According to Shoemaker, the anti-restrictionists outpolled the restrictionists by a margin of "at least seven to one and perhaps nine or ten to one" in the state as a whole (131).

41. *St. Louis Enquirer*, May 10, 1820, also in *Niles' Weekly Register*, June 10, 1820. For other warnings to the "closet emancipationists," see the *St. Louis Enquirer* for May 10, 1820.

42. Missouri Constitution of 1820, Article III, section 26. The constitution is reprinted in Shoemaker, *Missouri's Struggle*, Appendix: 3. For calls to exclude free blacks from Missouri, see, e.g., *Missouri Intelligencer*, April 15 and April 22, 1820; and *St. Louis Enquirer*, April 29, 1820. This provision created a second Missouri Controversy in Congress in 1820 and 1821.

43. Freehling, *Road to Disunion*, 39–58, 98–196; Ford, "Making the 'White Man's Country' White"; Ford, "Popular Ideology of the Old South's Plain Folk"; Watson, "Conflict and Collaboration."

5. "Hot Times about Slavery and Republicanism"

1. Thomas Worthington to Albert Gallatin, September 18, 1802, in Clarence E. Carter, ed., *Territorial Papers of the United States*, 28 vols. (Washington, DC, 1934–1975), 3:244; Abraham Shepherd to Thomas Worthington, February 13, 1799, and George Granger to Thomas Worthington, December 27, 1804, TWP, OHS. For politics in early Ohio, see Andrew R. L. Cayton, *The Frontier Republic: Ideology and Politics in the Ohio Country, 1780–1825* (Kent, OH, 1986); Andrew R. L. Cayton, "Land, Power, and Reputation: The Cultural Dimension of Politics in the Ohio Country," *William and Mary Quarterly* 47 (April 1990): 266–86; and Donald Ratcliffe, *Party Spirit in a Frontier Republic: Democratic Politics in Ohio, 1793–1821* (Columbus, OH, 1998).

2. *Scioto Gazette* (Chillicothe, OH), September 4, 1802.

3. "Blue Jacket," *Scioto Gazette,* September 11, 1802; Duncan McArthur, "To the Electors of Ross County," *Scioto Gazette,* September 11, 1802; "Plain Truth and Very Plain Dealing," *Scioto Gazette,* September 18, 1802.

4. Jacob Burnet, *Notes on the Early Settlement of the North-Western Territory* (Cincinnati, 1847), 302. Historians rely too heavily on Burnet's claim to explain the supposed lack of interest in slavery. They also tend to accept Eugene Berwanger's claim that "the slavery issue in the Buckeye State was not a matter of public discussion" (Eugene Berwanger, *The Frontier against Slavery: Western Anti-Negro Prejudice and the Slavery Extension Controversy* [Urbana, IL, 1967], 12–13). For brief examinations of the Ohio debates over slavery, see Peter S. Onuf, *Statehood and Union: A History of the Northwest Ordinance* (Bloomington, IN, 1987), 113–16; Cayton, *Frontier Republic,* 56–58; and Ratcliffe, *Party Spirit in a Frontier Republic,* 53–54, 66, 70–71.

5. *Liberty Hall and Cincinnati Mercury,* July 7, 1806. For the early "democratization" of politics in Ohio, see Ratcliffe, *Party Spirit in a Frontier Republic,* 13–74.

6. For early white settlements in the Northwest Territory, see Cayton, *Frontier Republic,* 12–67; and R. Douglas Hurt, *The Ohio Frontier: Crucible of the Old Northwest, 1720–1830* (Bloomington, IN, 1996). For the Northwest and Ohio Indians' efforts to beat back white settlement, see Richard White, *The Middle Ground: Indians, Empires, and Republics in the Great Lakes Region, 1650–1815* (Cambridge, 1991), 413–76; and Gregory Evans Dowd, *A Spirited Resistance: The North American Indian Struggle for Unity, 1745–1815* (Baltimore, 1992).

7. For Fallen Timbers and the Treaty of Greenville, see Dowd, *Spirited Resistance,* 111–15; White, *Middle Ground,* 413–76; and Andrew R. L. Cayton, "'Noble Actors' upon 'the Theatre of Honour': Power and Civility in the Treaty of Greenville," in *Contact Points: American Frontiers from the Mohawk Valley to the Mississippi, 1750–1830,* ed. Andrew R. L. Cayton and Fredrika J. Teute (Chapel Hill, NC, 1998), 235–69. For the important role of federal power in opening the Northwest for white settlement, see Andrew R. L. Cayton, "'Separate Interests' and the Nation-State: The Washington Administration and the Origins of Regionalism in the Trans-Appalachian West," *Journal of American History* 79 (June 1992): 39–67. For white migration to Ohio, see Cayton, "Land, Power, and Reputation"; John Barnhart, *Valley of Democracy: The Frontier versus the Plantation in the Ohio Valley, 1775–1818* (Bloomington, IN, 1953), 121–43; and Beverly W. Bond Jr., *The Civilization of the Old Northwest: A Study of Political, Social, and Economic Development, 1788–1812* (New York, 1934).

8. Stephen Aron, *How the West Was Lost: The Transformation of Kentucky from Daniel Boone to Henry Clay* (Baltimore, 1996), 58–81; Craig Thompson Friend, "'Work & Be Rich': Economy and Culture on the Bluegrass Farm," in *The Buzzel About Kentuck: Settling the Promised Land,* ed. Craig Thompson Friend (Lexington, KY, 1999), 125–52.

9. For land sales in Ohio, see Malcolm J. Rohrbough, *The Land Office Business: The Settlement and Administration of American Public Lands, 1789–1837* (New York, 1968), 13–21. For lands, speculation, and settlement in the Virginia Military District, see Cayton, *Frontier Republic*, 51–57; and Cayton, "Land, Power, and Reputation," 274–81.

10. David Barrow Diary, June 28, 1795, Typescript, Special Collections, KHS; *Journal of the House of Representatives of the territory of the United States northwest of the river Ohio: At the first session of the General Assembly, 1799*, 17, 19, OHS. For the 1799 Kentucky constitution, see Aron, *How the West Was Lost*, 89–100.

11. *Journal of the House of Representatives of the territory northwest of the river Ohio*, 17, 19, OHS.

12. *Journal of the House of Representatives of the territory northwest of the river Ohio*, 108, OHS.

13. *Journal of the House of Representatives of the territory northwest of the river Ohio*, 117–19, OHS; "Blue Jacket," *Scioto Gazette*, September 11, 1802. The petitions apparently created some concern that slavery might be permitted in Ohio despite Article VI (see "the Humane Society, north west of the River Ohio," which was formed to "repel any and every attempt for the introduction of slavery into this territory," in the *Western Spy and Hamilton Gazette* [Cincinnati] for March 12, 1800; and "Querist," in the *Freeman's Journal* [Cincinnati] for March 5, 1799).

14. For the full range of issues and conflicts that gave rise to the increased resentment directed toward Federalists in Ohio, the movement for statehood, and partisan competition, see Ratcliffe, *Party Spirit in a Frontier Republic*, 13–74; and Cayton, *Frontier Republic*, 68–80. Ohio became a territory separate and distinct from the remainder of the Northwest Territory in July 1800.

15. *Scioto Gazette*, October 2, 1802; "Frank Stubblefield," *Western Spy*, August 7, 1802. For the issues involved in the 1802 election, along with an analysis of its partisan dimensions, see Ratcliffe, *Party Spirit in a Frontier Republic*, 44–74. Voters and delegates faced two critical questions in the 1802 elections. First, should the territory accept the terms of the 1802 Congressional Enabling Act, which permitted the people of Ohio to draft a constitution and apply for statehood? Most candidates recognized that the overwhelming majority of voters favored statehood and ran as candidates supporting statehood. The second issue facing the delegates and voters involved what type of constitution the Chillicothe convention would adopt if the delegates opted for statehood, which most voters and candidates expected they would. This is where slavery entered into politics.

16. "Speech of Governor St. Clair at Cincinnati, [August or September 1802], ASP, OHS; "A Hamilton Farmer," *Western Spy*, November 11, 1801; "Frank Stubblefield," *Western Spy*, August 7, 1802. For Federalist opposition to slavery, see Linda Kerber, *Federalists in Dissent: Imagery and Ideology in Jeffersonian America* (Ithaca, NY, 1970), 23–66; and Paul Finkelman, *Slavery and*

the *Founders: Race and Liberty in the Age of Jefferson*, 2nd ed. (Armonk, NY, 2001), 105–28. For a more critical analysis of Federalist antislavery, see Matthew Mason, *Slavery and Politics in the Early American Republic* (Chapel Hill, NC, 2006).

17. "A Hamilton Farmer," *Western Spy*, November 11, 1801; "Frank Stubblefield," *Western Spy*, August 7, 1802.

18. "Republicanus," *Western Spy*, August 7, 1802, reprinted (allegedly) from the *Ohio Gazette* (Marietta) for July 6, 1802; "The Dayton Association," *Western Spy*, June 26, 1802; "Frank Stubblefield," *Western Spy*, August 7, 1802.

19. Lewis Kerr, "To the Republican Corresponding Society at Cincinnati," in the *Western Spy* for July 24, 1802. For interpretations stressing the important role of racism in keeping slavery out of Ohio, which also tend to equate antislavery politics with antiblack racism, see Berwanger, *Frontier against Slavery*. For general claims that racism figured prominently in early northwestern opposition to slavery, see William W. Freehling, "The Founding Fathers and Conditional Antislavery," in *The Reintegration of American History: Slavery and the Civil War* (New York, 1994); Finkelman, *Slavery and the Founders*, 37–80; and Stephen Middleton, ed., *The Black Laws of the Old Northwest: A Documentary History*, Contributions in Afro-American and African Studies, No. 152 (Westport, CT, 1993), 3–5, 15, 159. The strongest claim that northern Republicans were generally proslavery racists and northern Federalists were generally opposed to slavery on humanitarian grounds is Finkelman, "The Problem of Slavery in the Age of Federalism," in *Slavery and the Founders*, 105–28. These works incorrectly read antebellum racism backward into this earlier period. The essay by the Federalist "Hamilton Farmer," in the *Western Spy* for November 11, 1801, is the only one I can find in the Cincinnati papers that associates the exclusion of slavery with the exclusion of blacks, whether free or enslaved. For a similar piece, also written by a Federalist, see "For Liberty Hall: Reflections," in the *Liberty Hall* for October 22, 1805.

20. *Western Spy*, September 18, 1802. For the Republican corresponding societies in Hamilton County, see Ratcliffe, *Party Spirit in a Frontier Republic*, 26–27, 55–57, 60–62. According to Ratcliffe, Cincinnati Republicans' "outlook was akin not so much to that of the leading Virginia Jeffersonians as to the more radical, democratic ideology of New York and Philadelphia, inspired by Thomas Paine and the French revolutionaries" (27).

21. "To the Members of the several REPUBLICAN SOCIETIES, in the north western territory, from the Friends of Humanity," *Western Spy*, July 31, 1802; "A Farmer" *Western Spy*, July 24, 1802; Lewis Kerr, "To the Republican Corresponding Society at Cincinnati," *Western Spy*, July 24, 1802.

22. For opposition to slavery on similar grounds but at a later period, see Paul Goodman, *Of One Blood: Abolitionism and the Origins of Racial Equality* (Berkeley, 1998); Daniel Feller, "A Brother in Arms: Benjamin Tappen and the Antislavery Democracy," *Journal of American History* 88 (June 2001): 48–74; Sean Wilentz, "Slavery, Antislavery, and Jacksonian Democracy," in *The Market*

Revolution in America: Social, Political, and Religious Expressions, 1800–1880, ed. Melvyn Stokes and Stephen Conway (Charlottesville, VA, 1996), 202–23; and Jonathan H. Earle, *Jacksonian Antislavery and the Politics of Free Soil, 1824–1854* (Chapel Hill, NC, 2004). My reading of the Cincinnati Republicans' understanding of the American Revolution owes much to Gordon Wood, *The Radicalism of the American Revolution* (New York, 1991).

23. "A Republican," *Western Spy,* September 25, 1802; "The Friends of Humanity," *Western Spy,* July 31, 1802; "A Farmer," *Western Spy,* July 24, 1802; Statement of John Browne, *Western Spy,* October 2, 1802.

24. Andrew Badgley, John Gossett, George Medsker, "An Address," *Western Spy,* August 22, 1802; *Scioto Gazette,* July 17, 1802. For their status as middling farmers, see Ratcliffe, *Party Spirit in a Frontier Republic,* 69–70. Among other things, the three called for universal manhood suffrage, including the vote for African Americans, and no property qualifications for office.

25. "Some Short Observations on Slavery," *Western Spy,* July 3, 1802; Andrew Badgley, John Gossett, George Medsker, "An Address," *Western Spy,* August 22, 1802.

26. "Some Short Observations on Slavery," *Western Spy,* July 3, 1802. For the importance of Independence Day celebrations in forming national, regional, local, and partisan identities, see Simon P. Newman, *Parades and the Politics of the Street: Festive Culture in the Early Republic* (Philadelphia, 1997), 83–119; and David Waldstreicher, *In the Midst of Perpetual Fetes: The Making of American Nationalism, 1776–1820* (Chapel Hill, NC, 1997), 177–293.

27. "Some Short Observations on Slavery," *Western Spy,* July 3, 1802.

28. *Western Spy,* July 10, 1802; "Some Short Observations on Slavery," *Western Spy,* July 3, 1802. See also "A Christian," in the *Western Spy* for July 17, 1802. In addition to defending black equality and rights, various essayists assured readers that Ohio slaves, like those in the Atlantic states, would rebel. Remarkably, the writers were all adamant in their defense of slaves' rights to rebel. "The Friends of Humanity" equated rebelling slaves with the "American Heroes" and "their struggles for liberty in the revolutionary war."

29. "A Republican," *Western Spy,* September 25, 1802; "The Friends of Humanity," *Western Spy,* July 31, 1802.

30. "A Republican," *Western Spy,* September 25, 1802; "The Friends of Humanity," *Western Spy,* July 31, 1802. For the slave trade, see the following pieces in the *Western Spy and Hamilton Gazette:* "Something New," which claimed that slave traders in North Carolina and Virginia were setting prices for slaves "by weight, at three and one third dollars per pound" (July 24, 1802); and "Extract from a letter from a member of the Humane Society of Virginia, to his friend, dated February 3d, 1791," which decried that the domestic slave trade broke up families (September 4, 1802). For essays on the horrors of the international slave trade, see "On the Slave Trade," in the *Western Spy* for July 10, 1802; and "From London," in the *Western Spy* for August 14, 1802.

31. "A Farmer," *Western Spy,* July 24, 1802; "The Friends of Humanity,"

Western Spy, July 31, 1802; "A Republican," *Western Spy,* September 25, 1802; Andrew Badgley, John Gossett, George Medsker, "An Address," *Western Spy,* August 22, 1802.

32. "An elector and friend to the County," *Western Spy,* September 25, 1802; "Statement of Stephen Wood," John Browne, "To the Electors of Hamilton County," *Western Spy,* October 2, 1802. In his memoirs, Ephraim Cutler claimed that Browne introduced a proposal to allow slavery under the new constitution; see Julia Perkins Cutler, ed., *Life and Times of Ephraim Cutler, Prepared from his Journals and Correspondence* (Cincinnati, 1890). Ratcliffe believes it possible that Browne might have indeed introduced the motion, in part because of its consistency with Jeffersonian principles of diffusion (*Party Spirit in a Frontier Republic,* 265n80). However, Browne's public pledges, along with the strong public pronouncements by the Republicans to prohibit slavery and the promise of "the Friends of Humanity" to expose candidates who voted against their pledges, make this highly unlikely.

33. "A friend of order and good government," *Western Spy,* October 9, 1802; "The Friends of Humanity," *Western Spy,* July 31, 1802. The Cincinnati Republicans also consistently opposed proposals, some of which passed the constitutional convention, restricting the rights and freedoms of free blacks in Ohio; see Ratcliffe, *Party Spirit in a Frontier Republic,* 71; and Helen M. Thurston, "The 1802 Constitutional Convention and the Status of the Negro," *Ohio History* 81 (Winter 1972): 15–37.

34. Nathaniel Massie to Thomas Worthington, October 1, 1802, TWP, OHS; *Scioto Gazette,* September 4 and September 11, 1802. For an analysis of the full range of issues involved in the 1802 election in Ross County, see Ratcliffe, *Party Spirit in a Frontier Republic,* 51–52, 62, 66. For the social, political, and cultural biases that underwrote Republicanism in Ross County, see Cayton, "Land, Power, and Reputation"; and Cayton, *Frontier Republic,* 51–59.

35. John Willis, *Scioto Gazette,* September 11, 1802; Nathaniel Massie, *Scioto Gazette,* September 18, 1802; Robert W. Finley, *Scioto Gazette,* October 9, 1802.

36. James Grubb, Edward Tiffin, Thomas Worthington, *Scioto Gazette,* September 11, 1802; *Scioto Gazette,* August 28, 1802; Plain Truth and Very Plain Dealing," *Scioto Gazette,* September 18, 1802. For similar sentiments, see the statements of James Crawford, Elias Langham, James Dunlap, and Samuel Finley in the *Scioto Gazette* for September 4, 1802; Abraham Claypool, *Scioto Gazette,* September 18, 1802; James Scott, *Scioto Gazette,* September 25, 1802; and "Blue Jacket," *Scioto Gazette,* September 11, 1802.

37. John Hopkins, *Scioto Gazette,* October 2, 1802; Michael Baldwin, *Scioto Gazette,* August 28, 1802; James Grubb, *Scioto Gazette,* September 11, 1802; Robert W. Finley, *Scioto Gazette,* October 9, 1802; Noble Crawford, *Scioto Gazette,* October 2, 1802; and "A Citizen," *Scioto Gazette,*" August 21, 1802.

38. "Yellow Jacket," *Scioto Gazette,* September 18, 1802. For similar defenses

of the natural rights of African Americans, see "A Citizen," in the *Scioto Gazette* for August 21, 1802.

39. Jacob Smith, *Scioto Gazette*, September 4, 1802; William Craig, *Scioto Gazette*, October 2, 1802. For the votes, see the *Scioto Gazette* for October 16, 1802. Smith placed ninth and Craig placed twenty-first out of the twenty-two candidates for Ross County's five seats to the convention.

40. *Scioto Gazette*, October 9, September 4, and October 2, 1802; Thurston, "The 1802 Constitutional Convention."

41. *Scioto Gazette*, September 4 and September 11, 1802.

42. "Yellow Jacket," *Scioto Gazette*, September 18, 1802; Duncan McArthur, "To the Electors," *Scioto Gazette*, September 11, 1802.

43. "Yellow Jacket," *Scioto Gazette*, September 18, 1802; Duncan McArthur, "To the Electors," *Scioto Gazette*, September 11, 1802. For the election results, see the *Scioto Gazette* for October 16, 1802. Electors cast 621 votes for James Grubb, the delegate with the least number of votes.

44. Jehial Gregory to Return J[onathan] Meigs Jr., August 8, 1802, in Julia Perkins Cutler, ed., *Life and Times of Ephraim Cutler* (1890; rpt., New York, 1971), 66n; Philip Gatch to Edward Dromgoole, February 11, 1802, in William Warren Sweet, ed., *Religion on the American Frontier, 1783–1840* (Chicago, 1931), 4:152; James Pritchard to Thomas Worthington, October 23, 1802, TWP, OHS. James Sargent, the other delegate from Clermont County, had also freed his slaves in Maryland before removing to Kentucky and, ultimately, Ohio; see John D. Barhart, *Valley of Democracy: The Frontier versus the Plantation in the Ohio Valley, 1775–1818* (Bloomington, IN, 1953), 153.

6. Slaveholding Nationalism and Popular Antislavery Politics

1. *Western Sun* (Vincennes, IN), December 15, 1810; Louis B. Ewbank and Dorothy Lois Riker, eds., *The Laws of the Indiana Territory, 1809–1816*, Indiana Historical Collections, Vol. 20 (Indianapolis, 1934), 138–39.

2. Paul Finkelman, "Evading the Ordinance: The Persistence of Bondage in Indiana and Illinois," and "Slavery and the Northwest Ordinance, 1787: A Study in Ambiguity," in *Slavery and the Founders: Race and Liberty in the Age of Jefferson*, 2nd ed. (Armonk, NY, 2001), 37–57, 58–80. The strongest argument that racism was the primary factor keeping slavery out of Indiana is Eugene Berwanger, *The Frontier against Slavery: Western Anti-Negro Prejudice and the Slavery Extension Controversy* (Urbana, IL, 1967), 7–29. For a Turnerian analysis stressing southern-born settlers' dislike of planters, see John D. Barnhart and Dorothy L. Riker, *Indiana to 1816: The Colonial Period* (Indianapolis, 1971), 334–35, 347–49, 358. For a more nuanced, but regrettably brief treatment which recognizes that the slavery issue involved larger questions and was quite contentious, see Andrew R. L. Cayton, *Frontier Indiana* (Blooming-

ton, IN, 1996) 226, 246–47, 258. Peter S. Onuf analyzes the debates over Indiana slavery as a question of settlement and development, but does not delve deeply into the political struggles (see *Statehood and Union: A History of the Northwest Ordinance* [Bloomington, IN, 1987], 116–23). In general, the literature on Northwest slavery does not address why Congress failed to suspend Article VI; see, e.g., Don Fehrenbacher, *The Dred Scott Case: Its Significance in American Law and Politics* (New York, 1978), 84–86; Don Fehrenbacher, *The Slaveholding Republic: An Account of the United States Government's Relations to Slavery* (New York, 2001), 256–59; and William W. Freehling, *The Road to Disunion,* Vol. 1, *Secessionists at Bay, 1776–1854* (New York, 1990), 138–43. Finkelman is nearly alone in trying to address why Congress failed to overturn Article VI in Indiana (see "Evading the Ordinance").

3. Congress created the Indiana Territory in 1800, which through 1805 included the remainder of the Northwest Territory less Ohio. In 1805, Congress created the Michigan Territory, and the Indiana Territory was reduced to present-day Illinois and Indiana. In 1809, Congress created a separate Illinois Territory.

4. Journal of John Breathitt's Tour to St. Vincennes, Indiana Territory, and John Breathitt's memorandum book and diary, 1804–1805, KHS; John Badollet to Albert Gallatin, January 1, 1806, in Gayle Thornbrough, ed., *The Correspondence of John Badollet and Albert Gallatin,* Indiana Historical Society Publications, Vol. 22 (Indianapolis, 1963), 59–60. For Indiana's population in 1801, see Cayton, *Frontier Indiana,* 178. My description of territorial Indiana relies heavily on Cayton, *Frontier Indiana;* and Barnhart and Riker, *Indiana to 1816.*

5. Harrison to Thomas Worthington, July 13, 1800, and Harrison to Thomas Jefferson, October 1801, WHH Papers, IHS. For the important role of territorial officials as diplomats charged with securing the interests of the United States in western territories, see Peter J. Kastor, "'Motives of Peculiar Urgency': Local Diplomacy in Louisiana, 1803–1821," *William and Mary Quarterly* 58 (October 2001): 819–48. For the problem of incorporating the trans-Appalachian West into the "union of interests," see Cayton, "'Separate Interests' and the Nation-State: The Washington Administration and the Origins of Regionalism in the Trans-Appalachian West," *Journal of American History* 79 (June 1992): 39–67. For military threats to the Northwest, see Gordon T. Stewart, "The Northwest and the Balance of Power in North America," in *The Northwest Ordinance: Essays on Its Formation, Provisions, and Legacy,* ed. Frederick D. Williams (East Lansing, MI, 1989), 21–38. For Illinois Country settlers' discontent with American rule, see, e.g., "Petition to Congress by Inhabitants of the Illinois Country," February 7, 1800 (which was forwarded to Harrison), in Clarence E. Carter, ed., *The Territorial Papers of the United States,* 28 vols. (Washington, DC, 1934–1975), 3:76–77.

6. For this interpretation of Harrison and slavery, see Finkelman, *Slavery and the Founders,* 68–72; Cayton, *Frontier Indiana,* 185–90; and, especially, Andrew R. L. Cayton, "Land, Power, and Reputation: The Cultural Dimension

of Politics in the Ohio Country," *William and Mary Quarterly* 47 (April 1990): 266–86.

7. For Harrison's early career, see Dorothy Burne Goebel, *William Henry Harrison: A Political Biography* (Indianapolis, 1926), 14–37. For the ways that military service convinced territorial officials of the importance of federal power in creating stable, prosperous communities in the American Union, see Cayton, "'Separate Interests' and the Nation-State." For Harrison's close association with Ohio Federalists, see Donald Ratcliffe, *Party Spirit in a Frontier Republic: Democratic Politics in Ohio, 1793–1821* (Columbus, OH, 1998), 35–36.

8. For a more complex picture of Harrison, which acknowledges his commitment to a strong federal presence in the Northwest, see Andrew R. L. Cayton, "Radicals in the 'Western World': The Federalist Conquest of Trans-Appalachian North America," in *Federalists Reconsidered*, ed. Doron Ben-Atar and Barbara B. Oberg (Charlottesville, VA, 1998), 77–97. For the 1840 campaign, see Michael F. Holt, *The Rise and Fall of the American Whig Party: Jacksonian Politics and the Onset of the Civil War* (New York, 1999), 89–113. For an example of Harrison's nationalist bent, see the Harrison Land Act of 1800, and his commentary on its importance to the West in the *Western Spy and Hamilton Gazette* (Cincinnati) for June 11, 1800, in Logan Esarey, ed., *Governor's Messages and Letters of William Henry Harrison, 1800–1811*, 2 vols., Indiana Historical Collections, Vol. 7 (Indianapolis, 1922), 1:13. For Harrison's decision to live in free Ohio rather than Kentucky, and his conversion to antislavery politics in 1816, see chapter 7.

9. Petition of Shadrach Bond Sr. et al., November 15, 1802, WHH Papers, IHS; "Proclamation: Calling a Convention to Petition Congress to Allow Slavery in Indiana Territory," November 22, 1802, in Esarey, *Governor's Messages and Letters*, 1:60–61. For earlier complaints about Article VI, see Barthelemi Tardiveau to Arthur St. Clair, June 30, 1789, ASP, OHS; Barthelemi Tardiveau to the Continental Congress, July 8, 1788, and Major John Hamtramck to General Josiah Harmar, August 14, 1789, in Clarence W. Alvord, ed., *Kaskaskia Records, 1778–1790* (Springfield, IL, 1909), 485–88, 508–9; and Arthur St. Clair to Thomas Jefferson, February 10, 1791, in Carter, *Territorial Papers*, 3:323–37. For the necessity of Harrison working through the leading local men from Illinois and Vincennes, see James E. Davis, *Frontier Illinois* (Bloomington, IN, 1998), 113–21; and Cayton, *Frontier Indiana*, 228–44. The leading men from the Illinois Country were persistently frustrated by what they believed was Harrison's failure to do enough to introduce slavery into the territory.

10. Memorial and Petition of the Indiana Territorial Convention to Thomas Jefferson, December 28, 1802, WHH Papers, IHS. For the early assumptions about settlement and development under Article VI, see Onuf, *Statehood and Union*, 109–13. For complaints about the slow settlement of Indiana, see, e.g., Robert Morrison to Joseph Morrison, January 26 and December 1, 1805, IHS; Harrison to Jonathan Dayton, January 12, 1803, WHH Papers, IHS; John Bad-

ollet to Albert Gallatin, December 16, 1804, in Thornbrough, ed., *Correspondence of Badollet and Gallatin*, 40.

11. "1803 Legislative Petition," in Jacob Piatt Dunn, ed., "Slavery Petitions and Papers," *Indiana Historical Society Publications* (Indianapolis, 1894), 2:443–529, quote at 462. For the problems with Kentucky land titles, see Stephen Aron, *How the West Was Lost: The Transformation of Kentucky from Daniel Boone to Henry Clay* (Baltimore, 1996), 58–81. For the problems with Tennessee lands, see John R. Finger, *Tennessee Frontiers: Three Regions in Transition* (Bloomington, IN, 2001), 202–38. For Harrison's reforms of the territorial government, see Barnhart and Riker, *Indiana to 1816*, 334–41.

12. "Legislative Resolutions of 1807," in Dunn, "Slavery Petitions and Papers," 2:507; see also John Badollet to Albert Gallatin, December, 21, 1807, in Thornbrough, *Correspondence of Badollet and Gallatin*, 93; "Eumenes," *Liberty Hall and Cincinnati Mercury*, June 2, 1806; and Harrison to Jonathan Dayton, January 12, 1803, WHH Papers, IHS.

13. Francis S. Philbrick, ed., *The Laws of the Indiana Territory, 1801–1809* (Springfield, IL, 1930), 42–44, 136–39, 203–4. The indentured servant laws, passed in 1803 and revised in 1805 and 1807, gave slaves from states like Kentucky the "choice" of agreeing to an indenture in Indiana for a period of years or removal to a slave state, where they would presumably remain a slave for life. This distinction often proved meaningless, as indentures ran anywhere from ten to ninety-nine years. For an example of an indenture, see Daniel Owen, "Circumvention of Article VI of the Ordinance of 1787," *Indiana Magazine of History* 36 (March 1940): 110–16.

14. Historians sometimes claim that "the indentured servitude system in Indiana amounted to de facto slavery"; see Stephen Middleton, ed., *The Black Laws of the Old Northwest: A Documentary History*, Contributions in Afro-American and African Studies, No. 152 (Westport, CT, 1993), 160. See also Finkelman, *Slavery and the Founders*, 58–80. This is correct, but only in a limited sense. For more nuanced interpretations that recognize the failure of indentured servant laws to create a secure system of slavery, see Freehling, *Road to Disunion*, 138–41; and David Brion Davis, "The Significance of Excluding Slavery from the Old Northwest in 1787," *Indiana Magazine of History* 84 (March 1988): 75–89. For the distinction between "slave societies" and "societies with slaves," see Ira Berlin's masterful analysis in *Many Thousands Gone: The First Two Centuries of Slavery in North America* (Cambridge, MA, 1998); and Ira Berlin, *Generations of Captivity: A History of African-American Slaves* (Cambridge, MA, 2003).

15. Emma Lou Thornbrough counts eighty-six indentures in Knox and Vincennes counties, home to the greatest number of settlers (*The Negro in Indiana before 1900: A Study of a Minority*, Indiana Historical Collections, Vol. 37 [Indianapolis, 1957], 8–21). The actual number of slaves or servants was probably higher because not all slaveholders registered their slaves. For examples of servants gaining freedom, see the file Indenture between the Archer family

and Sampson and Eve, April 17, 1816, IHS; Inhabitants of Madison Indiana to his excellency Thomas Posey, October 14, 1814, William H. English Collection, IHS. In 1812, the antislavery politician John Badollet implored Albert Gallatin to use his influence to have President Madison appoint northern judges to Indiana so that servants would receive a favorable hearing in their freedom suits; see Badollet to Gallatin, April 8, 1812, in Thornbrough, *Correspondence of Badollet and Gallatin,* 225.

16. "A Citizen of Vincennes," *Western Sun,* April 22, 1809; "Benevolensus," *Liberty Hall,* July 14, 1806. Harrison, especially, understood the limits and risks of the indentured servant laws; see Harrison to Frederick Ridgely, May 24, 1807, and Harrison to James Henry, May 10, 1806, WHH Papers, IHS.

17. "Eumenes," *Liberty Hall,* August 11, 1806. The only mention of the indentured servitude laws in the William Henry Harrison Papers at the IHS is Harrison to Frederick Ridgely, May 24, 1807, and Harrison to James Henry, May 10, 1806, where Harrison is attempting to purchase slaves or servants. Similarly, while Robert Morrison repeatedly asked his brother in Philadelphia to assist him in both working for congressional suspension and encouraging settlement in the Illinois Country, Morrison made no reference to the indentured servant laws, instead focusing on suspension of Article VI; see Robert Morrison to John Morrison, January 22, January 25, and December 1, 1805, HIS.

18. John Badollet to Albert Gallatin, December 21, 1807, in Thornbrough, ed., *Correspondence of Badollet and Gallatin,* 92. In the 1804 election, voters were asked to decide if Indiana should enter the second stage of territorial government. From 1801 through 1805, Indiana was at the first stage of territorial government, which consisted of Harrison and three appointed judges. In 1805, Indiana entered the second stage of territorial government. This included an appointed upper council of five men and an elected lower assembly. But between 1805 and 1807 the lower assembly only contained between five and seven members and the vote for representatives was limited to freeholders. For the "politics of patronage" and disputes between the Illinois men and Harrison, see Cayton, *Frontier Indiana,* 226–44; and Davis, *Frontier Illinois,* 113–21.

19. Finkelman, *Slavery and the Founders,* 70.

20. "Partial Voting List and Election Return," December 9, 1802, William H. English Collection, Special Collections, University of Chicago Library. For the few mentions of slavery or the indentured servant laws, see the *Indiana Gazette* for August 14, 1805, which reported that a committee had been established "to examine into the propriety of enlarging the privilege of introducing bond servants of colour into this territory." The only mention of the proslavery "conventions" is found in "The Letters of Decius," a series of articles written in 1805 by an Illinois politician critical of Harrison's control of patronage and office. The author mentioned the "convention" only briefly, and criticized Harrison for exploiting it to gain support for his reappointment as governor;

see John Barnhart, ed., "Letters of Decius," in *Indiana Magazine of History* 43 (June 1947): 262–96. For the annual exchanges between Harrison and the assembly, see the *Western Sun* for August 22, 1807; *Speech Delivered by William Henry Harrison, . . . the 18th August, 1807* (Vincennes, 1807); the *Liberty Hall* for September 10, 1805 and December 2, 1806; *Journals of the General Assembly*, 38–47, 135–36, 137–38; and Esarey, *Governor's Messages and Letters*, 152–59. For accusations of deceit with the proslavery legislative petitions, from an antislavery member of the assembly, see "Memorial of Clark County Inhabitants to the U.S. Congress," October 10, 1807, in Dunn, "Slavery Petitions and Papers," 2:518–20; and John Badollet to Albert Gallatin, August 31, 1805; March 7 and December 21, 1807, in Thornbrough, *Correspondence of Badollet and Gallatin*, 49, 91, 102. For the failure to record the petitions as part of the proceedings, see *Journals of the General Assembly*, 101–8. The only publication of the petitions and laws is to be found in the Cincinnati newspaper *Liberty Hall*, which criticized them; see the *Liberty Hall* for December 10, 1806, February 17 and March 10, 1807. In Illinois, where some settlers actually did support slavery, petitions regularly included upward of two hundred signatures, but none of the Indiana petitions contained signatures; see Dunn, ed., "Slavery Petitions and Papers," 2:455–61, 483–91. For a Cincinnati editor's claim that Indianans would learn of the proslavery movement only from him, see the *Liberty Hall* for March 31, 1806.

21. John Badollet to Albert Gallatin, March 7, 1807, in Thornbrough, *Correspondence of Badollet and Gallatin*, 91; see also Badollet to Gallatin, August 31, 1805, December 21, 1807, in Thornbrough, *Correspondence of Badollet and Gallatin*, 49, 102; Judge Thomas Davis to John Breckinridge, January 26, 1806, in Carter, *Territorial Papers*, 2:335; and "Memorial of Clark County Inhabitants to the U.S. Congress," October 10, 1807, in Dunn, "Slavery Petitions and Papers," 2:518–20.

22. Dunn, "Slavery Petitions and Papers," 2:476, 461, 462, 469, 507; *Letter from William Henry Harrison, Governor of the Indiana Territory, inclosing certain resolutions passed by the Legislative Council and House of Representatives of the said Territory, relative to a suspension, for a certain period, of the sixth Article of compact* (Washington, 1807), LOC.

23. Dunn, "Slavery Petitions and Papers," 2:448, 456, 462. For earlier warnings, see Barthelemi Tardiveau to Arthur St. Clair, June 30, 1789, ASP, OHS; Barthelemi Tardiveau to the Continental Congress, July 8, 1788, and Major John Hamtramck to General Josiah Harmar, August 14, 1789, in Alvord, *Kaskaskia Records*, 485–88, 508–9. For the larger problems of settlement and Union in the Northwest, see Onuf, *Statehood and Union*; and Cayton, "Radicals in the 'Western World.'"

24. Dunn, "Slavery Petitions and Papers," 2:469, 500–501, 511.

25. Memorial and Petition of the Indiana Territorial Convention to Thomas Jefferson, December 28, 1802, WHH Papers, IHS; "Petition to Congress by Inhabitants of the Illinois Country," February 7, 1800, in Carter, *Territorial*

Papers, 3:76–77. This petition was forwarded to Harrison, who served as territorial delegate to Congress for the Northwest Territory at the time. For the ways in which a lack of federal power in the West drove some leading men into the arms of the British or Spanish, see Cayton, "'When Shall We Cease to Have Judases?' The Blount Conspiracy and the Limits of the Extended Republic," in *Launching the "Extended Republic": The Federalist Era*, ed. Ronald J. Hoffman and Peter J. Albert (Charlottesville, VA, 1996), 156–89.

26. For Harrison's career, see Cayton, *Frontier Indiana*, 167–95, 226–44; and Goebel, *William Henry Harrison*, 36–59. For an example of Harrison using his connections to gain the support of leading men in Washington early in his career, see Carter B. Harrison [William Henry's brother] to the Secretary of State, August 5, 1802, in Carter, *Territorial Papers*, 7:64–65. Harrison boasted of his "friends" in both parties; see Harrison to Jonathan Dayton, January 12, 1803, WHH Papers, IHS. For Jefferson's confidence in Harrison, see Jefferson to Harrison, April 28, 1805, in Esarey, *Governor's Messages and Letters*, 126–28. When Jefferson had to choose five men to occupy the seats in the Indiana legislative council, Jefferson sent Harrison blank commissions, instructing him to pick the five ablest men in the territory who were not speculators or Federalists.

27. John Rice Jones to Judge Davis, January 21, 1804, in Carter, *Territorial Papers*, 7:168–69; Memorial and Petition of the Indiana Territorial Convention to Thomas Jefferson, December 28, 1802, and Jefferson to Harrison, February 28, 1803, WHH Papers, IHS. For evidence that Jefferson's cabinet discussed the matter, and (excepting Gallatin) supported suspension, see Albert Gallatin to William Henry Harrison. September 27, 1809, in Thornbrough, *Correspondence of Badollet and Gallatin*.

28. Harrison to Jonathan Dayton, January 12, 1803, WHH Papers, IHS. For Dayton and Harrison's friendship, see Harrison to Dayton, October 29, 1804, WHH Papers, IHS. This was the same Jonathan Dayton who so passionately defended slavery in the Louisiana Purchase Territory. For other letters and petitions to northern politicians, see, e.g., Harrison to George Clinton [vice president of the United States, president of the Senate], October 13, 1807, WHH Papers, IHS.

29. Harrison to Thomas Worthington, October 26, 1803, TWP, OHS; John Rice Jones to Judge Davis, January 21, 1804, in Carter, *Territorial Papers*, 7:168–69; *Annals of Congress*, 8th Cong., 1st sess., 779, 1023–24.

30. Robert Morrison to Joseph Morrison, January 26, 1805, December 1, 1805, IHS; Shadrach Bond to Harrison, April 14, 1806, WHH Papers, IHS. The Morrisons also tried to lobby for suspension through William Duane's *Aurora and General Advertiser* (Philadelphia), but the plan backfired when Duane strongly rebuked suspension and slavery in the West (October 21, 1803).

31. *Liberty Hall*, January 6, 1806.

32. For historians' oversight, see Fehrenbacher, *Slaveholding Republic*, 256–59; Fehrenbacher, *Dred Scott Case*, 84–86; Onuf, *Statehood and Union*,

116–23; Cayton, *Frontier Indiana,* 244–52; and Freehling, *Road to Disunion,* 138–43.

33. See, e.g., Freehling, *Road to Disunion,* 138–43, 585n34. Explanations that rely on the generalized antislavery sentiments of "the founding fathers," however, fail to consider important sectional and partisan distinctions.

34. Finkelman, *Slavery and the Founders,* 67. Similarly, Duncan MacLeod concludes that "the efficacy of the sixth article in maintaining the territory free of slaves was due less to any determination to enforce it than the inertia created by the accident of its passage" (*Slavery, Race, and the American Revolution* [New York, 1974], 54).

35. For the expanded franchise, see *Annals of Congress,* 10th Cong., 1st sess., 1434, 1615–17; for salaries, see *Annals of Congress,* 9th Cong., 2nd sess., 476, 527; and 10th Cong., 1st sess., 1011. For the division of the territory, see *Annals of Congress,* 10th Cong., 1st sess., 2067; and 10th Cong., 2nd sess., 971, 1808.

36. Robert Morrison to Joseph Morrison, January 26, 1805, IHS. For other opposition to Indiana slavery at the national level, most of it from northern Republicans, see *Annals of Congress,* 8th Cong., 1st sess., 783; William Henry Harrison to Thomas Worthington, October 26, 1803, TWP, OHS; the *Liberty Hall* for June 2, July 14, and August 11, 1806; the *National Intelligencer* for March 7, 1806, reprinted in the *Liberty Hall* for March 31, 1806; John Badollet to Albert Gallatin, August 31, 1805, Harrison to Gallatin, August 29, 1809, and Gallatin to Harrison, September 27, 1809, in Thornbrough, *Correspondence of Badollet and Gallatin,* 49, 107–12, 113–14; and Thomas Randolph, "To the People of Indiana," in the *Western Sun* for February 25, 1809.

37. Dunn, "Slavery Petitions and Papers," 2:515–17. For the growing divisions between Harrison and the Illinois politicians, much of which was unrelated to slavery, see *Journals of the General Assembly,* 147, 153–54; and Barnhart and Riker, *Indiana to 1816,* 351.

38. Dunn, "Slavery Petitions and Papers," 2:518–20.

39. *Annals of Congress,* 10th Cong., 1st sess., 816; *Annals of Congress,* 8th Cong., 1st sess., 783.

40. "House Report on Slavery in Indiana," November 17, 1807, in Esarey, *Governor's Messages and Letters,* 275–76; *Annals of Congress,* 10th Cong., 1st sess., 816.

41. "Senate Report on Slavery in Indiana," November 13, 1807, in Esarey, *Governor's Messages and Letters,* 274–75; *Annals of Congress,* 10th Cong., 1st sess., 22, 23–27, 31.

42. Randolph, "To the People of Indiana," *Western Sun,* February 25, 1809; "Citizens of Indiana," *Western Sun,* April 22, 1809.

43. Judge Thomas Davis to John Breckinridge, January 26, 1806, in Carter, *Territorial Papers,* 3:335; Robert Morrison to Joseph Morrison, January 22, January 26, and December 1, 1805, IHS. For the petitions calling for separation and suspension, see "Memorial from Randolph and St. Clair Counties, 1805,"

"Memorial of Randolph and St. Clair Counties, January 17–1806," and "Petition of Randolph and St. Clair Counties, February 20, 1807," in Dunn, "Slavery Petitions and Papers," 2:483–91, 498–506, 510–12. For a good, brief analysis of the Indiana and Illinois factions' battles over patronage, office, and power, see Cayton, *Frontier Indiana*, 228–44.

44. Harrison to Jefferson, July 16, 1808, WHH Papers, IHS. For their alienation from Harrison, see Badollet to Gallatin, October 13, 1807, and Harrison to Gallatin, August 29, 1809, in Thornbrough, *Correspondence of Badollet and Gallatin*, 80; and Cayton, *Frontier Indiana*, 226–52.

45. Badollet to Gallatin, November 13, 1809, in Thornbrough, *Correspondence of Badollet and Gallatin*, 121; *Journals of the General Assembly*, 191–92. For the antislavery petitions, see *Journals of the General Assembly*, 183, 188, 189–90, 191–92.

46. *Journals of the General Assembly*, 191–92, 225; Badollet to Gallatin, November 13, 1809, in Thornbrough, *Correspondence of Badollet and Gallatin*, 121–22.

47. *Journals of the General Assembly*, 222; *Western Sun*, December 17, 1808. General Washington Johnston, the most vocal antislavery member of the legislature, claimed that the antislavery petitioners outnumbered the proslavery petitioners by "a majority of 600 and odd persons" (*Western Sun*, November 12, 1808).

48. Harrison to Jefferson, July 16, 1808, WHH Papers, IHS; John Rice Jones to Peter Jones, month of June 1808, in Carter, *Territorial Papers*, 7:578–79; "Report of General W. Johnston, Chairman of the Committee to which the Petitions on the Slavery Question had been Referred," in the *Western Sun* for December 17, 1808, also in Dunn, "Slavery Petitions and Papers," 2:522–27. Though Badollet had probably authored the report, the antislavery men attributed it to Johnston, who was a member of the assembly. For Badollet's authorship of the report, see Badollet to Gallatin, March 7 and November 13, 1809, and Harrison to Gallatin, August 29, 1809, in Thornbrough, *Correspondence of Badollet and Gallatin*, 104–5, 121, 107–8.

49. The assembly passed a bill repealing the indentured servant laws, but it died in the council, where the Harrison and proslavery Illinois men still held sway; see *Journals of the General Assembly*, 257, 289, 301; and the *Western Sun* for November 12, 1808.

50. "General Washington Johnston," *Western Sun*, February 4, 1809.

51. "A Citizen of Vincennes," *Western Sun*, May 13, 1809. For the transformation of territorial politics in neighboring Ohio, which stresses the importance of an expanded electorate and the primacy of issues and party over faction and personality, see Ratcliffe, *Party Spirit in a Frontier Republic*. For interpretations that stress the importance of competing elites and the underlying cultural assumptions that formed their appeal to voters, see Cayton, *Frontier Indiana*; and Andrew R. L. Cayton, *The Frontier Republic: Ideology and Poli-*

tics in the Ohio Country, 1780–1825 (Kent, OH, 1986). My understanding of territorial politics owes much to these two contrasting—though not necessarily incompatible—approaches.

52. "Electors Attend," *Western Sun,* November 19, 1808. See also General Washington Johnston's Circular Address, special edition to the *Western Sun* for November 15, 1808; "An Elector of Knox," in the *Western Sun* for November 26, 1808; and the antislavery petitions in the *Western Sun* for December 17, 1808.

53. "A Citizen of Vincennes," *Western Sun,* January 28, 1809. The letters signed by "A Citizen of Vincennes" appeared in most issues of the *Western Sun* between January and June 1809. Elias McNamee, John Badollet's brother-in-law, was apparently the main author of the pieces, with Badollet and Johnston providing assistance; see Thornbrough, *Correspondence of Badollet and Gallatin,* 119n6.

54. John Hadden, "To the Citizens of Knox County," *Western Sun,* March 25, 1809; "D. Sullivan," *Western Sun,* February 18, 1809. For an antislavery candidate's pledge, see William Bruce, "Fellow Citizens of Knox," in the *Western Sun* for May 6, 1809. For a proslavery attack on his pledge to oppose slavery, see Chrisley Crum, "To William Bruce," in the *Western Sun* for May 13, 1809.

55. "A Citizen of Vincennes," *Western Sun,* May 13, 1809; "Thomas Randolph," *Western Sun,* April 15, 1809. For the Harrison party's attempts to avoid the slavery question entirely, see Randolph, "To the People of Indiana," *Western Sun,* February 25, 1809; Amyntor," *Western Sun,* February 18, 1809; and "A Voter," in the *Western Sun* for April 22, 1809. General Washington Johnston's pledges to oppose slavery took the form of extended essays signed by him and "A Citizen of Vincennes"; see the *Western Sun* for February 4, February 11, and February 18, 1809, as well as March 11, April 22, and May 6, 1809. For the duel, see *Western Sun,* June 10, 1809; and Badollet to Gallatin, November 13, 1809, in Thornbrough, *Correspondence of Badollet and Gallatin,* 119–20.

56. "A Citizen of Vincennes," *Western Sun,* January 28, 1809; "A Farmer," in the *Western Sun* for January 28, March 4, and April 22, 1809; "General Washington Johnston, *Western Sun,* February 4, 1809; "Citizens of Indiana," in the *Western Sun* for May 13, 1809. For more on how the charges of Federalism infuriated Harrison, see Harrison to Gallatin, August 29, 1809, in Thornbrough, *Correspondence of Badollet and Gallatin,* 109–10.

57. "A Citizen of Vincennes," in the *Western Sun* for January 28, April 22, June 24, 1809; Randolph, "To the People of Indiana," *Western Sun,* February 25, 1809. Harrison also attributed defeat to the slavery question; see Harrison to Wilson Cary Nicholas, November 21, 1809, WHH Papers, IHS.

58. "Slim Simon," and "To G. W. Johnston," in the *Western Sun* for February 11, 1809; "A Citizen of Vincennes," *Western Sun,* February 11, 1809. For an additional defense of slavery that probably repelled far more voters than it attracted with its aristocratic overtones, see "Pop Gun," in the *Western Sun* for February 11, 1809.

59. "Slim Simon," and "To G. W. Johnston," *Western Sun*, February 11, 1809; "A Citizen of Vincennes," in the *Western Sun* for January 28, 1809; General Washington Johnston, February 18, 1809, *Western Sun.*

60. "An Elector of Knox," in the *Western Sun* for November 26, 1808; "A Citizen of Vincennes," *Western Sun*, May 6, 1809.

61. In 1809 Congress approved the division of the territory, creating separate Indiana and Illinois territories. This required creating new electoral districts in Indiana. Also, Randolph and Harrison charged Jennings with fraud and contested his election. The 1809 meeting of the legislature spent the better part of the session dealing with these two issues; see Barnhart and Riker, *Indiana to 1816*, 355–60.

62. Jonathan Jennings to John K. Gorham, December 24, 1809, in Dorothy Riker, ed., "Some Additional Jennings Letters," *Indiana Magazine of History* (June 1932): 149–278; Jonathan Jennings, *An Address to the Citizens of the Indiana Territory* (Chillicothe, OH, 1810), Pamphlet Collection, IHS.

63. "Constitution of the State of Indiana," *Niles' Weekly Register* (Baltimore), October 4, 1817. For the request and the Enabling Act, see the *Niles' Weekly Register* for January 20, 1816; the *Western Sun* for January 27, 1816; and Charles Kettleborough, ed., *Constitution Making in Indiana: A Source Book of Constitutional Documents . . . , 1780–1851*, Indiana Historical Collections, Vol. 1 (Indianapolis, 1916), 69–77. By 1816, antislavery literature unconnected to the Jennings party was circulating in Indiana; see A Citizen of Ohio [Alexander Mitchell], *An Address to the Inhabitants of the Indiana Territory, on the Subject of Slavery* (Hamilton, OH, 1816), IHS; Benjamin Whitson, *African Slavery Turned Upside Down* (Lexington, IN, 1815), IHS; and *Constitution of the Columbian United Abolition Society, . . . Held at Eaton, 1816 . . . To which is prefixed, An Address to the People of the States of Ohio and Indiana, On the Subject of Slavery* (Cincinnati, 1816), OHS. For a weak plea to permit slavery in the state, which focused exclusively on the "charity" of diffusion, see "A Citizen of Gibson," in the *Western Sun* for March 2, 1816.

64. Matthew Lyon to James Madison, January 26, 1810, in Carter, *Territorial Papers*, 14:365. For slavery in late-territorial and early-statehood Illinois, see Onuf, *Statehood and Union*, 123–30; Finkelman, *Slavery and the Founders*, 74–77; Suzanne Cooper Guasco, "'The Deadly Influence of Negro Capitalists': Southern Yeoman and Resistance to the Expansion of Slavery in Illinois," *Civil War History* 47 (March 2001): 7–29; James Simeone, *Democracy and Slavery in Frontier Illinois: The Bottomland Republic* (Dekalb, IL, 2000); Davis, *Frontier Illinois*, 165; and John Reda, "Illinois Slavery Reconsidered: The Significance of the Northwest Ordinance," paper delivered at the Society for Historians of the Early American Republic Conference, Columbus, Ohio, July 2003.

65. "One of the People," *Western Intelligencer* (Kaskaskia, IL), April 15, 1818. The few vocal antislavery whites in Illinois opposed statehood for this reason; see "Caution," in the *Western Intelligencer* for April 15, 1818. For the battles over slavery in late-territorial and early-statehood Illinois, see Onuf, *Statehood and*

Union, 123–30; Finkelman, *Slavery and the Founders*, 74–77; Guasco, "'Deadly Influence of Negro Capitalists'"; Simeone, *Democracy and Slavery in Frontier Illinois*; Davis, *Frontier Illinois*, 165; and Reda, "Illinois Slavery Reconsidered."

66. *Annals of Congress*, 15th Cong., 2nd sess., 306–11.

7. Making the "Free Northwest"

1. *National Intelligencer* (Washington, DC), September 16, 1816, from the *Compiler* (Richmond, VA); *National Register* (Washington DC), September 28, 1816; for its reprinting in the Northwest, see, e.g., *Express and Republican Standard* (Zanesville, OH), October 31, 1816.

2. Daniel Drake, *Natural and Statistical View, or Picture of Cincinnati and the Miami country* (Cincinnati, 1815), 170, 26, 27, and Daniel Drake, *Notices Concerning Cincinnati* (Cincinnati, 1810), 30, UKSC; Alfred Tischendorf and E. Taylor Parks, eds., *The Diary and Journal of Richard Clough Anderson, Jr., 1814–1825* (Durham, NC, 1964), 31–32, 68. Anderson made these observations in 1815 and 1817.

3. Through the early 1820s, Illinois remained markedly different from Ohio and Indiana with regard to slavery, as many white settlers in Illinois continued to support efforts to introduce slavery there. Public debate over slavery in Illinois tended to focus on the best way to evade Article VI so that Illinois could introduce slavery. It was only between 1818 and 1824 that a sizeable number of Illinois settlers began vocally opposing slavery. Furthermore, settlers in Ohio and Indiana tended to self-consciously ignore Illinois in their celebrations of the "free Northwest." This chapter, therefore, excludes Illinois and focuses on Ohio and Indiana instead. For the prevalence of proslavery sentiment in late-territorial and early-statehood Illinois, and challenges to slavery after 1818, see Paul Finkelman, *Slavery and the Founders: Race and Liberty in the Age of Jefferson*, 2nd ed. (Armonk, NY, 2001), 74–77; Suzanne Cooper Guasco, "'The Deadly Influence of Negro Capitalists': Southern Yeoman and Resistance to the Expansion of Slavery in Illinois," *Civil War History* 47 (March 2001): 7–29; James Simeone, *Democracy and Slavery in Frontier Illinois: The Bottomland Republic* (Dekalb, IL, 2000); James E. Davis, *Frontier Illinois* (Bloomington, IN, 1998); and John Reda, "Illinois Slavery Reconsidered: The Significance of the Northwest Ordinance," paper delivered at the Society for Historians of the Early American Republic Conference, Columbus, Ohio, July 2003.

4. In the many histories of the trans-Appalachian West, historians stress both the differences and similarities characterizing the states north and south of the Ohio River. Though these works tend to assume a natural animosity toward slavery among settlers in the Northwest, they often trace this animosity to sources other than slavery. For a Turnerian analysis, which attributes the emergence of "democratic values" like individualism and local control in the Northwest to the weakness of the plantation system, see John D. Barhart's still

valuable *Valley of Democracy: The Frontier versus the Plantation in the Ohio Valley, 1775–1818* (Bloomington, IN, 1953). For an examination of regional identity from the perspective of commerce, see Kim M. Gruenwald, *River of Enterprise: The Commercial Origins of Regional Identity in the Ohio Valley, 1790–1850* (Bloomington, IN, 2002). For the impact of upland southerners on the Northwest's antebellum political culture, along with important differences within the Northwest itself, see Nicole Etchison, *The Emerging Midwest: Upland Southerners and the Political Culture of the Old Northwest, 1787–1861* (Bloomington, IN, 1996). For the ways that contrasting northern and southern cultural styles clashed, see Andrew R. L. Cayton, "Land, Power, and Reputation: The Cultural Dimension of Politics in the Ohio Country," *William and Mary Quarterly* 47 (April 1990): 266–86. For the important ways in which a stronger federal presence created a unique Northwest, see Andrew R. L. Cayton, "'Separate Interests' and the Nation-State: The Washington Administration and the Origins of Regionalism in the Trans-Appalachian West," *Journal of American History* 79 (June 1992): 39–67; and Andrew R. L. Cayton, "Radicals in the 'Western World': The Federalist Conquest of Trans-Appalachian North America," *Federalists Reconsidered*, ed. Doron Ben-Atar and Barbara B. Oberg (Charlottesville, VA, 1998), 77–97. For northern and southern settlers' shared racism, see Eugene Berwanger, *The Frontier against Slavery: Western Anti-Negro Prejudice and the Slavery Extension Controversy* (Urbana, IL, 1967), 7–29. For historiographical summaries of the literature on regional identity in the Ohio Valley and the Northwest, see Andrew R. L. Cayton, "Artery and Border: The Ambiguous Development of the Ohio Valley in the Early Republic," *Ohio Valley History* 1 (Spring 2001): 1–19; and Andrew R. L. Cayton and Peter S. Onuf, *The Midwest and the Nation: Rethinking the History of an American Region* (Bloomington, IN, 1990), 17–24.

5. On the construction of local, regional, and national identities in the early republic, see David Waldstreicher, *In the Midst of Perpetual Fetes: The Making of American Nationalism, 1776–1820* (Chapel Hill, NC, 1997), 246–94; and Andrew R. L. Cayton's review of *In the Midst of Perpetual Fetes*, "We Are All Nationalists, We Are All Localists," *Journal of the Early Republic* 18 (1998): 521–28.

6. For the tendency to explain hostility toward slavery as a combination of upland southerners who hated both blacks and planters, and northerners who possessed a general bias against slavery, see Berwanger, *Frontier against Slavery*; Barnhart, *Valley of Democracy*; Etchison, *Emerging Midwest*; and Stephen A. Vincent, *Southern Seed, Northern Soil: African-American Farm Communities in the Midwest, 1765–1900* (Bloomington, IN, 1999). These works tend to read antebellum racism backward into the early nineteenth century. For a cautionary note against overgeneralizing about the importance of settlers' sectional origins, see Cayton and Onuf, *Midwest and the Nation*, 25–29. For farmers and slavery in Missouri and Kentucky, see chapter 4. For northern migrants readily adapting to slavery in Kentucky, see *Annals of Congress*, 15th

Cong., 2nd sess., 1190; and John Corlis Jr. (Bourbon County, Kentucky) to John
Corlis Sr. (Providence, Rhode Island), March 14, July 29, August 1, September 6, and September 19, 1816, Corlis-Respress Family Papers, FHS. Indiana's
proslavery territorial delegate to Congress, Benjamin Parke, hailed from New
Jersey. Robert Morrison, one of six brothers who settled in Kaskaskia and led
the Illinois proslavery group, was from Philadelphia.

7. Carlos R. Allen Jr., ed., "David Barrow's Circular Letter of 1798," *William
and Mary Quarterly* 20 (July 1963): 440–51, quote at 450; James Smith, "Tours
into Kentucky and the Northwest Territory: Three Journals by the Rev. James
Smith of Powahatan County, Va., 1783–1795–1797," *Ohio State Archeological
and Historical Quarterly* 16 (1907): 375, 376–77, 381. For evangelicals' inability
to force passage of some type of gradual abolition in Kentucky, see Stephen
Aron, *How the West Was Lost: The Transformation of Kentucky from Daniel
Boone to Henry Clay* (Baltimore, 1996), 89–95; and Andrew Lee Feight, "James
Blythe and the Slavery Controversy in the Presbyterian Churches of Kentucky,
1791–1802," *Register of the Kentucky Historical Society* 102 (Winter 2004):
13–38. For background on southern evangelicals in the Northwest, see James
David Essig, *The Bonds of Wickedness: American Evangelicals against Slavery,
1770–1808* (Philadelphia, 1982); and Andrew Lee Feight, "The Good and the
Just: Slavery and the Development of Evangelical Protestantism in the Ameri-
can South, 1700–1830" (Ph.D. diss., University of Kentucky, 2001), 247–78. For
the numerous antislavery congregations in early Ohio, see Ellen Eslinger, "The
Evolution of Racial Politics in Early Ohio," in *The Center of a Great Empire:
The Ohio Country in the Early Republic*, ed. Andrew R. L. Cayton and Stuart
D. Hobbs (Athens, OH, 2005), 81–104.

8. David Barrow Diary, June 15, 1795, Typescript, Special Collections, KHS;
Smith, "Tours into Kentucky and the Northwest Territory," 376; William Williams, *Journal of the Life, Travels, and Gospel Labours of William Williams*
[Indiana, 1828], 171, UKSC; Frederick Bonner to Edward Dromgoole, July
19, 1807, in William Warren Sweet, ed., *Religion on the American Frontier,
1783–1840* (Chicago, 1931), 4:170–71; William Warren Sweet, ed., *The Rise of
Methodism in the West, being the Journal of the Western Conference, 1800–1811*
(Nashville, TN, 1920), 16. For other evangelicals who expressed deep gratitude for being led into a region free of slavery, see John Sale to Dromgoole,
February 20, 1807, Peter Pelham to Dromgoole, June 20, 1807, and Frederick
Bonner to Dromgoole, July 19, 1807, in Sweet, *Religion on the American Fron-
tier*, 4:159, 165, 171. For the antislavery appeal of the Northwest to southern-
born "Quakers and other religious professors" opposed to slavery, see Thomas
Ashe, *Travels in America performed in 1806, for the purpose of exploring the
rivers, Alleghany, Monongahela, Ohio, and Mississippi* (Newburyport, MA,
1808), 90. For the contrasting experiences of evangelicals who remained in the
South, see Christine Leigh Heyrman, *Southern Cross: The Beginnings of the
Bible Belt* (Chapel Hill, NC, 1997), 68–69, 92–94, 138–39, 155–56; and Feight,
"The Good and the Just," 247–78.

9. John Cleves Symmes to Charles W. Short, April 9, 1810, Short-Henry Papers, IHS; John Badollet to Albert Gallatin, December 21, 1807, in Gayle Thornbrough, ed., *The Correspondence of John Badollet and Albert Gallatin*, Indiana Historical Society Publications, Vol. 22 (Indianapolis, 1963), 93; *Memorandums of a Tour Made By Josiah Espy in the States of Ohio and Kentucky and Indiana Territory in 1805* (Cincinnati, 1870), 23.

10. "A Citizen," *Scioto Gazette* (Chillicothe, OH), August 21, 1802; "To Slim Simon," in the *Western Sun* (Vincennes, IN) for February 18, 1809; A Citizen of Ohio [Alexander Mitchell], *An Address to the Inhabitants of the Indiana Territory, on the Subject of Slavery* (Hamilton, OH, 1816), IHS, 19; "Memorial of Clark County Inhabitants to the U.S. Congress," October 10, 1807, in Jacob Piatt Dunn, ed., "Slavery Petitions and Papers," *Indiana Historical Society Publications* (Indianapolis, 1894), 2:518–20; "Charge to the Grand Jury," in the *Scioto Gazette and Fredonian Chronicle* for September 24, 1819. For preachers' appeals to southern migrants, see, e.g., Philip Gatch to Edward Dromgoole, February 11, 1802, in Sweet, *Religion on the American Frontier*, 4:152.

11. "Petition to the Territorial Legislature," October 19, 1808, in Clarence E. Carter, ed., *Territorial Papers of the United States*, 28 vols. (Washington, DC, 1934–1975), 7:603–5; Drake, *Natural and Statistical View*, 27; John Melish, *Travels through the United States of America, in the Years 1806 & 1807, and 1809, 1810, & 1811* (rpt., Philadelphia, 1818), 428.

12. Daniel C. [Hopkins?] to Daniel C. Banks, March 5, 1817, Daniel C. Banks Papers, FHS; William M. Meigs, *Life of Josiah Meigs* (Philadelphia, 1887); *Western Spy and Hamilton Gazette* (Cincinnati), July 10, 1813.

13. See, e.g., Andrew Miller, *New States and Territories . . . , in 1818* (Keene, NH, 1819), OHS; Samuel R. Brown, *The Western Gazetteer; or, Emigrant's Directory, Containing a Geographical Description of the Western States and Territories* (Auburn, NY, 1817), UKSC; Joseph Scott, *A Geographical Dictionary of the United States of North America: Containing a General Description of Each State. With a Succinct Account of Indiana, and the Upper and Lower Louisiana Territories* (Philadelphia, 1805), HSP/LCP; Jedidiah Morse, *The American Geography, or, a View of the Present Situation of the United States of America* (London, 1794), 463.

14. Amos Stoddard, *Sketches, Historical and Descriptive, of Louisiana* (Philadelphia, 1812), 343, HSP/LCP. For similar claims that the absence of slavery promised greater prosperity and freedom, see, e.g., Drake, *Natural and Statistical View*; Drake, *Notices Concerning Cincinnati*; Thaddeus Mason Harris, *The Journal of a Tour into the Territory Northwest of the Allegheny Mountains; Made in the Spring of the Year 1803* (Boston, 1805), UKSC; E[dmund] Dana, *Geographical Sketches on the Western Country: Designed for Emigrants and Settlers* (Cincinnati, 1819); Melish, *Travels through the United States*; John Bradbury, *Travels in the Interior of America, in the Years 1809, 1810, and 1811; including a description of upper Louisiana, together with the states of Ohio, Kentucky, Indiana, and Tennessee, with the Illinois and western territories*

(London, 1817), UKSC; Morris Birkbeck, *Notes on a Journey in America: From the coast of Virginia to the Territory of Illinois* (London, 1818), UKSC; Ashe, *Travels in America performed in 1806;* James Tongue, *A letter addressed to the people of Maryland, giving a short account of the country on the south shore of Lake Erie, . . . showing the advantages it offers to the middling people of Maryland to emigrate* (Washington, 1807), LCP; the *Evening Fireside* (Philadelphia), December, 21, 1805; and *Historical Register of the United States,* Vol. 1, *Of the State Governments* (Philadelphia, 1812), 11.

15. Estwick Evans, *A Pedestrious Tour of Four Thousand Miles through the Western States and Territories during the Winter and Spring of 1818* (Concord, NH, 1819), 173; John Stillman Wright, *Letters from the West: Or a Caution to Emigrants* (Salem, NY, 1819), 40–41. For similar portraits of slavery, see Ashe, *Travels in America performed in 1806,* 90, 182–83; Stoddard, *Sketches, Historical and Descriptive,* 331–38; and Birkbeck, *Notes on a Journey in America,* 6–19, 22–23, 49.

16. For Wheeling's importance in the domestic slave trade in the early republic, see Allan Kulikoff, "'Uprooted Peoples': Black Migrants in the Age of the American Revolution, 1790–1820," in *Slavery and Freedom in the Age of the American Revolution,* ed. Ira Berlin and Ronald Hoffman (Charlottesville, VA, 1983), 143–71. For the ways that witnessing the horrors of slavery contributed to northerners' opposition to slavery, see James L. Huston, "The Experiential Basis of the Northern Antislavery Impulse," *Journal of Southern History* 56 (November 1990): 609–40. For Lundy, see Merton L. Dillon, *Benjamin Lundy and the Struggle for Negro Freedom* (Urbana, IL, 1966), 5. For Ohio newspapers and the slave trade, see, e.g., the *Western Spy* for July 10, 1802, July 25, 1817; and the *Liberty Hall and Cincinnati Mercury* for January 15 and January 22, 1805, January 13, 1806.

17. *Western Spy,* August 26, 1801; Jonathan Basset to Beriah Tilton, March 25, 1815, Manuscripts, CHS. For a similar incident where slaves murdered slave traders on the Ohio, see the *Scioto Gazette* for November 12, 1803.

18. Harris, *Journal of a Tour into the Territory Northwest,* 357–58; Nathaniel Dike to John Dike, July 4, 1816, Nathaniel Dike Letters, 1816–1818, OHS; James McBride, "Journey to Lexington, Kentucky, by James McBride of Hamilton, Ohio, Related in a Letter to Margaret Poe, 1810," *Quarterly Publication of the Historical and Philosophical Society of Ohio* 5 (1910): 21–26, quote at 25.

19. Daniel C. Banks Diary, December 13, 1815 (Ohio), January 20, 1816 (Louisville), Daniel C. Banks Papers, FHS.

20. [Jas.?] W. Pearce to General Jonathan Clark, March 30, 1811, Bodley-Clark Papers, FHS; Daniel Drake, *Pioneer Life in Kentucky, 1785–1800* (Cincinnati, 1870; rpt., New York, 1948), 206–7; Samuel Meredith to John C. Breckinridge, October 24, 1800, BFP, LOC; Philip Gatch to Edward Dromgoole, June 1, 1805, in Sweet, *Religion on the American Frontier,* 4:155–56. For middling families' hiring of slaves from planters, see Drake, *Pioneer Life,* 93; John Corlis Jr. to John Corlis Sr., July 29, August 1, and September 6, 1816,

Corlis-Respress Family Papers, FHS. For Kentuckians advising relatives to purchase slaves in Virginia before migrating to Kentucky, see the undated journal entries written sometime before 1804 in the Journal of Charles Julian, 1800–1818, UKSC. For an excellent description and analysis of the traumas and hardships experienced by slaves forced to the West, see Ira Berlin, *Generations of Captivity: A History of African-American Slaves* (Cambridge, MA, 2003), 159–244.

21. Abel Westfall to Thomas Worthington, December 27, 1801, TWP, OHS; Daniel Symmes to Nathaniel Massie, February 20, 1803, Nathaniel Massie Papers, OHS; David Dodge to William Lytle, September 28, 1803, Lytle Papers, CHS; Lee Ludwell to William Lytle, March 5, 1809, Lytle Papers, CHS; Robert P. Henry to John F. Henry, January 10, 1815, Short-Henry Papers, IHS.

22. John Corlis Jr. to John Corlis Sr., March 14 and September 16, 1816, Corlis-Respress Family Papers, FHS; Robert Todd to William Lytle, January 4, 1808, Lytle Papers, CHS.

23. John Lorain, *Hints to Emigrants, or, A Comparative Estimate of the Advantages of Pennsylvania, and of the Western Territory* (Philadelphia, 1819), 77–79, HSP/LCP; Elias Pym Fordham, *Personal Narrative of Travels in Virginia, Maryland, Pennsylvania, Ohio, Indiana, Kentucky; and of a Residence in the Illinois Territory: 1817–1818* (rpt., Cleveland, 1906), 209–11.

24. Edouard de Montule, *Travels in America, 1816–1817*, trans. Edward D. Seeber (Bloomington, IN, 1950), 129.

25. This self-image of a free Northwest accorded closely with the democratic world described in Gordon Wood, *The Radicalism of the American Revolution* (New York, 1991), 229–369.

26. Waller Taylor, "To The People of the Indiana Territory," June 17, 1812, Broadside Collection, ISL; James Crawford, in the *Scioto Gazette* for September 4, 1802; "A Citizen," in the *Scioto Gazette* for August 21, 1802; "Another Citizen of Gibson," in the *Western Sun* for March 30, 1816; [Mitchell], *An Address to the People of the Indiana Territory*, 9; the *Liberty Hall* for July 21, 1806; "A Lover of Truth," in the *Liberty Hall* for June 2, 1806.

27. Badollet to Gallatin, January 1, 1806, in Thornbrough, *Correspondence of Badollet and Gallatin*, 64–65; General Washington Johnston's Report, *Western Sun*, December 17, 1808; John Cleves Symmes to Charles W. Short, April 9, 1810, Short-Henry Papers, IHS; Drake, *Notices Concerning Cincinnati*, 30; Drake, *Natural and Statistical View*, 167.

28. Smith, "Tours into Kentucky and the Northwest Territory," 376–77, 381.

29. John Sale to Edward Dromgoole, February 20, 1807, and Philip Gatch to Edward Dromgoole, June 1, 1805, in Sweet, *Religion on the American Frontier*, 4:160, 157; Ephraim Brown to Silas Brown, November 19, 1807, Silas Brown Papers, 1805–1817, LOC.

30. "The Friends of Humanity," in the *Western Spy* for July 31, 1802; "Yellow Jacket," in the *Scioto Gazette* for September 18, 1802; "Nathan Guilford's address at the Presbyterian Church, July 4, 1817," in the *Western Spy* for July 11, 1817.

31. "A Friend to Truth," *Western Sun,* August 26, 1809; *Niles' Weekly Register,* January 20, 1816; *Western Sun,* January 27, 1816; Drake, *Natural and Statistical View,* 26–27.

32. For the importance of territorial politics and constitution-making in shaping the Northwest's political institutions and culture, see Cayton and Onuf, *Midwest and Nation;* and Cayton, "Land, Power, and Reputation." For popular politics and the importance of political rituals in shaping political culture, along with regional and national identities, see Simon P. Newman, *Parades and the Politics of the Street: Festive Culture in the Early American Republic* (Philadelphia, 1997); and Waldstreicher, *In the Midst of Perpetual Fetes.* For the importance of racism in northwestern antislavery politics after 1820, see Guasco, "'Deadly Influence of Negro Capitalists'"; and Berwanger, *Frontier against Slavery.*

33. "A Lover of Truth," in the *Liberty Hall* for July 21, 1806; "Clark County [Indiana] Petition, October 10, 1807, in Dunn, "Slavery Petitions and Papers," 2:443–529, quote at 520. Abolitionist historiography has stressed the religious and social sources and expressions of abolitionism to the exclusion of politics and ideology. For three important exceptions that recognize what Charles Sellers deems an "uncompromisingly egalitarian credo" among abolitionists, see Daniel J. McInerney, "'A Faith for Freedom': The Political Gospel of Abolition," *Journal of the Early Republic* 11 (Autumn 1991): 371–93; Paul Goodman *Of One Blood: Abolitionism and the Origins of Racial Equality* (Berkeley, 1998); and Richard S. Newman, *The Transformation of American Abolitionism: Fighting Slavery in the Early Republic* (Chapel Hill, NC, 2002). For a more general discussion of changing religious beliefs and practices in the wake of the political changes produced by the American Revolution, see Nathan O. Hatch, *The Democratization of American Christianity* (New Haven, CT, 1989).

34. *Constitution of the Columbian United Abolition Society . . . Held at Eaton, 1816 . . . To which is prefixed, An Address to the People of the States of Ohio and Indiana, On the Subject of Slavery* (Cincinnati, 1816), 5, OHS; Thomas H. Genin, *An Oration, Delivered before the Semi-annual Meeting of the Union Humane Society, held in Mount Pleasant, Ohio, May 14th, 1818* (Mount Pleasant, OH, 1818), 5, UKSC; [Mitchell], *An Address to the People of the Indiana Territory,* 12–15. Antislavery literature from Kentucky also circulated in Ohio; see, e.g., "Minutes of the Kentucky Abolition Society," in the *Weekly Recorder* (Chillicothe) for June 7, 1815.

35. Genin, *An Oration,* 35, 36; [Mitchell], *An Address to the People of the Indiana Territory,* 8; Benjamin Whitson, *African Slavery Turned Upside Down* (Lexington, IN, 1815), IHS. For a similar, earlier critique of slavery that combined religious and political principles, see "A Lover of Truth," in the *Liberty Hall* for July 21, 1806.

36. *Constitution of the Union Humane Society, St. Clairsville,* 1816, n.p., CHS. The *Western Herald and Steubenville Gazette* published the Union Hu-

mane Society's constitution in three successive issues, April 5, April 12, and April 19, 1816; see also Union Humane Society, Proceedings, CHS.

37. Union Humane Society, Proceedings, CHS; "Corpus Collosom," *Liberty Hall*, July 14, 1806. In addition to the *Western Herald* publishing the Union Humane Society's constitution, the editor also encouraged subscribers to take subscriptions to Lundy's *The Philanthropist;* see the *Western Herald* for September 19, 1817. For Lundy, see Dillon, *Benjamin Lundy.* For other religious organizations opposed to slavery, see *Constitution of the Female Association of Cincinnati for the Benefit of Africans* (Cincinnati, 1817); Female Association of Cincinnati for the Benefit of Africans, Proceedings and Reports, CHS; *Weekly Recorder,* June 7, 1815; *Constitution of the Columbian United Abolition Society,* OHS; and "The Humane Society, north west of the River Ohio," in the *Western Spy* for August 18, 1800. For newspaper articles that can only be called abolitionist, see the long series of essays that appeared in the *Western Spectator* (Marietta) between March 5, 1811, and February 8, 1812; and "Agricola," in the *Western Herald* for July 25, 1807. For religious leaders marshaling their adherents into political contests, see *Constitution of the Columbian United Abolition Society,* 6, OHS; Genin, *An Oration;* and Philip Gatch to Edward Dromgoole, February 11, 1802, in Sweet, *Religion on the American Frontier,* 4:152.

38. "Querist," *Freeman's Journal* (Cincinnati), March 5, 1799; "The Humane Society, North West of the River Ohio," *Western Spy,* August 18, 1800; *Scioto Gazette,* July 10, 1802; "Statement of John Browne, in the *Western Spy* for July 31, 1802. For Republicans, see, e.g., "A Farmer," *Western Spy,* July 24, 1802; "The Friends of Humanity," *Western Spy,* July 31, 1802; and "A Republican," *Western Spy,* September 25, 1802. For Federalists, see "Speech of Governor St. Clair at Cincinnati," [August or September 1802], ASP, OHS.

39. *Liberty Hall,* January 13, 1806, January 15, 1805. For reprints of articles from other papers on the horrors of slavery, see the *Liberty Hall* for December 4, 1804, January 22, February 19, and December 2, 1805. Browne also printed antislavery books and pamphlets for sale at his printing office; see the *Liberty Hall* for November 19, 1805, January 6, 1806. For other antislavery pieces unrelated to Indiana or the slave trade, see, e.g., *Liberty Hall,* June 2 and July 21, 1806. Cincinnati's other major newspaper, the *Western Spy,* also reprinted articles detailing the horrors of southern slavery; for examples, see "On the Slave Trade," in the *Western Spy* for July 10, 1802; "Something New," *Western Spy,* July 24, 1802; "Extract from a letter from a member of the Humane Society of Virginia, 1791," *Western Spy,* September 4, 1802; and "Negro Slavery," in the *Western Spy* for July 25, 1817. The argument that northern and northwestern Republicans were the willing racist dupes of southern slaveholders who controlled the Republican Party needs qualification. For Northwest and northern Republican racism, see Berwanger, *Frontier against Slavery,* 7–29; and Finkelman, *Slavery and the Founders,* 105–28.

40. *Liberty Hall,* June 2, 1806. For slavery in Indiana see, e.g., the *Liberty*

Hall for December 2, September 17, 1805, January 6, March 31, June 2, July 14, July 21, August 11, and December 10, 1806, February 17 and March 10, 1807. For a Federalist essay cautioning against too rapid expansion, in part because it would increase the black population, see the *Liberty Hall* for October 22, 1805.

41. "Meeting of the citizens of Sycamore Township, in the town of Montgomery," *Liberty Hall,* July 28, 1807; "The Mechanics of Neville, Clermont County," in the *Liberty Hall* for July 21, 1817; *Liberty Hall,* July 7, 1807.

42. *Inquisitor and Cincinnati Advertiser,* July 7, 1818; *Western Spy,* August 7, 1807; *Western Herald,* July 12, 1816.

43. "To the Electors of the First Congressional District," broadside dated October 1, 1816, OHS; the *Liberty Hall* for July 14, 1816.

44. *Barret v. Jarvis* (1818), in Benjamin Tappan, *Cases Decided in the Courts of Common Pleas in the Fifth Circuit of the State of Ohio, Commencing with May Term, 1816* (Steubenville, OH, 1831; rpt., Norwalk, OH, 1899), 212–15; Daniel Feller, "A Brother in Arms: Benjamin Tappen and the Antislavery Democracy," *Journal of American History* 88 (June 2001): 48–74; *The Trial of Charles Vattier, Convicted of the Crimes of Burglary and Larceny, for Stealing from the Office of the Receiver of Public Monies, for the District of Cincinnati* (Cincinnati, 1807), 31, 56, UKSC; the *Liberty Hall* for April 28 and August 4, 1807, June 23, 1808. Historians have produced regrettably little work on free and runaway blacks in Ohio prior to 1820; see, e.g., Eslinger, "Evolution of Racial Politics in Early Ohio," which demonstrates that white Ohioans generally tolerated free black settlers and runaways who sought freedom.

45. "State of Ohio v. Thomas D. Carneal," in the *Liberty Hall* for June 16 and June 30, 1817.

46. *Liberty Hall,* June 16 and June 30, 1817; *Western Herald,* July 25, 1817; the *Muskingum Messenger* (Zanesville) for July 17, 1817.

47. Governor Gabriel Slaughter to Governor Thomas Worthington, September 4, 1817, UKSC; Worthington to Slaughter, October 23, 1817, KHS; and *Acts of Kentucky, 1816–1817,* 282, KHS. It was even more difficult to recover alleged fugitives in Indiana. The 1816 Act to Prevent Manstealing drastically exceeded the federal Fugitive Slave Act of 1793 and made the recovery of a fugitive slave in Indiana a long, costly, and difficult process that placed a much higher burden of proof on slave catchers than on alleged fugitives, who were required to provide testimony before a grand jury and judge who would decide their fate. This, not surprisingly, provoked a controversy between Indiana and Kentucky; see the *Indiana House Journal,* 1816–1817 (housed at the Indiana State Archives, Indiana Division, ISL), 11; *Laws of Indiana,* 1st sess., 1816, 150–52; *Laws of Indiana,* 3rd sess., 1819, 64; and *Indiana House Journal,* 1819–1820, 360–62. After a long-standing conflict with Kentucky, Indiana rescinded the law in 1824.

48. James Flint, *Letters from America, Containing Observations* (Edinburgh, Scotland, 1822; rpt., Cleveland, OH, 1904), 166–67; Hezekiah Conn, in

the *Western Herald* for April 12, 1816, January 31, 1817. For similar threats, see the warning of James Riddle in the *Western Spy* for June 27, 1817.

49. "Jacob Kounts v. ——," *Western Spy,* May 30, 1817; *Inquisitor and Cincinnati Advertiser,* July 14, 1818. For earlier concerns about kidnappings, see the *Western Spy* for July 17, 1802. For the increase in kidnappings in Indiana, along with resistance to it by both blacks and whites, see Wright, *Letters from the West,* 30–31; "Inhabitants of Madison Indiana to his excellency Thomas Posey, October 4, 1814," William H. English Collection, IHS.

50. *Muskingum Messenger,* September 24, 1817; *Liberty Hall,* November 10, 1817; *Ohio House Journal,* 1817–1818, 294, OHS.

51. *Muskingum Messenger* for May 30, 1816, July 18, 1816; *Western Herald,* July 19, 1816; *Liberty Hall,* July 5, 1816. See also the *Express and Republican Standard* for July 25, 1816; and "Ohio Governor's Message to the Legislator" in the *National Register* (Washington, DC) for January 4, 1817. Due to the greater strength of the proslavery forces in Illinois, Ohio newspapers remained largely silent about that territory's movement to statehood.

52. "An Elector of Knox," *Western Sun,* November 26, 1808; "A Citizen of Vincennes," *Western Sun,* February 11 and May 13, 1809.

53. "A Friend to Truth," *Western Sun,* August 26, 1809; "Petition to the Territorial Legislature," October 19, 1808, in Carter, *Territorial Papers,* 7:603–5; "General Washington Johnston's Report to the Legislature," in the *Western Sun* for December 17, 1808.

54. "Petition to Congress by Citizens of Harrison County," 1809, in Carter, *Territorial Papers,* 7:703–4. The Clark County petitioners requested Harrison's replacement by a governor, "who in Sentiment is opposed to Slavery"; see "Petition to the President and Senate by Citizens of Clark County, 1809," in Carter, *Territorial Papers,* 7:705–7.

55. Taylor, "To The People of the Indiana Territory," June 17, 1812, Broadside Collection, ISL; Thomas Posey to Gen[eral] Gibson, March 13, 1813, William H. English Collection, IHS; Thomas Posey to Fayette Posey, January 17, 1814, Posey Papers, IHS.

56. "Another Citizen of Gibson," *Western Sun,* March 30, 1816.

57. [Mitchell], *An Address to the People of the Indiana Territory,* 18–19.

58. *National Intelligencer* for September 16, 1816, from the *Compiler;* the *Western Spy* for July 10, 1813.

8. "The States or Territories Which May Hereafter Be Admitted into the Union"

1. For Lincoln's criticism of popular sovereignty, see Don Fehrenbacher, *The Slaveholding Republic: An Account of the United States Government's Relations to Slavery* (New York, 2001), 276–92.

2. The literature on the Missouri Controversy is immense. The standard,

but dated account remains Glover Moore, *The Missouri Controversy, 1819–1821* (Lexington, KY, 1953). For three accounts that challenge Moore on many important points, see Robert P. Forbes, "Slavery and the Meaning of America, 1819–1833" (Ph.D. diss., Yale University, 1994); Matthew Mason, *Slavery and Politics in the Early American Republic* (Chapel Hill, NC, 2006), 177–212; and Joshua Michael Zeitz, "The Missouri Compromise Reconsidered: Antislavery Rhetoric and the Emergence of the Free Labor Synthesis," *Journal of the Early Republic* 20 (Autumn 2000): 447–85. Mason contains a valuable survey of the many issues beyond expansion that the Missouri Controversy raised; see *Slavery and Politics*, 177–212. As recent works have demonstrated, northern Republicans initiated and led much of the opposition to slavery in Missouri. Moreover, while Federalists, like Rufus King of New York, tended to focus on extending the three-fifths clause to Missouri, Republicans instead tended to frame the conflict as a struggle between slavery and freedom. For the partisan dimensions of opposition to Missouri slavery, see Sean Wilentz, "Jeffersonian Democracy and the Origins of Political Antislavery in the United States: The Missouri Controversy Revisited," *Journal of the Historical Society* 4 (2004): 375–401; Sean Wilentz, *The Rise of American Democracy: Jefferson to Lincoln* (New York, 2005), 218–35; Leonard Richards, *The Slave Power: The Free North and Southern Domination, 1780–1860* (Baton Rouge, 2000), 52–82; and Jonathan H. Earle, *Jacksonian Antislavery and the Politics of Free Soil, 1824–1854* (Chapel Hill, NC, 2004). For an immensely valuable reading of the controversy as a conflict between slavery and freedom, see Major L. Wilson *Space, Time, and Freedom: The Quest for Nationality and the Irrepressible Conflict, 1815–1861* (Westport, CT, 1974), 22–48.

3. *Saratoga Sentinel* (Saratoga Springs, NY), December 22, 1819.

4. Following Moore in *Missouri Controversy,* historians narrowly focus on northern efforts to restrict slavery in Missouri; see, e.g., Don Fehrenbacher, *The Dred Scott Case: Its Significance in American Law and Politics* (New York, 1978): "Neither northerners nor southerners were at this point prepared to insist, on moral or constitutional grounds, that all federal territory should be uniformly closed or uniformly open to slavery" (115). However, northern restrictionists called for a comprehensive ban on slavery in all new states and territories, while southern expansionists denied that the federal government possessed any authority to restrict slavery. In short, the Missouri Controversy became a fundamental debate about the place of slavery in an expanding continental Union. See also "Town Meeting," in the *Liberty Hall and Cincinnati Gazette* for December 21, 1819.

5. George Hay to James Monroe, February 12, 1819, James Monroe Papers, LOC.

6. "Representative William Hendricks to His Constituents," *Western Sun* (Vincennes, IN), April 25, 1818; "A Bill for the Government of the Territory of Louisiana," February 7, 1805, and "An Act for the Government of the Territory of Louisiana," March 3, 1805, in Clarence E. Carter, ed., *The Territorial Papers*

of the United States, 28 vols. (Washington, DC, 1934–1975), 13:87–89, 92–95; *Annals of Congress*, 12th Cong., 1st sess., 1248; *Annals of Congress*, 16th Cong., 1st sess., 336–37; Carter, *Territorial Papers*, 14:552–59.

7. The postwar prospects for the Union and expansion are well covered in James E. Lewis Jr., *The American Union and the Problem of Neighborhood: The United States and the Collapse of the Spanish Empire, 1783–1829* (Chapel Hill, NC, 1998), 69–125; and Reginald Horsman, "The Dimensions of an 'Empire for Liberty': Expansion and Republicanism, 1775–1825," *Journal of the Early Republic* 9 (Spring 1989): 1–20. For the generally optimistic postwar mood among white Americans, see C. Edward Skeen, *1816: American Rising* (Lexington, KY, 2003). For the Fourteenth Congress's ambitious agenda, which gave the federal government a more active role in promoting economic development to strengthen the bonds of union further still, see John Lauritz Larson, *Internal Improvement: National Public Works and the Promise of Popular Government in the Early United States* (Chapel Hill, NC, 2001), 109–48; and Charles Sellers, *The Market Revolution: Jacksonian America, 1815–1846* (New York, 1991), 34–102.

8. Lewis, *American Union and the Problem of Neighborhood*, 69–125. As Lewis cautions, statesmen, diplomats, and leading congressmen like Henry Clay continued to express concerns about the still unstable future of the Union in the West.

9. In general, the best analysis of increased attention on slavery between 1815 and 1818 is Mason, *Slavery and Politics*, 75–176. For the Middle Atlantic Antislavery Societies' efforts to secure black freedom, see Richard S. Newman, *The Transformation of American Abolitionism: Fighting Slavery in the Early Republic* (Chapel Hill, NC, 2002), 39–85. For similar efforts in the Ohio Valley, see the works cited in chapter 7, as well as Minutes of the February 14 and May 14, 1817, meetings, Union Humane Society, Proceedings, CHS. In December 1818, after it was discovered that slave traders were conning and coercing New Jersey free blacks and term slaves into Louisiana slavery, two New Jersey Republicans proposed legislation restricting the sale of slaves out of states with gradual abolition laws; see *Annals of Congress*, 15th Cong., 2nd sess., 75–76, 336–37; and Frances D. Pingeon, "An Abominable Business: The New Jersey Slave Trade, 1818," *New Jersey History* 109 (Fall–Winter 1991): 15–35. For the larger concerns about the spread of slavery in the nation that the New Jersey smuggling incident generated, see the *National Intelligencer* (Washington, DC) for December 21, 1818. For the popularity of James Riley's *Authentic Narrative of the Loss of the American Brig Commerce*, see Donald Ratcliffe, "Captain James Riley and Antislavery Sentiment in Ohio, 1819–1824," *Ohio History* 81 (Spring 1972): 76–94. For Amelia Island, see Fehrenbacher, *Slaveholding Republic*, 150–52. For the Fugitive Slave Law, see *Annals of Congress*, 15th Cong., 1st sess., 225–26, 231–38, 241–54, 257–58. For congressional attention on the international slave trade, see *Annals of Congress*, 15th Cong., 2nd sess., 442–43, 2544–45; and the *Richmond Enquirer* for January 9, 1819.

10. *Annals of Congress,* 15th Cong., 1st sess., 1675–76; *Annals of Congress,* 15th Cong., 2nd sess., 305–11. For other concerns about slavery in the West, see *Annals of Congress,* 15th Cong., 2nd sess., 547; *Minutes of the Proceedings of . . . Fifteenth American Convention for Promoting the Abolition of Slavery and Improving the Condition of the African Race . . . December, 1818* (Philadelphia, 1818), 42–43; *National Intelligencer,* September 16, 1816; and *National Register* (Washington, DC), September 28, 1816.

11. Tallmadge's motives were far less sordid and political than Moore claims in *Missouri Controversy,* 36–40; see Richards, *Slave Power,* 52–54; and Forbes, "Slavery and the Meaning of America," 140–41.

12. Moore wrongly claims that the Missouri question was of little interest to the nation as a whole, except for the brief enthusiasm that the Federalists generated and then used as a cloak to regain power (see *Missouri Controversy*). For correctives, see Mason, *Slavery and Politics,* 177–212; and Zeitz, "Missouri Compromise Reconsidered." For a northern Republican calling for "freely expressed" public discussion of the question, see, e.g., Ephraim Bateman to his constituents, *New Jersey Journal* (Elizabethtown), April 27, 1819; and *Washington Whig* (Bridgeton, NJ), March 15, 1819. For actual public discussions of the question, see, e.g., "Petition & Memorial, of a Committee appointed by the Republican electors of Woodbridge Township . . . October 18, 1819," *Washington Whig,* November 22, 1819.

13. For references to an empire for slavery, see, e.g., "Meeting at New York," in the *Niles' Weekly Register* (Baltimore) for February 20, 1819; and *Annals of Congress,* 15th Cong., 2nd sess., 1207.

14. *Annals of Congress,* 16th Cong., 1st sess., 335; *Centinel of Freedom* (Newark, NJ), December 28, 1819; *Niles' Weekly Register,* August 14 and October 2, 1819. For other warnings that unrestricted slavery in Missouri would soon extend the institution across the entire trans-Mississippi West, see, e.g., "From the Rhode Island American," in the *Niles' Weekly Register* for December 20, 1819; "Resolution of the Legislature of Pennsylvania," in the *Niles' Weekly Register* for January 1, 1820; the *Niles' Weekly Register* for August 14, 1819; the speech of James Tallmadge, *Annals of Congress,* 15th Cong., 2nd sess., 1206; the speech of John Sergeant, *Annals of Congress,* 16th Cong., 1st sess., 1214; the *American Watchman* (Wilmington, DE) for December 22, 1819; and the *Patriot* (Concord, NH) for December 28, 1819.

15. *Patriot,* November 30, 1819; *Centinel of Freedom,* December 28, 1819. For other suggestions that halting expansion in Missouri was the first step toward slavery's "speedy and gradual abolition," see, e.g., the *Aurora and General Advertiser* (Philadelphia) for November 23, 1819.

16. *Western Herald and Steubenville Gazette,* July 1, 1820; *Aurora,* May 16, 1820; *Annals of Congress,* 16th Cong., 1st sess., 1182, 1180; *Centinel of Freedom,* November 30, 1819. For other references to the "principles of slavery" and the "principles of republicanism," see, e.g., the *Centinel of Freedom* for December 28, 1819; the *Niles' Weekly Register* for March 11, 1820; "Meeting at Boston," and

"From a Philadelphia Paper," in the *Niles' Weekly Register*, Supplement, vol. 17, 242; "Benjamin Rush," in the *National Intelligencer* for November 9, 1819; "The Meeting at New York," in the *National Intelligencer* for November 22, 1819; "From a Philadelphia Paper," in the *Niles' Weekly Register* for December 11, 1819; *Niles' Weekly Register*, November 27, 1819; *Liberty Hall*, December 3 and December 21, 1819; and the *Connecticut Courant* (Hartford) for December 7, 1819. For southern expansionists' acceptance that they defended the "principles of slavery," see the Kentucky legislature resolution in the *Kentucky Reporter* for January 4, 1820; and in the *Niles' Weekly Register* for January 22, 1820. For criticisms that the South had strayed from its republican and antislavery principles, see Jonathan Roberts to Matthew Roberts, February 16, 1820, Jonathan Roberts Papers, HSP; *Niles' Weekly Register*, January 8 and January 29, 1820; and the speech of New Hampshire Republican William Plumer, *Annals of Congress*, 16th Cong., 1st sess., 1430.

17. John Eppes to James Barbour, May 3, 1820, in Lyon G. Tyler, ed., "Missouri Compromise: Letters to James Barbour, Senator of Virginia in the Congress of the United States," *William and Mary Quarterly* 10 (July 1901): 5–24, quote at 23.

18. [New Hampshire Senator David Morril], *Annals of Congress*, 16th Cong., 1st sess., 294; [Pennsylvania Representative William Darlington], *Annals of Congress*, 16th Cong., 1st sess., 1375; A Philadelphian [Robert Walsh], *Free Remarks on the Spirit of the Federal Constitution, the Practice of the Federal Government, and the Obligations of the Union, Respecting the Exclusion of Slavery from the Territories and New States* (Philadelphia, 1819), 99; Daniel Raymond, *The Missouri Question* (Baltimore, 1819), 3–4.

19. *Annals of Congress*, 15th Cong., 2nd sess., 1210.

20. *Annals of Congress*, 15th Cong., 2nd sess., 1171–74; *Annals of Congress*, 16th Cong., 1st sess., 164, 243, 279–93, 322, 1029, 1174–1222, 1282–87, 1506. For southern attacks on Article VI and the Northwest Ordinance more generally, see *Annals of Congress*, 15th Cong., 2nd sess., 1001–2, 1179, 1198; and *Annals of Congress*, 16th Cong., 1st sess., 322. Southern claims that Article VI and the Northwest Ordinance amounted to "an act of illegitimate power" on the part of the federal government made the threat of expansion seem far more local and immediate in the Northwest. For fears that southern congressmen might try to force slavery on the Northwest, see, e.g., the *Western Herald* for October 21, 1820; and *Annals of Congress*, 16th Cong., 1st sess., 1174–1201, 1205–18.

21. *Annals of Congress*, 16th Cong., 2nd sess., 281–82. For similar praises of Article VI by northwestern congressmen, see, e.g., *Annals of Congress*, 16th Cong., 1st sess., 1205–18.

22. "Resolutions of the Pennsylvania Legislature," in the *Niles' Weekly Register* for January 1, 1820; "Benjamin Rush," in the *National Intelligencer* for November 4, 1819; the *Centinel of Freedom* for November 23, 1819. The Pennsylvania legislature, among others, directed its congressmen to apply the exact wording of Article VI to all future states or territories admitted to the Union,

beginning with Missouri. For congressional attempts to apply Article VI to the trans-Mississippi West, see *Annals of Congress*, 16th Cong., 1st sess., 158, 732, 733–34, 801–4, 1566–67.

23. [Walsh], *Free Remarks*. For a synopsis and praise of Walsh's *Free Remarks*, see the *Niles' Weekly Register* for January 8, 1820. For King's speech, see the *Niles' Weekly Register* for December 4, 1819. This was not exactly a novel argument. Geographers and others who wrote about the West prior to the Missouri Controversy often concluded that the federal government permitted expansion only out of necessity, and only where slavery already existed; see, e.g., John Melish, *Travels through the United States of America, in the Years 1806 & 1807, and 1809, 1810, & 1811* (rpt. Philadelphia, 1818), 388; A Citizen of Ohio [Alexander Mitchell], *An Address to the Inhabitants of the Indiana Territory, on the Subject of Slavery* (Hamilton, OH, 1816), 19; and Amos Stoddard, *Sketches, Historical and Descriptive, of Louisiana* (Philadelphia, 1812), 338, HSP/LCP.

24. [Walsh], *Free Remarks*, 6, 9, 43; *Annals of Congress*, 16th Cong., 1st sess., 179; *Niles' Weekly Register*, January 8, 182. For other examples of an antislavery and anti-expansionist past, see, e.g., *Annals of Congress*, 16th Cong., 1st sess., 125, 126, 141–42, 1349–51; "The Missouri Question," in the *Observer* (Concord, NH) for February 14, 1820; "Report of a Committee of the Delaware Society," in the *American Watchman* for December 15, 1819; "Legislature of Pennsylvania," in the *Niles' Weekly Register* for January 1, 1820; [Lemuel Shaw], "Slavery and the Missouri Question," *North American Review*, January 1820; and *Memorial to the Congress of the United States, on the Subject of Restraining the Increase of Slavery in New States . . . the Inhabitants of Boston* (Boston, 1819).

25. *Annals of Congress*, 16th Cong., 2nd sess., 1395; *Annals of Congress*, 15th Cong., 2nd sess., 1182; [Walsh] *Free Remarks*, 24, 32, 33. For other appeals to the principles of the Declaration of Independence, see, e.g., "From a Philadelphia Paper," *Niles' Weekly Register*, December 11, 1819; and *Annals of Congress*, 15th Cong., 2nd sess., 1210. Northern congressmen also used Jefferson's *Notes on the State of Virginia* (1781–82) to oppose slavery; see *Annals of Congress*, 16th Cong., 1st sess., 150, 155–56, 957, 1011–12, 1135, 1399–1402, 1427–28. Northern use of the Declaration of Independence and Jefferson's *Notes* especially rankled southern expansionists; see, e.g., *Annals of Congress*, 16th Cong., 1st sess., 227, 269, 301, 325, 405, 1004, 1071. For restrictionists' creation of an antislavery constitution, see *Annals of Congress*, 16th Cong., 1st sess., 1189, 1379, 1395–97, 1423; the *Western Herald* for September 9, 1820; *Memorial to the Congress of the United States*, 15; and [Walsh], *Free Remarks*. The best analysis of the Constitution's "open-ended" stance on slavery, which allowed such wildly divergent readings of the Constitution, is Fehrenbacher, *Slaveholding Republic*, 15–48. For an insightful reading of northern Republicans' understanding of constitutionalism and slavery, see Wilson, *Space, Time, and Freedom*, 23.

26. "Resolutions of the Pennsylvania Legislature," *Niles' Weekly Register*,

January 1, 1820; *Annals of Congress,* 16th Cong., 1st sess., 281, 292; *Annals of Congress,* 15th Cong., 2nd sess., 1208; *Saratoga Sentinel,* December 1, 1819.

27. "Wilmington Meeting," and "The Delaware Resolutions of the Delaware General Assembly," in the *Niles' Weekly Register* for January 22, 1820. For resolutions from northern public meetings and state legislatures calling on Congress to prohibit the "further extension of slavery in all states and territories hereafter admitted to the Union," see, e.g., "From the Rhode Island American," in the *Niles' Weekly Register* for December 20, 1819; "Resolutions of the Pennsylvania Legislature," in the *Niles' Weekly Register* for January 1, 1820; "From a Philadelphia Paper," in the *Niles' Weekly Register* for December 11, 1819; "Resolutions of the New Jersey Legislature," in the *Niles' Weekly Register* for January 22, 1820; "Resolutions of the House of Assembly of New York," in the *Niles' Weekly Register* for February 5, 1820; "Resolutions of the New Hampshire Legislature," in the *Niles' Weekly Register* for July 8, 1820; "The Citizens of the State of New Jersey at a meeting at Trenton," in "Benjamin Rush," in the *National Intelligencer* for November 9, 1819; *Memorial to the Congress of the United States;* "Town Meeting," in the *Liberty Hall* for December 21, 1819; "From the Connecticut Mirror: Slavery," in the *Connecticut Courant* for December 7, 1819; "Petition & Memorial, of a Committee appointed by the Republican electors of Woodbridge Township . . . October 18, 1819," in the *Washington Whig* for November 22, 1819; "Meeting at Camden," in the *Washington Whig* for December 20, 1819; "Meeting at Westchester, Pennsylvania," in the *American Watchman* for December 18, 1819; "Meeting at Keene, New Hampshire," in the *Concord Observer* for December 20, 1819; "Resolutions of New Haven, Connecticut," *Annals of Congress,* 16th Cong., 1st sess., 69–70; "Memorial of Newport, Rhode Island," *Annals of Congress,* 16th Cong., 1st sess., Appendix: 2454–58; Horton Howard to Micajah T. Williams, December 31, 1819, Micajah T. Williams Papers, OHS; *Ohio Senate Journal,* 1820, 145–147, 154, 169, OHS; *Ohio House Journal,* 1820, 166, 176, 198–99, OHS; and "Public Meeting; Respecting Slavery, Trenton, New Jersey," Broadside, TJP, LOC. For congressional proposals "prohibiting by law the introduction of slaves into the territories of the United States west of the Mississippi," see *Annals of Congress,* 16th Cong., 1st sess., 158, 732, 733–34, 801–4, 1566–67.

28. "Meeting at New York," *National Intelligencer,* November 22, 1819. "Meeting at New York," *National Intelligencer,* November 22, 1819.

29. *Annals of Congress,* 15th Cong., 1st sess., 1672, 1675–76; *St. Louis Enquirer,* February 5, 1820. For southern disgust with mass meetings in the North, see, e.g., the *National Intelligencer*'s comments on a New York City restrictionist meeting in the November 20, 1819 issue; the *Richmond Enquirer*'s comments on meetings in various New England towns in the December 16, 1819 issue; and the speech of Mississippi representative Christopher Rankin, *Annals of Congress,* 16th Cong., 1st sess., 1343.

30. John Tyler to Dr. Henry Curtis, February 5, 1820, John Tyler Papers, Presidential Papers Series, LOC; *Annals of Congress,* 16th Cong., 1st sess., 303.

Southern expansionists were well aware that northern restrictionists called for prohibiting expansion throughout the remainder of the United States; see, e.g., the *Richmond Enquirer* for November 20 and December 3, 1819; "Ego Tism," in the *Richmond Enquirer* for December 16, 1819; *Annals of Congress*, 16th Cong., 1st sess., 832; and George Hay to James Monroe, February 12, 1820, James Monroe Papers, LOC. For southern politicians' belief that the silence of the southern white electorate reflected widespread public support against restrictions, see *Annals of Congress*, 16th Cong., 1st sess., 99, 1457–58.

31. For efforts to consolidate and strengthen white control over slavery prior to the Missouri Controversy, see Mason, *Slavery and Politics*, 158–76; Ira Berlin, *Many Thousands Gone: The First Two Centuries of Slavery in North America* (Cambridge, MA, 1998), 217–356; Ira Berlin, *Generations of Captivity: A History of African-American Slaves* (Cambridge, MA, 2003), 97–158; Jeffrey Young, *Domesticating Slavery: The Master Class in Georgia and South Carolina, 1670–1837* (Chapel Hill, NC, 1999); Christine Leigh Heyrman, *Southern Cross: The Beginnings of the Bible Belt* (Chapel Hill, NC, 1997); Phillip Hamilton, "Revolutionary Principles and Family Loyalties: Slavery's Transformation in the St. George Tucker Household of Early National Virginia," *William and Mary Quarterly* 55 (October 1998): 531–56; Douglas R. Egerton, "'Its Origins Are Not a Little Curious': A New Look at the American Colonization Society," *Journal of the Early Republic* 5 (Winter 1985): 463–80; Douglas R. Egerton, *Charles Fenton Mercer and the Trial of National Conservatism* (Jackson, MS, 1989); and Douglas Ambrose, "Of Stations and Relations: Proslavery Christianity in Early National Virginia," in *Religion and the Antebellum Debate over Slavery*, ed. John R. McKivigan and Mitchell Snay (Athens, GA, 1998), 35–67.

32. "Cato," *National Intelligencer*, December 4, 1819; *Annals of Congress*, 16th Cong., 1st sess., 162. For other defenses of slavery and southern republicanism, see, e.g., the speeches of Representatives Benjamin Hardin of Kentucky and Ballard Smith of Virginia, and Senator William Pinkney of Maryland, *Annals of Congress*, 16th Cong., 1st sess., 1071–72, 1005–6, 408–10. For an extreme defense of slavery and slave society, see the speech of Senator William Smith of South Carolina, *Annals of Congress*, 16th Cong., 1st sess., 266–70. For a defense of slavery as a Christian institution that only strengthened great republics, see "An American," in the *Richmond Enquirer* for January 1, 1820.

33. "Limner," *National Intelligencer*, November 3, 1819; *Annals of Congress*, 16th Cong., 1st sess., 412. The concept of the United States as a slaveholders' republic is best developed in Fehrenbacher, *Slaveholding Republic*.

34. Randolph Macon to Bolling Hall, February 13, 1820, Hall Family Papers, Alabama Department of History and Archives; *Annals of Congress*, 16th Cong., 1st sess., 303, 407, 1004; Linn Banks to James Barbour, February 20, 1820, in Tyler, "Letters to James Barbour," 20. Again, for the Constitution's ambiguous commitment to slavery, see Fehrenbacher, *Slaveholding Republic*, 15–47.

35. *Annals of Congress*, 16th Cong., 1st sess., 322–23, 165, 263–65, 1029–30; "Missouri Question," *Richmond Enquirer*, February 26, 1820; *Annals of Con-*

gress, 16th Cong., 1st sess., 262–63, 229. For other southern congressmen's claims that precedent in no way favored restriction, see, e.g., *Annals of Congress,* 16th Cong., 1st sess., 319, 1071–73, 1221.

36. *Annals of Congress,* 15th Cong., 2nd sess., 1188; *Annals of Congress,* 16th Cong., 1st sess., 165. For similar arguments, see, e.g., the *Richmond Enquirer* for February 25, 1819, February 10, 1820; "An American," in the *Richmond Enquirer* for January 18, 1820; and the speech of Thomas Cobb of Georgia, *Annals of Congress,* 15th Cong., 2nd sess., 1436.

37. For Jefferson and diffusion during the Missouri Crisis, see William W. Freehling, *The Road to Disunion,* Vol. 1, *Secessionists at Bay, 1776–1854* (New York, 1990), 150–57. While Jefferson certainly seems to have hoped that diffusion would lead to gradual emancipation, Freehling greatly overstates the support this position received among other southern politicians. James Madison was the only other southern politician who devoted any serious attention to the links between diffusion and gradual emancipation; see Drew R. McCoy, *The Last of the Fathers: James Madison and the Republican Legacy* (New York, 1989), 253–322.

38. *Western Monitor* (Lexington, KY), February 8, 1820; *Annals of Congress,* 16th Cong., 1st sess., 133; "An American," *Richmond Enquirer,* November 23 and November 30, 1819; see also, "Cato," in the *National Intelligencer* for December 4, 1819; the *National Intelligencer* for August 25 and November 27, 1819, January 29, 1820; and "From the National Intelligencer," and "State of Missouri," in the *Richmond Enquirer* for February 25, 1819. See also George Hay to James Monroe, December 24, 1819, James Monroe Papers, LOC. Hay, the author of the "American" essays, was President Monroe's son-in-law, and he wrote the essays with Monroe's knowledge. For the reality of forced western migration for slaves, see Berlin, *Generations of Captivity,* 159–243.

39. *Annals of Congress,* 15th Cong., 2nd sess., 1184–91; *Annals of Congress,* 16th Cong., 1st sess., 133, 335, 1024–25; "An American," *Richmond Enquirer,* November 23 and November 30, 1819; "Cato," *National Intelligencer,* December 4, 1819. For some southern politicians' repudiation of federal power after 1815, which extended far beyond slavery and focused on matters like internal improvements and the Bank of the United States, see Larson, *Internal Improvement,* 109–48; and Sellers, *Market Revolution,* 103–71.

40. *Annals of Congress,* 16th Cong., 1st sess., 1211.

41. George Hay to James Monroe, February 12, 1820, James Monroe Papers, LOC. For the deals, pressures, and haranguing that led to the two compromises, see Forbes, "Slavery and the Meaning of America," 202–90; Richards, *Slave Power,* 83–88; and Wilentz, "Missouri Crisis Revisited." Forbes shows that southern politicians, including President James Monroe and the director of the Bank of the United States, Langdon Cheves, put intense pressure on certain northerners like Jonathan Roberts to support the compromises.

42. *Statutes at Large,* 16th Cong., 1st sess., 548; *Annals of Congress,* 16th Cong., 1st sess., 732, 733–34, 801–4, 1566–67. For expansionists' doubts that

the phrase "forever prohibited" was binding, see, e.g., John Quincy Adams's discussion of the cabinet meeting, in Charles Francis Adams, ed., *Memoirs of John Quincy Adams: Comprising Portions of His Diary from 1795 to 1848*, 12 vols. (Philadelphia, 1874–77), 5:14–15; the speech of Senator Joseph Hemphill of Pennsylvania, *Annals of Congress*, 16th Cong., 1st sess., 1133; and the *Richmond Enquirer* for March 7, 1820. See especially the efforts of *Niles' Weekly Register* to convince northerners that the restriction would indeed be "forever" (see February 26 and March 11, 1820).

43. *Richmond Enquirer*, March 7, 1820.

Epilogue

1. Don Fehrenbacher, *The Slaveholding Republic: An Account of the United States Government's Relations to Slavery* (New York, 2001), 292–94.

2. "Governor Sargent's Address to the Inhabitants of this Territory," August 18, 1798, in Dunbar Rowland, ed., *Mississippi Territorial Archives, 1798–1819* (Nashville, TN, 1905); John W. Gurley to the Postmaster General [forwarded to Jefferson], July 14, 1804, in Clarence E. Carter, ed., *The Territorial Papers of the United States*, 28 vols. (Washington, DC, 1934–1975), 9:305.

3. For the ways that federal officials became agents of the slaveholders' regime in the lower Mississippi Valley, see Ira Berlin, *Generations of Captivity: A History of African-American Slaves* (Cambridge, MA, 2003), 163–65; and Adam Rothman, *Slave Country: American Expansion and the Origins of the Deep South* (Cambridge, MA, 2005), 37–70, 119–62.

4. James M. McPherson, *Battle Cry of Freedom: The Civil War Era* (New York, 1988), quote at 106. For southern interest in the Caribbean and the "Golden Circle," see McPherson, *Battle Cry of Freedom*, 105–16; Robert E. May, *The Southern Dream of a Caribbean Empire* (Baton Rouge, 1973); and Robert E. May, *Manifest Destiny's Underworld: Filibustering in Antebellum America* (Chapel Hill, NC, 2002). For slaveholders' designs for southern California, see Fehrenbacher, *Slaveholding Republic*, 292–94.

INDEX

61; Enabling Bill (1819), 154;
River, 63; River Valley, 3, 58, 62;
Territory, 53, 55, 57–58, 148, 152,
156; whites, 55–57, 58–59, 64, 65,
66, 68, 69, 70, 71, 73, 74–75
Missouri Compromise, 8, 171
Missouri Controversy, 3–4, 5, 6, 7,
8, 42–43, 56, 65, 66–67, 125, 126,
148, 151, 153, 154, 155, 156, 157,
161–62, 164, 165, 167, 170, 171, 172,
201n42, 228n4
Missouri Crisis, 53, 67–68, 75, 150–
51, 195–96n59
*Missouri Gazette and Public
Advertiser* (St. Louis), 68–69
Missouri Intelligencer (Franklin),
69, 70
Morris, Robert, 99
Morrison, Joseph, 108, 213n30
Morrison, Robert, 108, 211n17,
213n30, 219–20n6
Monroe, James, 235n38
Mount Pleasant: Baptist Association,
70–71; Quaker community, 145
Mulatto Militia Battalion, Louisiana,
47

Natchez (Miss.), 31, 33, 121;
conspiracies, 19–20; Country,
15; Indian Rebellion, 16, 33;
Northwest Ordinance in, 21, 23;
whites, 15, 21, 22, 23, 29. *See* also
Mississippi, Territory
Natchez Indian Rebellion, 16, 33
Natchez Indians, 16
National Intelligencer (Washington,
D.C.), 124, 141, 166
Native Americans, 11, 102, 147; and
British allies, 79, 105; nations, 6,
16, 28, 32, 101, 105. *See also under
names of Indian nations*
New Market Township Republican
Society, 86–87

New Mexico Territory, 171–72
New Orleans, 31, 32, 33–34, 35,
40, 47, 48, 49, 54, 152. *See also*
Orleans Territory
New York, 63, 101
Niles' Weekly Register, 70, 153
non-slaveholders, 17, 42, 43, 72, 74,
128, 128, 132, 135. *See also* settlers:
non-slaveholding
North Carolina, 2, 10, 11, 17, 58, 59;
Cession Act (1789), 10, 11
northern: politicians, 7–8, 110,
111, 122–23, 138, 151, 155, 158,
159–60, 162, 166–67, 171;
states, 2; sympathizers, 68.
See also Federalists, northern;
Republicans, northern;
restrictionists; settlers, northern
northerners, 65–66, 69, 127, 131–32,
151, 154, 155, 156, 158, 159–61, 163,
164, 166, 167; antislavery, 97
Northwest, 3, 4, 5, 6, 7, 24, 32, 58–59,
95, 99, 100, 101, 105, 106, 110, 111,
121, 122, 133–34, 158, 165, 169–70;
borderlands, 100, 104–5; free, 58–
59, 111, 124, 125, 127, 133, 134, 135,
218n3; Old, 77, 155, 158; Territory,
17, 27, 28, 36, 52, 79, 80, 81, 106,
195–96n59, 203n14, 208n3
Northwest Ordinance (1787;
including Article VI), 1–2, 3, 4,
9, 10, 11, 13, 23, 26, 28, 31, 32, 39,
42–43, 46–47, 50–51, 52, 57, 61,
78, 80, 81–82, 95, 96, 97–98, 99,
101–2, 103, 105, 106, 107, 108, 109,
110–11, 112, 113, 115, 116, 120, 121,
122, 123, 125, 127, 128, 129, 136, 137,
140, 143, 148, 157–58, 159, 163, 169,
171, 218n3
northwesterners, 132, 134, 137–38,
148
Northwest Indian confederacy,
78–79, 99

Jeffersonian America

Jan Ellen Lewis and Peter S. Onuf, editors
Sally Hemings and Thomas Jefferson: History, Memory, and Civic Culture

Peter S. Onuf
Jefferson's Empire: The Language of American Nationhood

Catherine Allgor
*Parlor Politics: In Which the Ladies of Washington Help Build a City and a
    Government*

Jeffrey L. Pasley
"The Tyranny of Printers": Newspaper Politics in the Early American Republic

Herbert E. Sloan
Principle and Interest: Thomas Jefferson and the Problem of Debt (reprint)

James Horn, Jan Ellen Lewis, and Peter S. Onuf, editors
The Revolution of 1800: Democracy, Race, and the New Republic

Phillip Hamilton
*The Making and Unmaking of a Revolutionary Family: The Tuckers of
    Virginia, 1752–1830*

Robert M. S. McDonald, editor
Thomas Jefferson's Military Academy: Founding West Point

Martha Tomhave Blauvelt
The Work of the Heart: Young Women and Emotion, 1780–1830

Francis D. Cogliano
Thomas Jefferson: Reputation and Legacy

Albrecht Koschnik
*"Let a Common Interest Bind Us Together": Associations, Partisanship, and
    Culture in Philadelphia, 1775–1840*

John Craig Hammond
Slavery, Freedom, and Expansion in the Early American West